A Gentle Death

This Booklet Distributed By:

Dying With Dignity Canada
#802 – 55 Eglinton Avenue East | Toronto, ON
416. 486. 3998 | 800. 495. 6156
www.dyingwithdignity.ca | info@dyingwithdignity.ca

A
Gentle
Death

Marilynne Seguin

R. N.

KEY PORTER BOOKS

Excerpt from *At the Will of the Body* by Arthur W. Frank, copyright
© 1991 by Arthur W. Frank and Catherine E. Foote. Reprinted by
permission of Houghton Mifflin Company. All rights reserved.

Excerpt from "The Shulman Case and the Right to Refuse Treatment"
by Prof. Barney Sniderman, reprinted from *Humane Medicine 7*,
vol. 1: no. 1 (Winter 1991), by permission of the publisher.

Canadian Cataloguing in Publication Data

Seguin, Marilynne
A gentle death

ISBN 1-55013-553-8

1. Terminal care.   2. Death – Psychological aspects.
3. Physician and patient.   I. Title.

R726.8.S44 1994   362.1'75   C94-930046-2

Key Porter Books Limited
70 The Esplanade
Toronto, Ontario
Canada M5E 1R2

The publisher gratefully acknowledges the assistance of
the Canada Council and the Ontario Arts Council.

Printed and bound in Canada
94 95 96 97 98 6 5 4 3 2 1

CONTENTS

To Marie, Mark and Jim
who have completed their journey with dignity

PREFACE

This is a book about choice—about your right to choose the time and manner of your death. It would be both moral and just for our society to recognize this right, yet at present our laws do not do so. You may not ever need to make such a choice, but what if you do? What if you find life-threatening or terminal illness making continued life unendurable? What can or will you be able to do about it?

Advice for the individual and advice for society, therefore, are two important streams in the book.

A third, non-prescriptive stream is my own story—the experiences with death that formed and, I suppose, dictated my personal preoccupation with these issues, as well as some of the many hundreds of personal involvements I have had with people who are confronting their own choices about death, or their lack of them.

My seminal experiences with dying were, in order:

- positive and negative episodes during my formative years of nursing people who were to go on to enjoy the gifts of life and those for whom life was no longer endurable and who wished to die. Both types of experiences informed and shaped my present attitudes;
- confronting my own death. I was not supposed to be alive, but I

fought disease, the medical establishment and traditional medical practices to keep from being ushered conveniently away;
- a younger brother's death. He faced death with a courage that continues to provide solace to our lives and strength to fight the odds;
- my mother's death. She chose to live, with joy and sacrifice, every minute available to her;
- my father's death. It was time.

The theme of each chapter will be illustrated by true stories that show both the difficulties of trying to prepare in advance and the possible consequences of a failure to do so, as well as the joys and benefits of clear action to preserve personal choice.

In some cases, the stories will illustrate the harm that well-meaning interventions—whether by relatives, doctors or the law—can do to people striving for dignity as they die. In one chapter I will talk about one intriguing aspect of modern health practice—the fact that AIDS sufferers seem to have greater access to help in ending their lives than others who suffer from ailments that are at least as devastating. (Is this ageism? Homophobia? Do we want homosexuals "out of the way"? A conspiracy? A simple result of the fact that doctors are seldom dealing with the family members who are also heirs to the person who is dying?)

I also examine some of the history of the issue of choice. When did dying start to be seen as somehow unnatural? What role have hospitals, doctors and high technology played in it all? How have the laws governing what one is or is not permitted to do about own's own life changed over the years, and where do these laws stand now in Canada? What remedies are most urgently needed?

But, to emphasize what I said at the beginning, the main focus of this book is not on doctor-assisted dying but on your right to make choices about your own death. Although I am personally a strong proponent of changes in the law that will permit Canadian physicians to follow their patients' directives in this regard, I choose to act with discretion for the moment, to allow the citizens of Canada to decide this issue through the proper forum—Parliament. It is up to each person to determine, according to his or her personal values, how the issue of doctor-assisted dying will be met. It is my sincere belief that by helping you to walk in the shoes of those who have suffered and made their choice, you will be better able to make your own more informed decision and thereby influence our political leaders wisely and with compassion.

I use true case histories to demonstrate the plight—the suffering, anxiety and joys—of those with life-threatening or terminal illness and of those who have, for one reason or another, reached a rational decision that to end their life "prematurely" is a "fitting choice". I examine the alternatives available to these people, describe the choice they made, and discuss, where relevant, the role of others (including myself) in the final decision—to live or to die. My uncompromising belief in the right to privacy of the dying, their families and their caregivers has made it necessary for me to use pseudonyms and to alter other details of these people's stories.

Relived in print for you are the true facts of each "case". However, I must keep faith first and foremost with every patient, family member, friend and caregiver whose anonymity I am pledged to protect. I believe that in caring for the dying I must respect their wishes, values and beliefs, even when that wish is to die before natural death would allow. This involves a devout personal commitment to confidentiality and discretion.

How does the struggle develop for each person in his or her unique situation? What is each one's limit of tolerance? When does suffering become intolerable? What makes one person choose to live through the most horrendous situation and another to seek an accelerated death? How does a friend, advocate or counsellor decide the correct response? Is the right answer sometimes to back away? What dynamic makes my involvement—and my decision to risk a great deal—different in the case of Michael, Analise, Danny or Margaret?

In my experience, for every hundred or so persons who initiate conversations about wanting to die, about three ultimately make a decision for suicide, assisted suicide or euthanasia. Why do the rest accept other options? In the final analysis do the ill person and his or her advocate always decide in favour of the principles of self-determination and autonomy as appropriate?

The medical profession is frequently hypocritical and inequitable in its treatment of people like those described in this book. If you are in the right place at the right time; if someone is willing to challenge "the system"; if your caregivers are sympathetic, you have a chance. If they profess to be "pro-life", this may mean life at all costs—the cost of your agony, not theirs. It may also mean intense scrutiny and exposure, a risk not all wish to or can accept. Do not blame them. Put your frustration and anger where it will do the most good. Help the persons you have the opportunity to care for, and continue to protest laws that the majority of people believe have ceased to be fair and just.

There is in progress a revolution by patients and an evolution by health-care providers. What is it like to be on the "firing line" of such a struggle in Canada? The issues are both complex and sensitive. We cannot shift the power base presently in force overnight. *But, the people who need a more compassionate way to die need an answer NOW.* Do we seek the holes in the law and use them, or struggle for change in the broader picture? Or do we do both? Can we do both simultaneously and safely? Where does the Supreme Court of Canada stand on the issue? And where do we go from here?

While I believe we must always think clearly and with calm rationality, I do not apologize for the deep passion between the lines. There is a quote by St. Augustine that says it all: "Hope has two lovely daughters, anger and courage. Anger at the way things are and courage to change them."

ACKNOWLEDGEMENTS

D ying With Dignity, A Canadian Society Concerned With The Quality of Dying was formed in 1980, about halfway along the journey I will explore in this book. This organization's leadership role is paramount in advancing the knowledge, debate and social change in end-of-life issues.

The founding members of this society, of which I am one, have had as our goal always to be a responsible, compassionate, rational voice of those who seek to improve the quality of living and dying in Canada. We realized it would take both time and patience to develop a strong informed public and also to prove to the recognized authorities in the health-care and legal communities that our goals for change were both credible and reflective of a national social value.

It is our belief that the welfare of individuals is the core of the society's mission. It is Dying With Dignity's mission "to improve the quality of dying for all Canadians in accordance with their own wishes, values and beliefs". Our "hands on" approach to meeting specific needs through counselling and advocacy of all who seek our help—the ill, their family and friends, and the health-care providers—put action to the philosophy of Dying With Dignity.

Dying With Dignity has grown from a few dedicated members in 1980 to over 7000 committed supporters in 1994. Our active participation in the World Federation of Right-to-Die Societies reflects our belief that this is truly an issue of worldwide importance and that through cooperation and sharing of knowledge in a sensitive and constructive manner, individuals as well as all of society will benefit.

Of those vital contributors to the development and success of Dying With Dignity I wish to particularly acknowledge: Jean Skelhorne, Prof. Patrick Nowell-Smith, Prof. Graham Parker, David Forsee, Don Elliott, Lidy Hogan, Gretta Riddell-Dixon, Margaret Norquay, Stella McMurran, Dr. Sid Saunders, Clem Finney, Marcie Smordin, Jack Bell, George Frank, Sheilagh Hickie, Isobel Dunning, Joan Stephenson, Olaug Smith, Margaret Baker, Irene Birch, Clara Muskat, Sue Thompson, Catherine Trim, Gerda and Rudi Tismer, Monique and Pierre Leon, Ina Simpson, Audrey White, Rose Wilner, Shirley Yamada, Nancy Mills, Bill Rapsey, Cooper Campbell, Lexie Miller, Jacqueline Voutt and Shirley Gibson, and certainly at the top of the list in more ways than one, DWD's president, Dr. Doug Campbell. There are so many, others who are not listed here but who remain close to my heart.

I would like to express my gratitude here to special colleagues who have encouraged and enlightened along the way: Chris Axworthy, MP; Norm Sterling, MPP; Harry van Bommel; Dr. Peter Singer; Dr. Willie Molloy; Derek Humphry; Prof. Barney Sneiderman; Eugene Sutorius; Hans van Delden; Prof. Bernard Dickens; Dr. Maria Verhoef; Yvon Bureau; Arthur Frank; Chris Docker; Doug Scott; Doris and Charles Clapham; Prof. Arthur Schafer; Dr. Rob Buckman; Rev. John Oldham; The Venerable John Moore; Sheila Power and Rev. Jim Dickey.

For strength and daily sustenance in my chosen work I single out Kathy Mills, DWD's Administrative Assistant, that special person who makes the impossible less so. And most especially my colleague, confident, chauffeur, critic and constant support, Sheilagh Hickie, who meanders with me intellectually and spiritually through thick and thin as we take delight and solace in glimpsing into the world of birds and nature to soften the edges of frequent sadness.

Forever thanks to a few of those who have offered gifts beyond value: Jeane Tromp-Meesters, who shared with me the lessons, joys and pain of counselling those at the end of life; Dr. Pieter Admiraal, who reassures me it is all right to cry for the dying and for ourselves; and Martin Campbell—counselor, colleague and friend—all these have helped me to listen to and learn with and through the many friends I have been privileged to help complete their journey in peace and dignity.

To "Nancy B" and Sue Rodriguez, two courageous women who shall not be forgotten as pioneers in the freedom-to-choose-to-die movement in Canada, we all own a debt of sincere gratitude.

Finally I wish to thank my family and extended family who helped mold my values, shared with me their love and confidence, and trusted me to return theirs.

To Anna Porter, Jonathan Webb and Margaret Allen I express my thanks for your confidence and gentle guidance.

OUTLINE OF CASES

The ideas expressed in this book are the author's own
and do not necessarily represent those
of Dying With Dignity.

All readers who wish to share thoughts, experiences
or opinions with the author, please write care of
Dying With Dignity
600 Eglington Avenue East, Suite 401
Toronto, Ontario M4P 1P3

CHAPTER ONE

The Journey Begins

This is the story of a journey—a physical, intellectual and also frequently very emotional journey—from the certainties and the absolutes of youth to the greyer world of middle age with its more tolerant, kinder and more truthful outlook.

And as I—Marilynne Seguin—grew and changed so did the world around me. Previously unquestioned moral certainties became blurred. Reality and the maturity of true compassion, born and nurtured through circumstance and experience, affected the person I have become and how I respond to the needs of those at the end of life in the 1990s. So have many grown and matured, acquiring more tolerant and selfless beliefs and attitudes and learning an acceptance of death, including physician-assisted death.

But back in 1956 I was a long way from these enlightened views. As a young student immersed in an exciting, progressive career, on the front lines of life and death, I had the world on a string, or so I thought. And then I met Hans and Erica.

The Case of Hans and Erica

Twenty-one is an invincible age. The whole world is a fresh, exciting kingdom of possibilities. Hans and Erica had been married on his twenty-first birthday in a quiet ceremony in Holland. Their parents, his brother and a few close friends attended. For Erica and Hans, however, this was just the beginning of so much more to come.

The day after the wedding, heads still a little fuzzy with wine, the couple left for Canada. First on their list of things to do was to search for an apartment—not anything grand for now, just a simple little place with a garden and lots of trees or perhaps a park nearby. Hans would be going into partnership with an old school chum who had emigrated to London, Ontario, a few years earlier. The electronics firm he had started was doing so well they needed another professional engineer. Hans was superbly qualified and also had a bit of money to invest in his and Erica's future. Erica did not have a job lined up, but she was a practical nurse and knew that there were job openings in London at that time. She also had plans to enter nursing school in the fall and train to become a registered nurse in Canada.

Two weeks after their arrival the world caved in on them. The sun was shining and it was a perfect day to bike into the country, share a picnic and some time together making love in the grass. The honeymoon would officially end tomorrow, but both were sure that for them it really would go on forever.

Hans had heard from a friend about a lovely swimming spot, with a bridge for diving into a deep, cool spring-fed river. But either they were in the wrong spot or something had happened to change the river bed; as Hans described later, it was only when he was in the air, plunging head first in a dive, that he realized the terrible mistake he had made. "I could see the stones just under the surface of the water and I knew this was very bad. In those few seconds my only thought was, 'Erica will be so lonely here in Canada without me.'

"The next thing I knew I woke in a strange room with lights glaring in my eyes and the sound of many people scurrying around speaking about things I did not understand or associate with myself. In fact I could not feel myself at all. And then it all came flashing back and I wondered how I was still alive, or *was* I alive? I tried to move my hands and my feet. Not only would they not move, they were not even there. I tried to lift my head, but it too did not seem a part of me."

It was a long time before the full truth of Hans's situation came to him. Certainly no doctors or nurses would tell him that he was almost totally paralysed and there was no hope he would ever be any different. The first image Erica had of Hans's real condition was when she was admitted briefly into the private hospital room "just to reassure her he was still alive", but not long enough to "be in the way". This fleeting image will haunt Erica the rest of her life. "There he lay," she told me two years later when I first met her, "with these ice-tong–like things jammed into his skull. I thought they were piercing right through his brain. And there were ropes and pulleys everywhere stretching him in a way I had only seen before in pictures of medieval torture chambers. The only thing different was the attendants were dressed in white and wore white caps and masks instead of medieval costumes and carrying leather thongs to tie him down. No, this was truly twentieth-century medicine—everything sanitary, sterilized, with no time or place for me."

When I was assigned to care for Hans I was in my second year of nurse's training. Long before this time the callipers and tension devices had been removed from his body. Now he lived in a Stryker frame, encased like the filling in a sandwich in a very narrow apparatus with a top and a bottom that would be bolted and strapped together when it was time to flip Hans from his front to his back. Arm boards could be added rather like wings to stretch his upper limbs in an attempt to prevent the inevitable contractions—permanent bending—of his arms, wrists and hands. He had a catheter in place to drain his urine and was on a rigid routine to empty his bowel. Hans could do nothing for himself except think and dream and talk.

And talk he did—sometimes very softly and gently but also sometimes with great anger and frustration. Hans was the first person to ask me to let him die. I was shocked! No, more than that, I was in stunned disbelief. How could this young man with a brilliant mind and a beautiful, loving wife truly want to die? And Erica was magnificent—with peaches-and-cream complexion; long, flaming amber hair; and a wit to match. Of course, I told myself, it was all just a clinical depression resulting from the ongoing effect of the trauma he had received. Of course it was difficult to imagine myself strapped to a stretcher, able to see only the ceiling or the floor, twenty-four hours a day year in and year out. But then, I also told myself, there was always "hope".

One of the fundamental principles of nursing—never allow "the patient" to lose hope. One never knows what miracles are just around the corner. Never give up and never, under any circumstances, let patients know that there really is no hope—that we have done all we can. If you can keep "them" alive just one day longer, you are a Hero with a capital H; you have done your job well. You go home after a shift and feel great, knowing it is a job honestly done, a professional performance. You are exhilarated. Of course, we were also taught that some days and some cases will be more demanding, but a good nurse can handle it.

And so, I did as I had been taught to do. Every time Hans asked me to let him die (and this became almost a daily ritual), I jollied him along; I looked for a new book or a new piece of music to amuse and distract him; I collaborated with the other nurses and doctors, the team leader, the social worker, the chaplain, and sometimes even the room cleaners to find some new way to take Hans's mind off his depression. After all, he really could not mean it.

Finally, Erica asked me for a meeting. We went to the

cafeteria for coffee and she spoke to me with utmost sincer-
ity, the tears—and the pain—pouring out of her eyes. "Miss
Seguin," she said, "please believe Hans knows and fully un-
derstands what he is saying. He is not a stupid or a frivolous
man. We both know the score. Hans will never improve. He
can only lie there and think what this sentence he endures
means to him and to me. We love each other as much today
as we did long before we took our marriage vows. He has
asked me to divorce him. I cannot do that. So then he pleads
with me to just stop visiting him. [Erica came every day to
feed him whenever she was not on duty, for she had succeeded in entering nursing school.] It pains him so to see me
and know we will never have a life together, we will never
make love again, that he cannot even feel my touch on almost
all of his body, that he will never be able to touch me or feel
my skin against his. Yes, he can feel my kiss on his face and
lips, but he has not allowed me to kiss him for more than a
year now. He tells me it only reminds him of what cannot be.

"We also both know that whenever his bladder becomes
infected [as happens frequently in persons with in-dwelling
catheters and with a lowered resistance to infection], when
he gets the sudden high fevers and convulsions, he could easily die. But no one will allow this to happen. The nurses rush
about and the doctors come running and once again the
struggle begins to prolong his life—to prolong his agony.
Please, could you not just once allow nature to take its
course? I know this is a Catholic hospital and you too are a
Catholic, but surely no caring person can look on Hans and
truly believe he is living a life that has any joy or dignity, that
he is living in any but the most mechanical sense. Please, I
beg you, Miss Seguin, the next time this happens, let him
die."

I could not. Nor, in 1956, with my limited experience of illness,
particularly the complexities of chronic, irreversible illness, could I

5

even imagine how anyone, certainly not any health-care professional, could consider allowing a patient to die when it could be
prevented. Such an action was unthinkable—quite beyond my
realm of comprehension. I was fully "conditioned" in the "life at all
costs" philosophy, yet not sufficiently exposed to the concepts or
practical reality of suffering to realize that it was always someone
else who paid the price.

Now in 1994 I listen to those pleas begging me not only, "Please
let me die," but, "For mercy's sake, please *help* me to die." "If there is
such a thing as compassion, if you care at all, I beg of you, help me
to die." I cannot count the number of times I have heard and continue to hear this cry for mercy.

The Case of David

Even tonight, as I am working on this book, a young man,
David, phones to ask me to visit him tomorrow. Our friendship began more than a year ago. At that time he appeared to
be quite well, was still working three days a week and was living with two other friends with AIDS. Both have since died.
David, now at Casey House, a free-standing hospice in
Toronto for persons with AIDS, lingers on in a half life that
has become intolerably burdensome.

"I know that I will die, Marilynne. No one has yet survived AIDS. Only today, the doctor told me it could take another two to three months. I eat as little as possible, hoping
that starvation will make the end come sooner. Today I
weigh eighty-nine pounds, down from my original one hundred and thirty-five. I'm comfortable here at Casey House
and could not ask for better care, but I want to die now, and
they cannot help me do this."

I inquire about all the usual things. What about his family? "Yes, they visit when they can. Mom is too frail to come
all the way from Thunder Bay very often, but she calls every

second night. My brother and one sister take me to their house for a day or two when they can, but this is a holiday weekend and they all have company coming. I'm not the most presentable decoration to have around, as you can see. They tell me I can come to visit next week if I feel up to it."

"Have you made any friends at Casey House, David? People with whom you can help pass some time during the weekend? As you know I am three hundred miles away right now and can't get back to Toronto until Monday. What about staff or other patients to talk with?"

"Marilynne," he answers patiently, almost as if talking to a child, "the staff are great, but they only have so much time and I guess I'm just too depressing to stick around with very much. As for other patients—there is no time to get to know anyone, nor do I want to. Many of them are fortunate enough to come in one day, and when I go down the hall in my wheelchair the next morning to say hello, the bed is already empty. Or maybe they have been moved to the second floor where the really serious cases are. Aren't they lucky? No, I don't even try to spend time getting to know other 'inmates'. It makes me too depressed. All I want is to die. Please try to find a way to help me soon—very soon?"

We talk a while longer and I share some thoughts and stories with him. This is all it is possible to offer right now. I help him "put in a bit of time". There is only so much one can discuss on the telephone. For the conversation David and I need, we must be face to face. We need that all-revealing eye contact to see the truth in each other's words. We must separate need from want. We plan to get together next week for a real visit to try to sort out a remedy for David.

But let us return to the beginning of the journey. It is a jagged trip through myriad convolutions of life and death. In the thirty-eight years between nursing Hans and meeting David there are a few things I have learned.

When you are eighteen, the issues are simple. Here you are, learning to be a professional in what you consider to be one of the most gentle, generous and noble callings available to women in the middle of the twentieth century. Your portrait of life is clear and simple—there is right and there is wrong. There is white and there is black—and no space in between. It is only after repeated exposure to some of the "life" you have fought so diligently to preserve, the deaths so successfully and deliberately prolonged, that greys slowly creep into the periphery of your vision, knocking your picture askew.

Somewhere along that road the first doubt intrudes into your perfect world of "doing good" and therefore "feeling good" about your performance. Eventually, you work up the courage to put into words some questions about the value of the deeds you perform. After some time—a long time, and many broken bodies and spirits later—you learn the real truth, that you must always question. That you must always listen and look for the underlying greys; the images, the feelings and the aches that provide a total picture of this life with which you are entrusted. And you must do this before coming to a decision, not just contemplate the justice or justify the "rightness" of your behaviour after the fact, when it is usually too late to change outcomes.

The other thing I have learned is equally critical: it is not my role to judge. It is for me to listen without prejudging to the free, uninhibited expression of each person's suffering. To listen with my whole self, not just to the words; many people find it difficult, if not impossible, to express themselves in words, especially when they are immersed in a crisis. Instead, I have to remind myself to really "walk in this person's shoes".

I must try to understand what it is like to fight for air as the person in respiratory failure is fighting; to endure the long hours of boredom and inactivity Lou Gehrig's disease imposes; to feel the constant tremors and insecurity of Parkinson's disease. I must also reach back into my own medical history and allow myself once again to feel the indescribable pain that I too suffered through operation after operation to heal wounds that resisted all surgical remedies. Finally, I must open myself to a little of the agony each person must endure alone in reaching his or her own treatment decisions.

The best thing I can then do for each person I am counselling is to provide an environment in which, together, we can explore all the alternatives possible, including the full implications of those options, and to listen with all of my being to hear the person's choice. Believe me, there are many times when you do not want to listen or hear, for the burden is great.

My role then becomes that of a friend and advocate totally committed to helping the person reach the goal he or she has chosen. Sometimes the best solution we can achieve in our current legal climate is a compromise, but much more often we find a way to honour each individual's wishes, even if it intrudes somewhat into the grey areas recognized by some "authorities".

In 1980, when "Dying With Dignity, A Canadian Society Concerned With The Quality of Dying" came into being, I still believed, somewhat shakily, in absolutes. But three experiences of long-term, life-threatening illness had exposed me to the harshness of illness and the realities of what "fighting for life" really meant.

In my final year of nursing I had contracted strep throat while caring for a darling, chubby but very sick two-year-old. He needed lots of cuddling, and I was just the person to enjoy fulfilling that need. It was a time of twelve-hour shifts and intense studying for final exams. My resistance was low, and at that time there was minimal understanding in the medical community of just how dangerously contagious this bug was. I caught it. The two-year-old recovered in a few days from his strep throat, but my own condition worsened into full-blown rheumatic fever, a trial that was to keep me bedridden in hospital for months, and with a lifelong price to pay.

Barely one year later this disease flared up again, only this time it had worsened to include inflammation of the lining membrane of the heart (subacute bacterial endocarditis). With this too I was months in hospital, and finally my physician told me to choose a less demanding career. I refused, and to my everlasting joy continued in the nursing profession. Finally, in 1980, I developed symptoms of uterine cancer. At age forty-two I was to face and make many life-altering decisions.

An important lesson I learned through my own illness and those of others was that the battle to survive is a solitary one. No matter how much support and love surround a person, the experience of serious illness is painfully lonely. Another revelation I was unprepared for was that at a certain point I would find myself considering that most difficult of all choices: whether to continue the struggle for life or to pursue the alternative—to choose to die.

Such a choice has, until very recent years, been a very private one, for it could not be discussed openly with either professionals or family and friends.

North Americans are fond of stories about the "brave" person who carries on against all odds. We glorify those who "set an example" for the rest of society with their choice of courageous deeds. Our heroes are the "winners" who beat disease or, alternatively, those who die only after prolonged "battles" with their particular disease.

But what of the others? Until very recently society did not tolerate the subject of suicide, physician-assisted death or euthanasia as an acceptable option for the very ill person. The end of life was that state automatically perceived to be predetermined by God or circumstance or the skill, personal attitude and philosophy of medical professionals.

The MD behind a doctor's name has come to stand for "Medical Deity" almost without our realizing it. For the most part, doctors did not choose this role; rather, it was forced upon them by our reluctance, as individuals and as a society, to assume responsibility for decision making. Of course, power is difficult to refuse or give up, and in many cases physicians came to accept that they held this power by right. Gradually, however, some health-care professionals are beginning to question if the power is worth the impossible burden it imposes.

In the early eighties, most members of the health-care professions—doctors, nurses and others—were overly enthusiastic in their battle for life at all costs. Most had not yet learned to listen to patients, although it was widely professed that this was a vital component of good patient care. Many consciously refused to "get involved" because it complicated their professional and personal lives beyond their willingness to make such an investment. Euthanasia was a dirty word, an evil, not a subject for rational scrutiny or debate.

In all fairness it must be stated that until very recently this issue was seldom considered to *require* debate. Death by choice, especially in the medical community, was always wrong. Euthanasia was part of the "harm" physicians had been instructed by Hippocrates *never* to do.

Even so, honest physicians and nurses have known, at least consciously, that physician-assisted dying has been practised for centuries. But such deeds almost always took place with great discretion and in private (see Chapter 11).

In the fourteen years since the founding of the "right to die" movement in Canada, there has been tremendous growth, not only in myself and immediate colleagues in this mission, but in other health-care workers, and in Canadian society. It is perhaps ironic that, through thinking about death, both patients and health-care professionals have acquired increased respect for human life. Many of the doctors, nurses, social workers, ethicists, chaplains and others with whom I come in contact daily are eager to discuss the quality not just the quantity of life. While we have developed our convictions at different paces—a pace that makes me very impatient at times—we have also vastly increased our respect for one another and for different points of view. In fact, the increasing ability and willingness on the part of the majority of health-care workers to struggle together with these monumental issues is remarkable.

At present, however, the professional faces a great personal dilemma. In acting compassionately to help a suffering patient to die sooner rather than later, a doctor or nurse risks all—the loss of the ability to earn a living, condemnation by their colleagues, even loss of their personal freedom under current Canadian laws. Meanwhile, the person whose life is already made unbearable by disease must continue to endure unspeakable suffering until a merciful solution can be either negotiated or achieved by some other means.

AUTONOMY

I recall a very independent lady who chose life and death on her own terms.

The Case of Betsy, "The Lady in Pink"

About five years ago, an extraordinary pink vision walked into my office. It was a lady dressed almost entirely in pink. She wore a pink snow-suit, a pink toque, had very pink cheeks, held a large pink carry-all and had a pink blanket bundled neatly under one arm. Only the old white runners on her feet broke the theme. I had heard her coming up the stairs to the office because of the swish, swish of the snow-suit fabric as she walked.

"Hi," she said, "my name's Betsy. Are you Dying With Dignity?" There was a twinkle in her eye and a bit of brogue in her rusty voice. "Not yet," I answered, "but I hope to some day." We both enjoyed the little joke and it seemed to ease some minor hesitation on her part. "Ah," she said, "I was afraid you'd be a glum lot up here, running such a business. It's sure a relief to know you're not. Now, would you have a cup of tea for a cold old lady, and time for a little chat?" "I have both," I said. "I'll just go put the kettle on while you make yourself comfortable."

When I returned with a battered tray holding tea, milk and sugar and a plateful of cookies, her eyes lit up and she hunkered down for a "wee stay" as she called it. "By the way, my name's Marilynne," I told her. "Well, I know that," she said. "I saw you on the TV the other day. How do you think I knew to look you up?" That seemed to settle that.

"What I want to know," she asked as she put milk and two spoonfuls of sugar in her tea and helped herself to two chocolate-chip cookies, "is, do you really believe what you said on that show? Can I die where and when I want? You see, I like to live my own way. I'm what they call a 'street person' and what some call 'homeless'. Balderdash, a lot they know. I'm not homeless. I have one of the best homes anyone could have. I've always hated being cooped up. When I was a kid my mother used to have to drag me in from the backyard come winter time. I had a little tent out there, and only when she was afraid I'd freeze to death did she put her foot down and insist I move back into the house for the winter months. Mom understood. She often whispered to me when the others couldn't hear that she wished she could live outside too. A restless pair, we two. Yes, I have a great home. Do you know, there are beautiful parks in Toronto, with stately trees and quiet places to sit and think. And there are lots of friends out there to share a chin-wag with if you get tired of being alone. No better place I can tell you—Toronto. I've tried lots of others, travelled the country from one ocean to the other, but I always come back here. This is home to Betsy."

And so she talked, reminiscing and sharing a part of herself while she sipped away at three cups of tea and a few more cookies, always asking first if we could afford it.

"Well," she said after a bit, "you have lots of other people to see so I'd better get down to what I came for. I'm in pretty good shape right now. I'm forty-five or thereabouts, always been healthy, eat well. I have some money you see. I'm not a bum or a vagrant. I live this way because that's how I choose to live. I don't drink or smoke. Never used drugs—that's for losers, and I'm not a loser. Just different. I like to help out a bit doing various things. And," she added with a grin, "I have my own charity work.

"A lot of my friends, you see, are not as lucky as me. They get into bad habits and with bad company. They get beat up by the tough kids, or they'll get into a brawl over a bottle, and I'll drop them off at Emerg', or see they get a bit of soup for a few days until they're feeling better. I don't do nothing special, like you. I just try to give back a little of the blessings I've been given. Dignity, you talk about. It's important for everyone. It's all I ask. You see, Marilynne, you quoted somebody or other on that TV show. You said, 'Most people die as they have lived.'"

(I had been quoting Dr. Rob Buckman, a friend and the author of a book called *I Don't Know What to Say*, about how people and their families and friends cope with life-threatening and terminal illness.)

"That's what I want," Betsy continued. "I want to die as I have lived—in the outdoors, plain and simple with no fuss, no tubes sticking out of me, no machines, no medicines, no nurses or doctors. Just as God intended. Free and natural. Can that happen? Can I make sure somehow I'll be let die as I choose when it's my time? What can I do to help make it happen?"

I explained to her about Living Wills (see Chapter 5 and Appendix B) and that I believed completing and signing such a document and carrying it with her would help. "Of course," I said, "nothing is foolproof in this world. Neither one of us can predict what course your life will take in the years to come. If you become seriously ill and fall unconscious will someone interfere and take you to hospital? Do you have a family member who will try to insist that you receive medical care? We cannot anticipate all the possible things that might happen to change even the best-thought-out plans. But this is a good start."

We talked a while longer, and she asked to take away a

copy of our Living Will, so she could study it and think about how she would want to word her specific personal requirements. Betsy left, after telling me a funny story, saying she would be back to visit again, thanking me for the tea and cookies and telling me she would find me a nicer tray "to impress the hoi polloi".

About two weeks later, once again early in the morning, there was Betsy, this time with a couple of friends in tow. "I came to sign my Living Will and thought I'd better bring a couple of witnesses with me. They can tell you I'm in my right mind," she said with her customary grin. She introduced me to her friends. One was a lawyer practising in downtown Toronto, near Betsy's favourite corner. The other was a friend who also lived on the street and who had known her for many years. She had figured out that such persons would be best able to testify, if ever it was necessary, that she was rational, thoughtful and capable of making her own decisions. When our business was concluded, Betsy made a generous donation to our society and said she would drop by occasionally "to make sure you're on the job and read the newsletters to see how DWD is doing. I don't have an address, so you can't mail them to me."

As the years went by, Betsy would telephone or visit occasionally, and whenever there was a public forum in Toronto, there she was with some of her friends. She would pick up brochures and pass them around to people she thought could use our help. She became a good friend. I admired her independence, her spunk in sticking to her principles, her insight and her ability to decide what she wanted and go about getting it while always respecting others in her goals and in her heart. She did quiet good works no one will ever know of or understand, and she did them for the best of all possible reasons. It was the right thing to do.

Early last winter, on a dreary day of wet snow flurries that dampened the rather deserted streets of downtown Toronto, a dear friend invited me to share "high tea" at the restaurant of an elegant downtown hotel. I was, at the time, suffering from a deep personal grief and on the brink of emotional collapse. This friend had sensed that I needed something very special to divert me from my anguish. There was no parking close to the hotel, so he dropped me off near the entrance and went to park farther along the street. As I sauntered toward the hotel door I spotted a familiar pink bundle half lying on the sidewalk, half leaning against the wall of a building.

Sensing a dire situation, I half ran along the street toward Betsy. Calling her name over and over, I squatted down beside her to examine her more closely. The signs were obvious—Betsy was dying. From what cause I could not tell, but dying nevertheless, and it would happen soon. Suddenly I became aware of movement around us and saw from the corner of my eye four or five of Betsy's chums moving toward us out of doorways and from around street corners.

"What are you going to do?" said a rather belligerent voice from behind me. "Are you going to call the cops?" "You're not going to move her to the hospital are you?" exclaimed another in obvious distress. "No," I assured these concerned people. "I'm just going to sit here and hold Betsy. No one should have to die alone." And so I sat on the sidewalk with my arms around this dear lady in pink, speaking softly in her ear. Very soon there was a last deep sigh and Betsy was still. She had died as she had lived, in freedom and dignity, exercising her right to choose what that dignity was for her.

Some time during all this, my friend had come upon our strange grouping on the street. He watched silently and patiently as Betsy's life came to an end. Only after Betsy died did he speak. "What should be done?" he asked. "Nothing," I replied. I put my card in Betsy's pocket, covered her gently with her pink blanket, and rose to leave. As I did so, John, a "grumpy old bastard", as he had always called himself, approached me, tears streaking his grimy face. "Thank you from all of us and from Betsy. She had asked us to call you, but we were afraid you might not understand. We should have known better. She looks peaceful don't she?" And slowly they all wandered off, back to the place each called home.

Those of us in the "right to choose to die" movement have learned tolerance and patience. The momentous changes we seek do not occur overnight. But we cannot and will not continue to be patient, for there is just too much unnecessary and unjustifiable suffering. As long as governments and politicians block the legal avenues, the dying and their families and caregivers will do what they can to circumvent "the system" in order to respond rationally and with compassion to an individual's need.

The Case of Michael

Dr. John looked casually around the room to see who was there. He had already examined Michael. He knew that AIDS would take Michael's life, in the normal course of events, within another six to eight weeks.

Garry, Michael's lover, was sitting on the side of the bed, unconsciously stroking Michael's almost pencil-thin forearm. We could hear Michael's daughters, Gail and Melissa, playing music in the other room, chatting on the phone and giggling occasionally. It was a very ordinary family setting. Of course the girls knew and understood that their father was going to die in a while, but it was not an immediate crisis. (They had already experienced many of those.) This was just another normal family evening. There were no great secrets within this household, except, of course, what Michael, Garry and I knew and, I am sure, Dr. John suspected. Michael and Garry and the girls had been together for fifteen years, and they had come to accept, respect, and love one another deeply.

Dr. John gave us a meaningful look, checked the top of the bedside table where all of Michael's medications were kept within arm's reach, and said, "I'm going away for the weekend and I wonder if there are enough medications here? I wouldn't want to see you run out. Well, here, I'll write another prescription in case you decide you want it. It's for thirty Seconal." Of course he could see there were at least a hundred capsules (two almost-full bottles) already sitting there. "And by the way," he added, "you must not run out of morphine, either. I know Michael has not used any for a while and must have some left." Once again he could see there were boxes of ampoules sitting right there beside the other drugs—more than could possibly be required even in a great emergency. But he wrote another prescription, leaving it conveniently on top of the first.

In the secret language of assisted suicide, Dr. John was giving Michael permission to overdose if that is what he chose to do. We all understood the message and we all played the game.

He went back over to the bed, looked at Michael and said with great calm. "Now, are you sure you're all right for the weekend? I could have an associate drop in to check you if you like."

"No, no," replied Michael and Garry almost simultaneously. "I'm feeling pretty good," Michael added. "The girls, their mother, and a few friends are coming over tomorrow afternoon and they'll move me out onto the back patio for a while. We're arranging a barbecue, you see—a real party. It's the fifteenth anniversary that Garry and I have been together. We would all like to celebrate. Then the girls will go to stay with their mother for the rest of the weekend. Marilynne, you will be joining us for the party, won't you? And perhaps you can stay after for another glass of wine with Garry and me." "Of course I will, Michael. I would be pleased to be part of the festivities," I replied.

I walked Dr. John to the door. Again there was that knowing look. He was not fooled by the words left unspoken. Then he paused quite deliberately and removed an envelope from his case. "Marilynne," he said, "I'm going to leave the death certificate with you. It is completed except for the date and time. You can take care of that."

"No," I responded. "You are not going to leave this document for me to complete. Especially one that has been falsified as to 'cause of death.' I have my role to play in this scenario and you have yours. Dammit, John, you have behaved courageously and well so far. You have gone farther than many palliative-care physicians in the same circumstances to ensure a peaceful end for Michael. Don't be a hypocrite now. You cannot simply abdicate the rest of your responsibility so casually. And I will not let you add your burden to mine." "Well," he said, "we'll compromise. I'll leave it here on the table in the sealed envelope. If you choose to use it, you know what to do. Goodbye and good luck."

Dr. John strode down the walkway and I watched him through the delicately coloured leaded-glass window-panes. For all his apparent callousness (and perhaps panic?) during this last brief exchange, I sensed the frustration and agony he felt. When he reached his car, John paused, leaned against the door for a few moments, then turned and gazed briefly at this lovely home in Forest Hill. Opening the car door, he placed his case behind the driver's seat, got in and slowly drove away—for the last time, he knew.

"Marilynne," Garry said as I came back to the bedroom, "do we need to fill these new prescriptions? I'd rather not bother if we don't need them. Michael has not used any of the previous supplies of these drugs. He has been saving them specifically for his death. What do you think?" "No," I answered, "let's just have a cup of tea and listen to some music, relax and talk a while, if you like. I'll go home in a little while and come back tomorrow as planned."

It was a sad but tranquil night for me. As frequently happens when I am preparing for a death, or have just come home from being with someone who has died, I usually think about my brother and the last months of his life. Just as if he knew I might need him that night, Jim appeared in my dreams. There he was as usual, sitting on the foot of my bed (except sometimes he was slouched in the old chair nearby), an impish smile on his face, as if to say, "Well, 'Lynne, I'm here. Let's talk it out." And so we do, and I waken the next morning either securely believing that my decision is fitting, or sometimes still with doubts, knowing I must think such-and-such a case through some more. This night was no exception. Jim and I schmoozed the night away, debating the implications of what the next twenty-four hours might bring.

Saturday was an exceptionally brilliant day. I called Michael and told him I was going to the market. Would he like me to pick up anything for the party? We confirmed our plans and later I met the family at the house, loaded with packages of fresh fruit and a nice bottle of Chardonnay.

The party was a great success. Michael seemed stronger than I'd seen him for ages. He was free from pain today and able to nibble some of the delicacies Garry, Monica (his wife) and the girls had prepared for this special anniversary. He ate little, however, so as not to interfere with the absorption of the drugs he would soon take. The garden paraded its best and brightest blooms. Debussy, Satie and a little Duke Ellington entertained us on the CD player—along with the girls, their close buddies and some feathered friends that came for treats to the garden bird feeder.

Everyone was happy, as though it was just another party, although I know that many at least suspected this was the "event" the close family members had discussed with us over the past few months. At nine o'clock, after first moving Michael back into the living-room, everyone went home. Even though it was really too warm for it, Garry lit the fireplace and the three of us sat together, quietly reviewing our plans. Eleven o'clock arrived. We calculated that it had been four hours since Michael had swallowed any food. He now had a little tea and a few Jacob's water biscuits (his favourite), followed soon after by one Gravol tablet. We waited some more, chatting as old friends do. Garry occasionally got up to nudge the fire or just sat close to Michael, holding on to him as if touch would give him the resources to carry on. I confess we all cried a bit as the time grew nearer.

At about five minutes to twelve Garry went into the kitchen and returned with three glasses. He and I were drinking wine and Michael sipped eagerly on a scotch with soda to help him swallow forty Seconal and ten Valium. Garry and I hugged Michael and within minutes could feel his spare, frail body relaxing. He continued to speak, gradually more slowly, of the love and peace of his life. "How privileged I am to be able to die now, while I am still whole in body, in spirit and in mind. Thank you, Garry—companion, lover, friend— the best part of me for fifteen wonderful years.

"Marilynne, these months of knowing you were nearby to listen and to negotiate for us with our families and Dr. John have given Garry and me the control and dignity we needed. Thank you for being our friend. Take care of Garry for me, will you—for a little while at least?"

At 1:30 a.m. on Sunday, we laid Michael gently on his bed, bathed him and dressed him in his favourite pyjamas. Then and only then did we call the physician's weekend service. Dr. John, we found, had stayed in town after all.

Four weeks later, Garry and I met for the last time in Winston Churchill Park. It had been an emotionally and physically exhausting time for him, helping the girls, their mother and his other friends to deal with their grief. Now, as we headed toward our favourite bench, he smiled through the fatigue lines around his eyes, and a glow came over his face. "You were right," he said with quiet amazement. "I had to call you today to tell you about it. It happened just as you said it would. This morning I woke up with this strange yet wonderful feeling. I did it! I did something that very few people ever have the chance to do. I helped Michael to die when and how he chose. That's really something isn't it?—and I feel so humble, yet proud. I know now deep in my spirit it was 'fitting,' as you always say. Marilynne, I feel great!"

Although he looked tired, I knew he would survive and would treasure this secret tight inside him. Garry knew it would be a long time, if ever, before he would be able to tell anyone of the rare gift he had given to Michael—a death of his own choosing.

None of this could I have envisioned when I was eighteen years old. Nor do we know what the next twenty or thirty years will bring. Certainly we will understand more about suffering and death. Let us hope that the future will also bring us a more reasonable, open and compassionate response to those who are at the end of life. We must allow each mature, competent person the freedom to choose the time and manner of his or her dying, and the assistance to do so in a gentle and dignified manner.

CHAPTER TWO

Patients
and Doctors

Finding a Balance of Power

Persons in a life-threatening situation usually feel vulnerable, wounded and, quite often, angry and helpless. It is natural and "normal" to experience such feelings. Life is seldom fair or just. The most we can hope for is to be able to direct our emotion and energy into a positive channel—one that will empower us to function as constructively as our abilities and the circumstances will permit.

Health-care providers, whether professionals or lay persons, experience the same feelings of helplessness and anger. Added to this is also the frustration of wanting to "do more", to "make it better" for those in their care. Frequently, however, the behaviour of even the most concerned health-care personnel seems brusque, callous and inconsiderate. To a person who is already smarting from the psychological and perhaps even physical scars of serious illness, such behaviour adds to the hurt and is totally unacceptable.

What is necessary for a therapeutic doctor-patient relationship is a level playing-field that encourages mutual respect and trust. No matter how long or brief the doctor-patient association, it is essential for both parties to use all the skills they possess to ensure that the "rules of the game" are fair to both. I can't say often enough that you must all talk to each other and *listen* to the answers.

It will soon be obvious whether such a partnership is possible or not. Do not hesitate. If both parties do not find considerable common ground and empathy fairly quickly, you should recognize the incompatibility and politely seek another source of support.

The Case of Annie

Annie was seventy-two, a cheerfully friendly but quietly determined lady. For more than thirty years, first as a teacher, then as assistant principal in one of the local grade schools, Annie had been a driving force in her community. A religious woman, she led the church choir for many years and took on a myriad of other charitable endeavours. She was a woman with an enthusiastic love of life.

Six months before I met her, Annie had been told she had cancer—a particularly painful, debilitating and fast-growing cancer that left her frail of body but as strong as ever in spirit. Although the pain was severe at times, Annie was confident she could manage, and wished to die at home.

Dr. Williams was new in town. Annie's old friend and family physician for as long as she could remember, Jacob Abramms, would have understood. But he had died of a stroke last year. Annie had not had the opportunity to get to know Dr. Williams very well, or to have Dr. Williams get to know her. She liked the new doctor well enough, but was tentative about whether or not she would respect her philosophy of care and preferred an old friend, Hermann, to hold her Power of Attorney for Health Care. Annie and Hermann had discussed her values at length, and Annie was confident that Hermann would act according to her clearly stated wishes.

Dr. Williams advised Annie that "she knew and would do what was best for her" and stated firmly that Annie must very soon be admitted to hospital. Such a decision was quite unacceptable to Annie. Annie understood that refusing to be hospitalized would probably mean less precise pain control and that there might be an increase of other unpleasant symptoms. Nevertheless, she was determined to die in her own bed.

Accustomed to making her own decisions, Annie investigated home-care services through a social-worker friend. She realized that these services alone would not be enough, but she believed that with the help of her friends, the church "caring committee" and dear Hermann, she had the makings of a good palliative-care team.

Having read a few good books on the subject, Annie felt reasonably confident that she had covered all the relevant possibilities, but she asked me to consult with her about some points Dr. Williams seemed reluctant to discuss. What was the probable course of events of her dying? Was it unreasonable to believe that she and her "team", as she calls them, could manage? Was she asking too much of good friends, neighbours and the health-care system? "In plain English, Marilynne, am I just being selfish?"

Would the Power of Attorney for Health Care Hermann held be enough to keep her here at home near her cat, the garden and the sea view that were such an important part of her life?

"What if Dr. Williams refuses to go along with my plans?" she asked as we talked one rainy spring morning, gazing out the window overlooking St. Mary's Bay. We were sitting in the homey kitchen where, as she put it, "all important conversations in this house seem to take place." I asked, "Would you like me to meet with Dr. Williams and find out her concerns?" "Yes, I certainly would, but what do I do if Dr. Williams will not cooperate? What if she decides to refuse me the pain medication I need or the social services a doctor must authorize? What choices do I have?"

The first priority, I assured her, was that she should feel secure and comfortable. "Annie", I reminded her, "you are in control here. My job is to make sure everyone recognizes that fact. We'll work it out."

Dr. Williams had not experienced caring for a dying person in the person's own home. She had moved to this part of Nova Scotia from Halifax and had not previously been directly involved with a patient using home services for terminal care. She was concerned about how a team made up mostly of volunteers could provide adequate care for this spunky patient she had come to admire. Young Dr. Williams needed support, information and reassurance that this was indeed an opportunity both to learn and to achieve the "balance of power" that is essential for good patient-doctor relationships.

I suggested Dr. Williams and I meet with Annie that evening, and Hermann too, as Annie's chosen surrogate decision maker, to discuss the plan of care. The doctor eagerly agreed. In her usual way, Annie organized everything and insisted Hermann pick up some sweets, even though she herself never indulged in them.

I visited with Annie for the next few days, and was able to meet with the home-care workers, the friends and church volunteers and Dr. Williams. Soon everything was in place, and Annie and I shared a teary goodbye.

Though our friendship was fairly brief, the next time I am out east I shall undoubtedly find my way again to "Annie's place". I shall also take time to share a cup of coffee and reminisce with Dr. Williams, who made sure my friend died as she wished, with the sunshine reflecting off the water up through her window, while many good people helped her with her final prayers.

FINDING THE RIGHT PARTNER
IN YOUR HEALTH CARE

Finding a sympathetic doctor is essential for putting together a health-care plan that is right for you. *You* have the responsibility for choosing a reasonable lifestyle; the *doctor* you choose has the responsibility to make sure you have all the help you need to maintain a healthy body, emotional well-being and peace of mind about your future.

This must be a true partnership. The decision making must be based on good communication between the parties, an acceptance of responsibility, respect for each other, and trust. If any of these qualities is missing, the relationship is unlikely to succeed and should be declined, politely but firmly, at the outset or as soon as either party realizes it is not working. Remember, a doctor does not have to accept you as a patient. You, however, need to make a private commitment in order to proceed. In the absence of compatibility and a feeling of comfort between you and your doctor, a long-lasting partnership is impossible.

Since you are making a choice of doctor for the primary purpose of helping you to stay well and healthy, it is important to remember that this is also the doctor's goal. Simply put, the best time to choose a doctor is when you don't really need one, when you are in good health. It is unwise to leave the choice until you are in a life-threatening situation. Of course, life does not always work so neatly, and if you are pressed for time, you should consider the following.

When we approach the end of life, our priorities may change. At this time most individuals need and desire their physician to understand and respond to their personal views about care versus cure. A person who has accepted the inevitability of death may find a continued aggressive fight for cure intrusive and unsympathetic. This is a time when the "one more for the Gipper" attitude is totally out of place.

We must also accept, however, that it may be very difficult for everyone—patient, doctor, nurse and family members—to switch their treatment goals at the same pace. Each person needs time to adjust and opportunities to talk with and *listen* to the others involved, so that a common understanding can be reached. Where the main players—patient and doctor—are dealing with life-threatening illness, it is critically important for their philosophies of caring

27

to be compatible. As the patient, you will need the reassurance that your expectations regarding care, as expressed in your Advance Health Care Directive (see Chapter 5), will prevail in any treatment decision.

I recall being in the audience when the primary-care physician caring for "Nancy B" (see Chapter 8) described the shock and trauma experienced by all the staff who were caring for this brave young woman when Nancy first expressed her wish to be taken off life-support equipment. As the doctor told the story, I was reminded of patients I had cared for, and with whom I had developed a close relationship—patients who had become friends in the fullest meaning of the word.

It is always a shock when a patient says he or she prefers death to merely existing as a helpless sufferer.

The Case of Harry

Many years ago when I was working on a film project about issues of medical ethics, I developed an important friendship with a person who was suffering from end-stage renal disease. He had twice undergone kidney-transplant operations, but both surgeries had failed. For the last four years he had existed by submitting to renal dialysis every second day.

After a period of time, Harry came to look on me as his sounding-board, his ever-ready shoulder to lean on and, finally, his advocate. He revealed to me on a number of occasions that he was considering discontinuing treatment. He fully understood that this would mean certain death within five to seven days. He also knew that it would be a difficult decision for his doctor and, especially, his nurses to accept. Not only did they work in a Roman Catholic hospital, they had all developed a closeness and true affection for each other. Harry was very easy to like.

He had fought his disability with all his strength and now

he decided it was time to rest. Over many weeks we would meet to debate this decision, backwards, forwards and every which way, as I played "devil's advocate" in Harry's case for the right to choose.

This was a long time ago. At that time no person on record had ever chosen to refuse this life-prolonging treatment. Finally Harry asked for a meeting with his doctor and explained his decision. Dr. X was aghast. What are we doing wrong? Where have we failed you, Harry? Do you know how hard this will be on the staff? The questions and challenges went on and on. Harry was very moved by the doctor's agonized opposition, but his decision was as irreversible as his disease.

I thought Harry very courageous when he then went to the nurses who had cared for him so long and well to explain his decision personally. As I took him home from the hospital, he told me that they had been too shocked even to respond. He wept to recall the pain and bewilderment in their eyes, so moved was he by their depth of caring.

Every member of the health-care team, without exception, took Harry's decision very poorly and quite unprofessionally, but, one has to admit, in a very human fashion. For the next three days I sat with Harry, comforting him as his condition quickly deteriorated. During that time we were inundated with calls and visits from the doctor and the nurses, begging Harry to come back for treatment. Harry drew the line, however, when two police officers arrived at the door to attempt to force him to return to hospital. At this point, on Harry's orders, we decided not to open the door to anyone but his family.

Harry suffered unbearably from a constant itching. This was not the usual sort of itch—on the surface of the skin— but an itch that was inside his whole body. He screamed aloud at times, but all our best efforts could not stop it.

Then, on the fourth day, Dr. X telephoned for the

umpteenth time. But this time when I answered he shouted, "Marilynne, please do not hang up. I know I've been wrong and that Harry must be suffering terribly. Please let me help." We were all grateful for his final act of compassion, when he sent over the medication Harry needed that would quell the itching, reduce the stress and allow him to die in peace.

Eventually, I was very proud of this health-care team. After Harry was buried (and almost all of them came to the funeral, weeping openly at the loss of their friend and patient), a team conference was called and I was invited to attend. Together we analysed the reactions of the staff and discussed where their concept of caring for Harry had gone wrong. It was a painful process for everyone, but an invaluable one. Only three weeks later another person receiving dialysis at this hospital also decided to make a rational choice to end treatment. This lady was treated with love and respect and was given all the care possible to permit a comfortable, dignified death.

Good, caring, compassionate doctors exist in abundance. But, as with any group, some who have chosen the profession are unsuited to it, while others have chosen it for the wrong reasons.

It is important to debunk some of the myths about doctors. While some physicians' performance and achievement are outstanding, courageous, bold and at times close to miraculous, all doctors are not heroes. Nor, in fact, are their deeds all heroic or unusual, or even, occasionally, adequate. Doctors are, after all, human beings, with all the frailties and vulnerabilities of our species. They can be brilliant, charming, erudite, wise, generous, sympathetic, humorous, gentle, organized, sensitive professionals. They can also be pompous, stupid, ignorant, boring, crass, distant, miserly in spirit and pocket, uncaring, cranky and, generally, subject to most human failings. We do not have a right to expect perfection. But because of the nature of the profession, we do have a right to expect every doctor to be an ethical, moral, honest, truthful and compassionate person.

Doctors may be male, female, gay or lesbian, black, yellow, brown, red or white. While some people have personal preferences about such things, for me the ability to trust a doctor does not depend on skin tone or sexual orientation. But I do think you the patient are entitled to know, in general, if a doctor's beliefs will be an obstacle to your obtaining the type of care you would choose to receive. You are also entitled to know, in general, what is his or her attitude toward life-prolonging treatments. You cannot reasonably expect any doctor to be able to give specific answers to hypothetical questions. If you are well now, as we presume you are, let the relationship develop for a while before you try to pin him or her down on this issue.

WHAT MAKES A "GOOD DOCTOR"?

Here are the guidelines I use. You can amend them to fit your own priorities, or add more if you choose.

The first things I look for in a doctor, once I examine the certificates authenticating his or her professional qualifications, is a person who will:

- be relaxed with me (after all it is the doctor's role to help you be comfortable in the situation);
- make eye contact with me;
- take a thorough medical and social history asking reasonable (but not overly invasive) questions;
- listen carefully to my answers and either record or remember them accurately (it's not out of line to test this a little with a few well-directed questions of your own);
- demonstrate respect for my intelligence and my time;
- welcome a signed, witnessed and dated Advance Health Care Directive, which I would present and discuss with him or her to begin to determine whether our philosophies of care are compatible;

31

- order only the diagnostic tests that are necessary to evaluate my health status properly;
- prescribe medications only if they are absolutely necessary (and then only after fully discussing their short-term and long-term risks and benefits);
- be accessible for both telephone consultation and office appointments, within realistic limits. If a particular doctor does not make house calls, I need to know what arrangements he or she has made to cover emergencies. Simply suggesting that I can go to a hospital emergency department is inadequate, and except on rare occasions, unacceptable. A reasonable, empathetic doctor would realize that I would not abuse such a service. Except for care as a terminally-ill person dying at home, my requests for a home visit would be unusual indeed. If, however, your choice of doctor includes home visits as part of routine practice, make sure you do not abuse this benefit.

It is up to you to explain to the receptionist when you make the first appointment that, as a potential new patient, you will require extra time. This way neither you nor the doctor will feel rushed or worried that you are delaying someone else's appointment. If such a request cannot be accommodated, I would not consider this person for my physician.

Another element I consider when choosing a doctor is waiting time. When I arrive for an appointment at the scheduled time, do I find that I am still sitting in a waiting-room thirty to forty minutes later along with one or two others who were scheduled for the same time? If so, either the physician's secretary is a poor planner (and do not accept this excuse too readily) or the physician's workload is too heavy (which means you will have limited access to his or her services), or this doctor has little respect for the value of your time ("patient" not "patience" is the correct terminology).

It is your responsibility to find out if a doctor has admitting privileges to one or more hospitals, which institutions they are and what is the limit of the doctor's involvement if you are admitted to hospital. If your family doctor does not have such privileges, you need to find out who is going to be responsible for your hospital care and what, if any, input you will have into this decision.

If your "in-hospital" care is turned over to a specialist, will your family doctor visit and maintain some guardianship and influence over your care? If the hospital to which your family doctor is affiliated is a teaching institution, what are the expectations and regulations regarding examinations, diagnosis, treatment, and ongoing evaluation and care of patients? Is your family doctor informed thoroughly and quickly, or does he or she receive only cursory reports weeks after treatment is completed?

When you leave hospital, who assumes responsibility for your ongoing care? Are you once again returned to your family doctor for all health care to be maintained in the style to which you have become accustomed? Or are you now to be treated like a collection of body parts—with your heart as the responsibility of the cardiologist, your lungs of the respiratory specialist or internist, your diabetes of the medical internist or endocrinologist, and so on.

Overall you must consider and decide what style and conditions of health care you are most comfortable with—subject, of course, to the peculiarities of a particular region and the regulations of the provincial health-care system. If you prefer to be referred to a myriad of specialists, if it makes you feel more secure to be seen and cared for by various experts, by all means follow this route. If, on the other hand, you wish to have one family doctor organize and monitor your total health regime, make sure your expectations are compatible with your family practitioner's philosophy of care.

Specialists are, of course, a vital component of thorough health care. If you need surgery, naturally you will seek a reputable surgeon. Many cancers, too, require the expertise of an oncologist. However, you are requesting the advice of the oncologist, including full disclosure of all possible risks and benefits. The responsibility for choosing among the various options offered is yours and yours alone. You may be wise, however, to discuss these options with your family doctor before making a final decision. Doing so provides you both with an opportunity to keep up to date and, more importantly, gives you a chance to test your thinking out loud and clarify it for yourself.

As patient/partner in your health care you cannot afford to adopt a passive attitude or to hand over responsibility for these decisions to anyone else. You may wish to seek assistance in making your choices, and probably should do so. But you must always keep in mind that it is you who will reap the benefits or bear the consequences of whatever treatment options you choose.

A good equation to keep in mind is that the benefits must always outweigh or exceed the risks. IT IS YOUR LIFE!

GOOD COMMUNICATION IS THE CORNERSTONE OF GOOD CARE

Clear, precise and generous communication is essential to a good patient-doctor relationship. Especially with serious or life-threatening illness, your doctor must be ready to "go that extra mile" in times of crisis, to ensure that you have been told and have heard and understood the diagnosis, the treatment options with all their implications and the prognosis for your recovery. You will probably not be ready to hear and assimilate all of this at one time, but the observant health-care professional will recognize that fact and arrange additional opportunities to repeat the information or give it in a different way, so that you are properly and completely informed.

SOME CAUSES OF COMMUNICATION BREAKDOWN

1. A person may have been feeling unwell for some time before consulting the family physician about the symptoms. By the time a person does decide to see a doctor, she or he may be under great stress and unable to absorb all the relevant information. As

well, there may be an uncomfortably long waiting period between the decision to see a physician and the actual appointment. Waiting time increases dramatically when patients are referred to specialists, who, it seems, have longer and longer waiting lists. Long waits for appointments further increase the patient's anxiety and interfere with the ability to take in what is being said. There are times when it is helpful to take a friend or family member with you to a difficult doctor's appointment. Two impressions are more reliable than one (see Chapter 6).

2. Many doctors are simply very poor communicators. They may think they have explained your diagnosis, choices of treatment and prognosis quite clearly, when in fact they have not done so. Or perhaps they have neglected to translate "medicalese" into everyday language that all patients can understand.

3. The human psyche has many defences against pain—particularly psychological and spiritual pain. When we fear serious illness, we may block out information that is too traumatic to accept at this particular time. Or we may simply refuse to acknowledge that the devastating words were ever spoken.

Perhaps the doctor has said, "Mrs. Smith, there is a lump in your left breast. It may be a simple cyst, or it may be more serious—possibly a tumour. If it is the former, a cyst, it can be dealt with quickly at minimal risk and discomfort. If, however, after a biopsy it is determined that the lump is a tumour, it could be a benign (harmless) growth or, it could be malignant (cancerous). In the case of a cancerous growth there are a number of treatment options ..." And so the physician proceeds to outline the various options available. However, the shock of this news has stopped you from hearing any words after "it may be more serious—possibly a tumour." At this point your defence mechanism kicked in and "saved" you from hearing what you were unprepared to accept at that time. This is a common reaction to bad news we are not yet ready to assimilate.

4. We do not all accept difficult news at the same rate, nor does everyone hear the message in precisely the same way. Each of us brings to the situation our own experiences, which colour the information we receive. If, for instance, your mother suffered and endured a painful death from breast cancer, you are going to hear your *potential* diagnosis quite differently from a friend who has not had your experience. It is quite possible that two people will hear exactly the same words from a physician, but will interpret the message in vastly different ways.

A lawyer friend often tells me that the decision a particular judge renders in a courtroom on any given day depends entirely on the state of his digestion. While this may be a slight exaggeration, it nonetheless highlights the conundrums of human frailty. We are all susceptible to outside factors that may sway our behaviour or affect the way we function on any given day, including the way we hear and communicate messages.

The Case of Susan and Andrew

Openness is something many doctors find difficult. Especially when the truth is that there is no further treatment they can offer you.

Hesitatingly, with halting pauses, a young man's voice said, "I don't know why I have been told to call you, but this is our story." And so he talked for some time one fall afternoon, his voice sometimes breaking with emotion. I listened carefully and as calmly as I could while he eloquently described their plight—his and his wife, Susan's.

Susan was thirty-two years old with ovarian cancer. She had first been diagnosed three years earlier, had undergone surgery and appeared to be symptom-free for almost a year. She had gone back to her career and volunteer work, and was trying to adjust to the idea that she and Andrew would never be able to have the children both so wanted.

The story of Andrew and Susan began years earlier. They had been a love match from their first date back in high school. Both had ambitions to be educators. Both came from similar backgrounds—professional parents, strong Protestant beliefs, an ethic of community service and everyday neighbourliness. They had been raised in the London area, growing up to love the simple things in life—skiing and skating in the winter, hiking and canoeing in the summer. The two families, although only casually acquainted before Susan and Andrew became "an item", became close after the marriage and frequently did things together in the evenings or on weekends. Everyone eagerly anticipated the time when these two would have a family of their own to add to the pleasure and closeness.

Susan's surgery had put an end to this last dream, but they accepted with faith and love that it must be part of God's greater plan and were grateful that it was not worse.

Quite early one morning, long before her usual waking hour, Susan was jolted awake by a sharp pain. She lay still but it came again. When Andrew wakened and was shaving to get ready for school (he had recently been promoted to assistant principal), Susan shyly told him about the pain. "That's that," said Andrew. "I will call the school to tell them I'll be late today and we'll get you over to see Dr. Brown immediately. It is probably nothing, something you ate, perhaps, but we are not taking any chances." Susan hesitated briefly, but she too was scared, and after a quick breakfast and a call to make sure Dr. Brown could fit them into his schedule, they were off to the emergency department of the local hospital to meet him.

Three years passed before Andrew's call to me. They were three years filled with chemotherapy, radium treatments, special diets and therapies galore. Susan had been faithful to every regime prescribed for her. She participated in the regional support group for persons with cancer. Being Susan, she had written about her experiences, so that others might share her hope and positive thinking about beating this disease, as she was sure she would. The oncologist (cancer specialist) had been absolutely positive that soon Susan would be well and back doing the special-education teaching she so loved. Perhaps she and Andrew could even adopt a child or two to receive all that love they had stored up.

As Andrew explained the situation I could not keep back tears. The story was one I had heard hundreds of times, yet it never ceased to anger and frustrate me. In Susan's case, she had gone to the hospital this afternoon for a routine check-up. Andrew said she looked the worst he had ever seen her. Either she was totally knocked out with morphine or she was in great agony. He would carry her downstairs whenever she felt strong enough, but mostly she lay in bed, listening to the tapes she loved and trying to stay alert enough to visit with family and friends. Her brothers had arrived last night from California, but she hadn't been able to do without the morphine long enough to talk with them for more than a few minutes. When she woke, Susan was devastated to think how far they had come, leaving busy jobs and their own families, when she could not stay awake long enough to visit.

It was this crisis that made Andrew ask the doctor whether her appointment, scheduled for the next week, could be moved forward. The doctor agreed and told them to come immediately. He examined Susan and then suggested to them that perhaps another short course of chemotherapy would be helpful to reduce the pain. Then he asked them to wait a minute and left the room. A few minutes later, as Andrew later told me, the doctor's nurse came into the room, handed Andrew a piece of paper and said, "Call this number. There is the name to ask for. Dr. Brown thinks this lady will be able to help you."

Written on the paper was: "Marilynne Seguin, Dying With Dignity." (And the office phone number.)

What was this all about? No one had ever talked to either of them about dying or even mentioned the word. Why did the doctor not come back or explain the message to them himself? Why did the nurse rush out and not offer to make an appointment for the chemotherapy if that was what Dr. Brown thought would help Susan's pain?

Andrew put Susan in the wheelchair and they went to the hospital waiting-room. Both were stunned. They talked briefly, and then Susan said, "Andrew, call the number please. I think we need to do this."

At first, after Andrew explained the situation to me, he offered to come to Toronto the next day, to bring Susan and have a meeting. I had given him my home number in case of an emergency—something I rarely do. My phone rang at 7:30 in the morning, just as I was about to leave for the office. It was Andrew.

"Susan is much too sick today to make the trip. I could come alone to Toronto. Her parents and brothers are here to stay with her and the home-care nurse is due at ten o'clock, so she would not be alone, but we would really be grateful if you could come to see Susan. Is there a chance?"

I thought about the magazine interview scheduled for early in the afternoon, the meetings booked and all the other plans already in place for the day. "How would it be, Andrew, if I came later this afternoon? I will ask one of the volunteers to drive me, and I can probably be there about six o'clock. It's about a two-hour drive and I could leave here about four. Would that be soon enough?" "Oh yes," he replied, "whenever you can make it will be just fine. Susan will be so pleased." He gave me the directions to their home and rang off to tell Susan.

Sheila, one of the many volunteers who put in so many hours for the society, did not hesitate when I called and explained the situation. "Of course," she said. "I can leave my office about three-thirty and that would get me to the DWD office about four. Do you need to pack any clothes? How will you get back to Toronto?" "Let's wait and see how it goes, Sheila," I replied. "Maybe this will just be a short first visit. After all, the doctor is suggesting more chemotherapy, so it may be some time yet before this lady needs extensive help. I may be able to drive back tonight with you. Or I can always catch a train later on. We'll play it as it comes."

This was not unusual. Sometimes only a short meeting is required to resolve a problem; other times it takes days or weeks of meetings and negotiations to find a solution for some clients.

Andrew was at the door to meet me. He introduced me to his parents and Susan's, and then we went directly upstairs to their bedroom.

This was a scene I had encountered so many times over the years. Susan's bed had been placed by the window so she could see outside, day and night. It is as though those persons losing their grasp on life hunger for nature—a touch of sunshine, a glimpse of birds flying. Flowers and trees, the stars, the moon in all its wondrous phases, even the rain and lightning refresh us and remind us of the power and beauty surrounding us like a warm cloak. Andrew had placed a cot close to the bed so he could hold Susan's hand as she slept, reassuring both of them through their touch that life and love endured. Daisies and cornflowers decorated the bedside table amidst the bottles of medicine, the water pitcher and the spouted cup that made it easier for Susan to drink without lifting her head.

At this moment, however, all my attention was on Susan's large, green eyes, smiling out at me somewhat worriedly from sunken sockets. Her face bore the marks of her great suffering. She held out her hand and smiled with lips so pale and parched one wondered how she was still alive at all. I approached the bed and quietly asked her if I could hug her ever so gently, for I knew how painfully sensitive her tissues and bones would be. "Oh yes," she answered, "please do. People are afraid to touch me, it seems, and I miss it so."

Andrew had already pulled a chair close for me. He moved to the other side of the bed and with exquisite tenderness lay down behind Susan, cradling her in his arms.

Their first question was, "What is Dying With Dignity and why did the doctor give your name and number to us?" We talked for some time about these matters, and then I explained to them that I would like to examine Susan before we continued our discussion. There was no hesitation on their part as I gently lifted the bedclothes, looked at and tenderly felt Susan's stomach, arms and legs, smelled her breath and listened to her chest and bowel sounds. All the while their eyes were on mine, watchful for any reaction I might show. Then I asked Susan a great number of questions that would give me further insight into her physical and emotional state.

John, Susan's dad, called us and asked if he could bring a tray of tea and cookies to the room. On the tray were also a sandwich and a bowl of soup, for he suspected my friend and I had driven right through without stopping for dinner. He reassured me that they were "taking care of Sheila downstairs", and in fact, she was "taking his wife for a walk at the moment".

Susan and Andrew and I spent a long time together. When she grew too tired and the pain was obviously intruding on her ability to concentrate, Andrew gave her an injection and we left her to rest for a while. Andrew and I strolled around the neighbourhood and he expressed to me the many fears that plagued him. He suspected she was going to ask me to help her to die. Or ask him for the same thing. He did not know if he could deal with this. Would he go to jail if he did help her? Did they have enough and the right kind of drugs to let her die peacefully? Both his parents were lawyers. Could they also get into trouble? Susan's parents and his were very religious. They had already asked him if I was coming to visit to help Susan end her life. What should he tell them? On and on he expressed questions and fears that shook him to the core. Some questions I answered, but many I told him I would discuss only when both he and Susan were present. She was my primary concern, and she had a right to hear my answers first, or at least at the same time as he did. There were to be no misunderstandings, no preconceived conclusions. No decisions of any kind were to be made without Susan's involvement.

He understood this and was patient, but finally the pent-up fear, anxiety, frustration and anger were just too much for him. As we sat on the stairs of the porch Andrew cried. For a long time it seemed as if the tears would never stop—as though he had struggled to be brave for so long but couldn't find the resources to get through this time. His mom and dad came out finally and put their arms around us both, whispering in Andrew's ear that Susan was awake and asking for us.

We went into the house, refreshed ourselves and then returned to Susan's room. She read in our faces the agony of this last hour and said quite calmly, "It is time for the truth. Will you tell us the truth, Marilynne?"

And so I did. I discussed with them both the status of the cancer and explained to them how I knew these things—the signs and symptoms that revealed her condition. I told them that I would speak in plain, simple straightforward language, as I had from the start. This was not the time for euphemisms or misunderstandings. Should she try more chemotherapy? No. In response to her direct question, should she take her own life? I paused and let the words hang in the air briefly to make sure we all absorbed the implications. This question was much harder to answer. Instead I said I needed to ask them some questions first and then, I promised, I would give a truthful, no-nonsense answer.

My first question was, "Susan, do you know you are dying?" More followed. When do you think you will die? How will you die? Do you want to know how the end will come for you? Have you taken care of all the "business" you want to do? Have you visited and shared your life with your family and friends? Is there anything left undone that is giving you feelings of anxiety? Do you believe that Andrew will be able to manage without you—that he will recover from his grief and have the help he needs to heal again? And then the final question, "Are you ready to die?"

She and Andrew answered each of my questions carefully, often gazing at each other as though to test the truth of their impressions and answers.

After a long pause I held Susan close in my arms and told her I believed she was ready to die—that the time was fitting. "If I believed, Susan, that the end was a long time away, a month or more, you have enough drugs to end your life by your own hand at any time. But, dear Susan, how would you feel if I said you cannot possibly live for another two weeks?" She asked, rather plaintively, "Will it be that long? I don't know if either Andrew or I can manage that long." "Susan," I asked, "what would you say if I told you I honestly believe you will die within days?"

Her eyes lit up and she smiled quietly, hugged me tightly and replied, "I would bless you and pray for you, my angel. You could give me no greater gift than this truth. We can both manage that, and Andrew will not need to live at risk for helping me die early." And with that she and Andrew wept—not with sorrow but with joy.

We talked a while longer, I kissed her and offered to stay until the end. "No, Marilynne. Others need your care and your honesty. Andrew and I will be all right now. We desperately needed to know the full truth. If we need you to be here, we know you will come, but I think we will be all right now."

I visited a while longer with the family downstairs. Many tears were shed, but these were tears of genuine, healthy sadness, not the tears of anger and frustration that come with uncertainty and lies. "Why had the oncologist offered her the false hope of improvement with more chemotherapy?" her mother kept asking in bewilderment. "Why did he not ever use the words of death and dying with Susan or Andrew? Surely he could see she had wasted away to nothing, her swollen belly, her toothpick-thin arms and legs, and her pain. Why? Why?" she asked, again and again. I tried to explain, but I knew in my heart, as did this loving, intelligent family, that there really was no explanation and no real excuse for the doctor's behaviour.

Just after midnight Sheila and I started back to Toronto. When I arrived home there was a message on my answering machine. "Marilynne, Susan fell into a sound sleep almost before you left the room. I have not seen her so peaceful since this whole ordeal started three years ago. Thank you, and I will call tomorrow."

The next day Susan woke bright and early and asked for the whole family, a few old friends, her family doctor and her favourite nurse to gather just as soon as possible. No, she did not need the priest. She was ready to face her God. Everyone came and one or two at a time visited with Susan to say goodbye. By two o'clock, Andrew told me later, she was exhausted but glowing with happiness. Very soon after she just fell asleep with Andrew's arms around her and her favourite music playing on the tape recorder.

Andrew phoned me to say she had not wakened and had died peacefully at eleven-thirty that evening. He was amazed that she had not had any pain at all since my visit and had died with such quiet dignity and peace.

We have kept in touch, Andrew and I. He often goes out to visit others who are nearing the end of life and calls me for help in sorting out problems that arise that need my expertise. He has returned to teaching and is moving on with his life.

THE DIAGNOSIS

Let's start with the basics.

Doctors are (or should be) taught in medical school first to differentiate the various signs and symptoms a person exhibits and expresses, beginning with the most simple and obvious and working toward the more complex. For example, if a patient has a cold, the doctor should not initially prescribe tests for possible lung cancer. He or she must first be sure the problem is not just a simple upper-respiratory infection. Other tests may follow, once again moving from the simple to the more complex. This method has the advantage of beginning with the least expensive tests—a benefit all taxpayers will appreciate. Another advantage, and a much more important one for the patient/consumer, is that the simplest tests are also the least invasive and therefore involve far less risk to you, the patient.

Both patients and the health-care providers have a role and a responsibility in this aspect of care. It is up to each individual in Canada to make reasonable demands on and reasonable use of health-care resources. Patients who insist on "high-tech" investigations that are not truly necessary place a financial burden on the system and reduce access to such services for others. Physicians can also place a strain on the system by ordering the most sophisticated diagnostic tests as part of a "defensive medicine" strategy. While perhaps psychologically reinforcing to the patient and legally comforting to the doctor, such interventions can place the patient at higher risk and increase the economic burden on all health-care consumers.

Suppose, for example, that you go to your doctor complaining of an occasional pain in your chest. The source of your discomfort could be a gas pain, a warning sign of heart disease, or a variety of other ailments. The first thing the doctor should do is to take a complete history not only of the pattern of the chest pain, but also of your eating and exercise habits, work and family-related stresses and so on. Then you should expect a physical, hands-on examination. And I do mean "hands-on". The most effective tool medicine has ever developed is the physician who knows how to perform a good physical examination using all his skills of vision, hearing, smell, touch, instinct and experience to detect signs of malfunction or disease. Only when these means are exhausted should the practitioner proceed to the laboratory tests and the "bells and whistles" approach to diagnosis.

Particularly in the case of severe, life-threatening illness, many physicians find it difficult to speak plainly when giving a patient the diagnosis. If you do not understand what your diagnosis is, ask the doctor to write it out on a piece of paper for you and to explain in full what it means in terms of lifestyle changes or modifications, treatment options and prognosis.

There are times when the message and the diagnosis combine to create a conundrum for both the giver and receiver of news—especially bad news. A friend, Arthur W. Frank, has survived two life-threatening illnesses in his young life—a heart attack and cancer. In his book *At the Will of the Body*, Arthur describes how the variables of circumstance and impression can affect how we receive news.

Another friend remembered the indignation she felt when the physician told her that "cancer was coursing through her body." His comment was devastating to her, but at times I would have found it validating. Whatever was happening in her body, what she was feeling was a tiny lump in her breast. My body was telling me that something awful was coursing through it—not a bad description. When I was hardly able to walk, but my family doctor was telling me simply to quit running and see a urologist in a couple of months, it was reassuring to have other physicians acknowledge that the problems were as real as I felt they were.

When I was finally told how sick I was, the essential difference between the diagnoses ... was in the support each gave me.

The two diagnoses were about the same, but the sports medicine physician involved himself in what he was telling me, while the other physician pronounced his diagnosis like a verdict. Differences proliferate: the same message can have different meanings for different ill persons, and the same content can become two different messages, depending on how it is delivered.*

THE SPECIALIST

The second and third quarters of this century have been a particularly exciting but also in some ways a devastating time in medicine. There are new drugs, new surgical procedures, new treatment modalities of all kinds popping up every day—some of them of enormous benefit to society. Whole new specialties in medicine have appeared. Many doctors still treat the whole person, but many others have became "experts" in caring for (and sometimes curing) only one part of the human being. Specialties have proliferated to what sometimes seems a ludicrous extent. The old joke about the doctor who could treat only the right large toe and not the left is too close to reality for comfort. Health care in the 1990s has become a conglomeration of parts specialists and subspecialists that can at times boggle the mind and also delay proper attention to ailments while the "right" person for a referral is selected from among a multiplicity of specialists.

Only recently when I suggested to a friend that she perhaps needed to be seen by a general internist (a specialist responsible for all internal medical systems, including heart, lungs, gastrointestinal organs, kidneys and blood) I was told that there are now very few such specialists in some parts of the country. This specialty was going the way of the dodo bird as "more specialized" doctors took over.

---

*Arthur W. Frank, *At the Will of the Body: Reflections on Illness* (Boston: Houghton Mifflin, 1991), pp. 44-45.

Apart from the family doctor, then, very few doctors consider the patient as a whole. Nor do many specialists consider it their responsibility to think about the social, psychological and spiritual aspects of the patient who has come to them for diagnosis and treatment. Paradoxically, it seems, the more "advanced" medical knowledge becomes, the greater the risk of incomplete care.

I am not anti-specialist. Far from it, for we know that complex human beings do require attention at times from more than one point of view. But it is important to remember that you and your family doctor need to work together to make sure that all of the various specialists report to one primary-care physician who has agreed to assume responsibility for coordinating all of your needs.

SECOND OPINIONS

Some patients make a practice of flitting from one doctor to another. These patients are usually accused of "doctor shopping". Sometimes there is a very valid and sensible reason to seek another opinion about your problems. It may be that you have not been referred to the correct type of specialist in the first place. For instance, with a back pain, it may not always be clear whether the patient should be seen by a bone specialist or a nerve specialist or a good chiropractor or a sports medicine specialist. Or, a person who has been diagnosed with a particularly serious or life-threatening illness for which radical treatment is proposed may wish to have the diagnosis confirmed by another specialist before agreeing to invasive or particularly drastic measures.

True "doctor shopping" is a different matter. It occurs when a person is seeking something other than what medicine can, or should, legitimately provide. The patient may want drug prescriptions in doses that are harmful, or may be convinced that a specific diagnosis should be made. The former may harm the patient, while the latter is expensive, a drain on the health-care system and possibly unrealistic and dangerous.

That said, if you are convinced that you have been under-treated or mistreated or that for some reason you and your doctor are not compatible, do not lose any time in looking for another physician. And if you have reason to believe you are being treated badly by any health-care professional, you should report the conduct immediately, in writing, to the appropriate college or disciplinary body.

It is a good idea to inform a doctor if you decide to transfer to another physician. You can do this with a polite phone call or in a letter. The reason for the change may be a simple matter of convenience. Perhaps you have moved to a different city or a distant part of town. Perhaps your employment schedule has changed and you need a doctor who sees patients at other hours. Or it may be that you are truly dissatisfied with his or her service. Conveying that message may help another person to receive better care.

THE INCOMPATIBLE PHILOSOPHY

Unfortunately there will always be some health-care workers whose philosophy or style of care is wrong for you. There may be an innocent reason for the incompatibility; or it may be caused by genuine incompetence or bad behaviour. Regardless of the cause, take immediate action.

The Case of Mary

"There is an urgent call for you from an MLA [member of the Legislative Assembly] in British Columbia," my assistant said. I was in the middle of a counselling session, and it was rare for her to interrupt me at such a time, so I knew this was a call I had to take immediately.

"Hello, Miss Seguin. My name is Mr. W. and I am the MLA for a district in British Columbia. I have a constituent's family in my office. If it's all right with you I will put us on the

49

speaker phone so we can all hear each other and they can confirm what I am telling you and participate in this conversation. The family present are Grace, sister of Mary, the person we will be discussing, and Paul and Rita, Mary's son and daughter. These people are very upset, and I believe we need your assistance with this problem. The story is this.

"Grace's sister, Mary, aged seventy-five, was admitted to the emergency ward of a small local hospital one week ago. The doctor on duty diagnosed that she had suffered a severe stroke and told the family she was unlikely to survive more than a day or two. He said the kindest thing they could do would be to 'let her go' without any medical intervention. At the time, they relied on his advice and prepared for the worst. The doctor admitted Mary to an acute care department of the hospital. No other treatment has been initiated or specified with the exception of a written order that she was to be given nothing to eat or drink.

"According to the family, Mary has some weakness in her left side and muscle distortion in her face. She was unconscious for a brief while and aphasic [unable to speak] for a couple of days. She is now talking, with difficulty, but she can be understood. In fact, I have just spoken with her myself on the telephone, with a nurse assisting her while the family are here. She tells me she is very thirsty and cannot understand why no one will give her some water. She is an intelligent woman and knows from experience with friends who have had strokes that it is important to get started on therapy very soon. She is asking to be sent home where she feels she will receive better care. She is also asking why the doctor refuses to answer her questions and has visited her only once since her hospitalization."

At this point in the conversation Grace and Rita both started to talk at once. They were obviously very agitated but calmed down quickly and told me the following story. "Mary has always been a healthy, energetic person, very much in control of her life. She is having some difficulty with speech at the moment, but certainly we, the nurses, and the doctor, too, if he tried, can understand her. She is pleading with us to let her have something to eat and drink. The nurses are very upset and have gone to the hospital administrator, but were informed their job was to follow the doctor's orders. Shortly thereafter a sign was taped to the wall over Mary's bed stating 'This patient is not to be given food or fluids. By order of the attending physician.'"

At this point Paul spoke up. "Marilynne, we do not know you but have been told you will help us to fight for our mother. She wants to live and deserves better treatment than this. We understand the nurses' dilemma, but surely something can be done. Mother is slowly starving to death and grows noticeably weaker every day. Please help us. What can we do?"

I requested the doctor's name and phone number, the hospital name and phone number, the name of the administrator, the head nurse's name and a few other relevant facts. We made arrangements to be in touch in two hours through another conference call. I further promised the family that if matters could not be sorted out to our satisfaction by telephone, I would fly out that day.

My first call was to Mary, who had been told to expect my call. She was not only able to pick up the telephone, she was able to speak fairly clearly with only a moderate slur in her speech. We talked only briefly, for she was very weak and the dryness of her mouth made it onerous for her to talk. I asked her if she wished me to act on her behalf, and she assured me most enthusiastically that she did. Mary expressed concern over the pressure her family was under and asked also that I try to help them through this. It was clear this was a woman after my own heart—concerned about others, though in the most dire straits herself.

A call to the head nurse verified the condition of Mary

and the orders the nursing staff had received. The situation was precisely as the family and MLA had described. I advised her to give Mary small sips of water immediately, for after all, in her professional judgement, this was the appropriate nursing action. As the nursing code of ethics stipulates, a nurse will always act in the patient's best interest, even if this means going against a physician's orders. A nurse's primary obligation is always to the patient. I reinforced that Dr. B would be contacted immediately, as would the hospital administrator, and that someone would get back to her as soon as possible. Tears of relief could be heard in the nurse's voice as I gave her the numbers where she could reach me in case she was dissatisfied with the results or she needed me again on a similar matter.

Upon calling Dr. B's number I was told by his receptionist that he wanted to know the reason for my call before he would speak with me. I explained who I represented and the purpose of my call. A few moments later she came back on the line to tell me the doctor had refused to speak with me, he was too busy and would treat his patients as he saw fit, "without the interference of either family members or their advocates". The receptionist was embarrassed and apologized but said there was no more she could do.

Next I phoned the hospital administrator. We had a pleasant if largely unsatisfactory conversation. He seemed to be very intimidated by the physician in question and then proceeded to explain to me how hard it was "to get doctors to work in regions outside of the big city hospitals". "After all," he explained patiently, "Dr. B is a well-qualified practitioner, admits many patients here and has examined this patient and made his diagnosis. Who am I to interfere?"

As politely, calmly and quietly as my growing frustration would allow, I explained to him that this patient in his hospital would survive only if he did interfere. Perhaps he should be more concerned about the patients entrusted to him and the hospital's reputation if this problem was not resolved immediately. Such a situation would surely merit further investigation. The implied threat seemed to hit the mark, for he immediately offered his full cooperation.

I asked for a conference call between himself, Dr. B and myself within the hour. He promised to try to make such arrangements and to call me back immediately.

Try he did, but Dr. B would have no part of it. The administrator did promise to support the nurses and to assist in finding another physician to take over Mary's care if she so directed.

To cut to the end of this story, Mary discharged Dr. B immediately, selected another physician, and with proper care was released home soon thereafter. In fact, about ten days later she telephoned me at my home one evening, chipper and ecstatic. She was back in her own home, getting around with the help of a walker, which she confided she would be able to throw away very soon, and had started to gain back some of the weight she had lost. The next day she would go to church and pray for "all the good people who saved her life".

This all happened three years ago. Mary, Grace, Paul and Rita are all strong supporters of DWD. And every once in a while I receive a note from Mary telling me which flowers are blooming in her garden or what birds have visited recently.

I do not know if the doctor in question was overworked, stubborn, just unable to deal with this situation or simply incompetent. That is for the disciplinary authorities to decide. Not all physicians are created equal. Whatever else you do, if you for any reason mistrust the care you or your family are receiving, seek out an advocate—another doctor or nurse or whomever it takes to remedy the problem.

CHAPTER THREE

Suffering

What Is It, and What Can I Do About It?

D r. Marcel Boisvert, one of the most sensitive, caring physicians I have ever met, wrote that pain "is what the patient says hurts."* This is the accurate, simple truth.

There are so many kinds of suffering (I prefer the all-encompassing word "suffering" rather than "pain") that it is impossible to catalogue them all. Indeed, to try to envisage such a list could be hazardous to your sanity. I will touch on only a few of the many examples I know of.

The Case of Matthew

Matthew is dying of respiratory and cardiac failure. Although he is only fifty-nine years old—about the age when many of us are realizing our greatest success in work and society—his dying has seemed slow and agonizing. Every day he feels himself suffocating just a little more. Every time he tries to walk to the bathroom or lean over to put on a slipper,

---

*Marcel Boisvert, "All Things Considered ... Then What?" *Journal of Palliative Care* 4, nos. 1, 2 (1988), p. 115.

he grows short of breath and becomes dizzy. Sometimes small seizures strike, and when he regains awareness seconds or minutes later he is confused and wonders what has happened. He only knows that for some unknown reason he feels lost, and damaged just a little more. Tonight or tomorrow his kidneys will stop working, and someone, perhaps the doctor, perhaps his loving wife, will suggest that he accept dialysis. But Matthew and his doctor have talked about it, and their decision is not to start any further medical intervention, but to let nature take its course.

A few weeks after I first saw Matthew, I visited him again. He told me that through his family physician he had found it easy to stockpile enough drugs to end his life. He told me this, as many others have done, watching and waiting to see my reaction. I asked him if there was some particular reason he was considering this option now? We discussed the details of his plan—who, if anyone, might be hurt by his decision—and we both came to the conclusion that this choice was fitting for Matthew. He realized that his wife would be saddened by his death, but he also knew she would accept that he needed peace from the daily struggle for life. I did not judge or advise or reveal his decision to anyone. I knew that Matthew had done his research well and that he would not fail to achieve his goal. My only regret, aside from the fact that he was determined to "do it alone", was that Matthew's death would be written up as "death by natural causes", for we do not have the courage—or audacity (depending on your point of view)—to state the truth in official records that death was due to physician-assisted suicide. While I knew full well that the physician was a willing partner in Matthew's decision and had, with full knowledge, supplied him with the drugs he needed, I also knew that Matthew's death would not be allowed to embarrass anyone. What games we all play under the present system! But Matthew found a reasonable solution to his suffering.

There are other sufferings that do not lend themselves to such solutions. Can you imagine an odour so strong that not even the most sophisticated treatment—or, for that matter, the most tried-and-true home remedy—can disguise it? During my days in nursing many nuns came into the hospital in such an advanced stage of breast cancer that the bones of their ribs and sternum protruded through the wounds. The smell of rotting flesh was almost overwhelming. Then there was the biker who had old suppurating wounds from partially decomposed leg injuries. The smell of putrefaction pervaded the entire ward. The sisters usually offered their pain up to God, making Him a gift of the suffering with which they had been "blessed". More often than not the biker would call on the devil, cursing us all in his agony.

The average person takes some suffering for granted as part of the normal course of living. But what if those everyday ailments are a thousand times worse than usual?—such as constant diarrhea that lasts for weeks or even months; constipation so severe it brings more pain than the disease that is causing it (or forces patients to reduce their pain-killing codeine or other analgesic because it is causing the constipation); a total lack of energy that goes far beyond normal lethargy; headaches that never go away; constant coughing, or, sometimes worse, hiccoughs that persist for weeks; vomiting; bloating; shortness of breath; nausea that cannot be remedied by any known drugs. This is just the beginning of a litany of physical sufferings few of us can picture. Can you imagine the feeling of itching inside your body? There is little hope of stopping it, but many people, particularly those in the final stages of kidney failure, experience this suffering.

There are more subtle changes, too, such as hoarseness, diminishing vision or hearing, neuropathy (a tingling in the hands and feet that grows progressively worse), anorexia (an inability to eat), or conversely, constant hunger frequently provoked by some life-prolonging medications.

The more visible and public the evidence of disease and treatment becomes, the more it adds to the sufferers' burden. A very dear friend dying of a rare blood disease used to joke that he was losing all his hair, but his weight was increasing proportionately. He gained sixty pounds in the last weeks of life. Can you imagine what that was like for him? He would smile weakly and say to me, "I know the skin is elastic, but this is ridiculous."

The Case of John

Picture another person, John, dying of chronic respiratory failure, in a busy intensive care unit of a hospital. We can understand the constant pressure of tightness in his chest, perhaps even the shortness of breath that tortures him and the frequent episodes when he gasps for air, never quite sure the air will be there this time. But can you also imagine the burning he feels in his lungs when it takes a little longer for the bronchi to fill with oxygen; the irritation of the constant sounds of his own life-prolonging equipment running twenty-four hours a day; the gagging feeling when the nurse must suction the secretions that have built up in his throat—and having nothing to say about whether or not this procedure is performed, because nurses must act quickly and there is not always "time" to ask his permission before doing so; the "heaviness" that builds up in his body as fluids accumulate faster than the kidneys can excrete them; the poking and prodding, sometimes many times a day, for samples of blood to evaluate his oxygen level or other aspects of his physiological status.

INSTITUTIONAL SETTINGS

For someone in hospital, a simple irritant such as lights being turned on and off just when you have finally dozed off to sleep is just one more instance of your lack of control over even the simplest functions. And then there are the disturbances caused by the institution's

"routines". There is the changing of shifts (and the hour or two before and after, when your nurse wakens you to check your intake
and output of body fluids, clattering about to empty this bag or
change that bottle); the routine check of "vital signs" that must be
performed according to the prescribed timing of each physician;
the feeding ritual—usually one of the easiest ways for patients in
hospital to orient themselves in time (whether you are capable of
eating or not there is still the sound of trays and the smell of food
that pervades the ward); the doctor's visit; the head nurse's rounds;
the bathing routine; the cleaning staff's time to wash the floors,
clean the bathrooms and empty the trash. Some institutions still
have a public-address system that summons "Dr. Smith to four
North" or announces "Code Blue on two South". When you are in
hospital, these and dozens of other events become a part of your
day, whether you are in a crisis or just having an average day. And
YOU HAVE NO CONTROL OVER ANY OF THESE EVENTS!

IF YOU'RE GOING TO BE SICK, MAKE SURE THE DISEASE IS INTERESTING

Particularly in teaching hospitals, you will receive more attentive
care if your stay is very short, or if you are sick enough to be an "interesting case". If you are too interesting, however, you may be sub-
jected to innumerable examinations and history-taking by curious
student doctors and nurses and to diagnostic tests of great variety
and number and possible risk to your health.

A bit of advice I offer is that you should do your best to remain
cheerful and cooperative. As one who has been there, I know the result of letting the staff see that your disease is "getting you down". If
such an "attitude" is seen to persist, health-care personnel may attempt to make you more tractable either with tranquillizers or with
behaviour-modification techniques, such as refusing to respond to a
call for help or responding more slowly than usual. The so-called

problem patient has more recently been labelled the uncooperative or non-compliant patient. Such labelling can mean isolation or even abandonment by hospital staff. It is not fair or right, but it happens.

HOME SETTINGS

For the sufferer who remains at home, irritants and drawbacks also exist, though of a different kind. Each person must have the ability and opportunity to choose what is best for him or herself. Sometimes it is like being asked to choose between two versions of hell. Home care can offer more privacy, but some may experience this as insecurity or loneliness. For those who choose to die at home, however, privacy is usually seen as a blessing.

With home care, there may be a variety of worries that do not arise in hospital. Who will be available to provide the necessary care? The patient may need everything from pain management to meal preparation, the fetching of a cool drink of water or a warm cup of tea to soothe during a restless night, a change of linen, or a sensitive, caring person to help when the patient is incontinent of urine and faeces. At home or in the hospital, everyone at some time needs a person to listen to that small voice of fear about how the future will unfold; or to allow the sufferer to whine and complain about the injustice of it all—even if only for three minutes—without showing impatience or, worse still, forbearance.

"How will I get all my financial affairs in order?" "Who can go to the bank for me this week?" "Are the bills being taken care of?"

A mother must worry about feeding her family, about sharing her good moments with them and, when necessary, hiding her fears, pain and loneliness from them. Or perhaps she may let them glimpse what she is feeling, so they can better understand her death after it has occurred.

Psychological sufferings are no less real because we cannot see them with the naked eye. Try to sit inside the skin for a few moments of people who experience just a few of the following:

nightmares each time they fall asleep, so that soon they do not want to sleep; sleep deprivation for those whose suffering is too great to permit it; exaggerated sexual interest or total lack of sexual interest, either of which may be physically or psychological damaging to one's partner and oneself; ambivalence; confusion; depression; anxiety; intermittent or constant sadness; loss of competence; tension; irritability.

I remember when I was trying to move back into the real world of well people after three and a half years of illness, almost all of it spent in a hospital. My sister was helping me to reorient myself. Each day I would ask her to assign me some small duty. It was our way of increasing my powers of concentration while giving me a goal and a feeling of contributing to the household and being less of a burden to others. It would just be a small thing at first—say, to go across the street to the store for a loaf of bread and a quart of milk. I remember the panic I felt the first time I tried this. I couldn't remember whether the family liked brown or white bread, or if it should be homo or 2 per cent milk. As my anxiety grew, so did my feeling of helplessness and guilt at being so inept. I sat down on a bench nearby and wept in utter frustration. Soon I felt the presence of someone near me. It was a very elderly and kind Chinese gentleman. He seemed to recognize my dilemma and my acute embarrassment. He spoke softly to me and said, "Don't worry, it happens to me too. Just give me your sister's number and I'll give her a call. We'll work it out." After the shopping was done he walked me to my door and gave me a tender pat on the cheek, saying, "Don't worry, little lady. You will be better soon." I realized afterward that, yes, it would get better for me, I would soon be well and vigorous again. But would he?

It is often the loneliness and fear of indignity at the time of dying that are most defeating to one's spirit. How many hundreds of times have I heard, "Please, just be here for me. I am so afraid that I will be alone, or that I will be a drain on my family and friends, that I will ask too much and drive them away. And yet I cannot bear the idea of dying alone. Please, stay with me." How often, too, have

I listened to people who fear someone will *interfere* in their death. "What if some doctor or nurse does not understand that I just want to die peacefully, with gentleness and dignity? What if someone decides at that last moment to beat on my chest to start my heart again, to fill me with heart stimulants and *succeeds*, only to leave me in a coma or a vegetative state? How do I know this won't happen to me? Please don't leave me alone."

We often talk about the fear of pain—physical pain. Fear of pain is a reality that every ill person must deal with—and every health-care provider. Both those at home and those in institutions share a fear of overwhelming physical pain. In most cases, however, there is no justification for allowing a patient to suffer uncontrolled pain.

With appropriate medication pain symptoms can be managed. In most cases, the provision of analgesics, tranquillizers and other drugs can be fine-tuned to allow both lucidity and pain control. Where this is not possible, other options are available, *if, and only if,* the health-care provider in the decision-making position is truly *listening* to the patient and is open to the use of such alternatives. Some are not. Even specialists in palliative care can be most unforgiving and misunderstanding of their patients' needs for pain management. These persons, I believe, should not have chosen to care for the dying and should leave end-of-life care to people who are more flexible and more concerned with the quality of dying.

Is physical pain dealt with and managed adequately in Canada? The answer is, only *some pain* and only in *some health-care situations.* Persons in palliative-care and hospice situations usually receive good pain management. And yet here, too, many patients have told me that they are in pain but feel intimidated into "playing the game", lest they be seen as "uncooperative" or "not trying their best" or "not working with the team". They are afraid they might be labelled non-compliant patients and become candidates for less attentive care.

For example, a patient I worked with in a large palliative-care centre was informed that "until his pain was under control, he could not participate in the music-therapy program." The patient told the nurse on the next shift that he was feeling okay even though the level of suffering was quite severe. He felt that the music therapy was potentially more important than getting more pain medication.

I have also acted as an advocate for patients who are under the care of a palliative-care physician but are being denied sufficient analgesia because, as the doctor has said, "There is a limit beyond which I will not go. We do not know how long this patient may live, and to increase the medication now would elevate their tolerance level. What would I do to meet even greater pain that is bound to develop later in the disease process?"

This is the old narcotic-dependence argument that health-care professionals were indoctrinated with years ago but that only the ignorant and uninformed now still accept. Up-to-date professionals know, through the work done by Kathleen Foley* and others, that there is almost no possibility of physical dependence on narcotics as long as there is real, physical pain to "use up" the drug. I have seen patients on enormous doses of morphine for weeks and months who are neither addicted nor in danger of dying from "overdoses" of the drug.

Another great fallacy is the belief that if too much morphine is given, the patient will die sooner. Any patient who is in chronic pain and has been given morphine to manage that pain on a regular basis will not die from increased morphine. If morphine were combined with another drug, such a death *could* result, but not because of the morphine alone.

Most physicians and nurses are trying to the best of their ability to deal with suffering as they understand it. Social workers, therapists, healers of all kinds and spiritual leaders also work very hard to meet the needs of those who are suffering. But so much of suffering is intangible, unmanageable and personal and cannot be entirely

---

*Kathleen M. Foley and Charles E. Inturrisi, "Opioid Therapy: General Principles, Advances, Controversies, Alternative Routes and Methods of Administration," paper present at Why Do We Care? Conference (New York, N.Y.: Apr. 2-4, 1992), p. 32.

resolved by presently accepted means of alleviating suffering. Despite all the goodwill of a caring community, we *cannot* and may never be able to eliminate each person's unique suffering.

It is essential, if we are to improve our ability to reduce suffering, to try to achieve a better understanding of suffering and pain. In his book *At the Will of the Body*, Prof. Arthur Frank goes far beyond simple autobiography to explore concepts and beliefs about illness and disease. As he defines it, "Illness is the experience of living through the disease."

CHOICES

Choices in preparing for the end of life are as varied as there are people in the world. No two people will face exactly the same circumstances. If six or ten persons have exactly the same diagnosis, all will experience their symptoms uniquely. This is difficult to conceptualize.

How often I have heard, "Aunt Mabel had disease X. She did not have the pain Cousin Mary has. The doctors just are not trying hard enough." Well, perhaps Aunt Mabel had a higher pain threshold than Cousin Mary. Perhaps Aunt Mabel had so many other concerns that she sublimated her pain so she could deal with the other problems. Maybe Cousin Mary's tumour is touching a particularly sensitive spot—pressing on a nerve near a localized site. It could be that Aunt Mabel had a particularly strong spiritual belief that made enduring pain in silence beneficial to her. What if Mary's treatment had also included chemotherapy and this had not been an option for Mabel? Would this change the pattern of pain for each? Mary has few friends to visit, while Aunt Mabel ended her life at home in an atmosphere of hustle and bustle, with neighbours dropping in for tea or to bring fresh treats for the family. Perhaps Cousin Mary's doctor is less empathetic and less caring than Aunt Mabel's doctor. Such differences may cause Mary to seek compassion elsewhere.

The Case of Sadie

Sadie is the centre of a large, noisy family. For seven weeks she has been a patient in a large metropolitan hospital, suffering from terminal cancer. Symptom management has been somewhat successful.

Sadie has made some compromises with herself in deciding the course of treatment she accepts, choosing to tolerate more pain as a trade-off for "quality time" with her grandchildren. Sadie also wanted a little more time to help Jake, her husband, get accustomed to her impending death. Sadie could see the confusion and panic in Jake's face when she was groggy or less than alert from the morphine injections. No, she decided, I'm going to die soon anyway, and I don't want Jake to remember me stupid with drugs. I owe it to both of us to just accept the physical hurting a bit longer. Anyway, I'm a tough old bird—I can take it.

Suddenly it's 6:30 p.m. on Friday night, and Sadie decides she must go home—now. She believes she will die very soon and wants to be at home with her family in familiar surroundings. The primary-care physician, Dr. Jones, has taken a rare holiday and left the city for a long weekend, leaving a new young doctor, Dr. Smith, in charge. This doctor states categorically, "I will not discharge Sadie from the hospital. Obviously Sadie's own physician wanted her in hospital, and I will not discharge this patient without a signed, properly witnessed Advance Health Care Directive or an order from Dr. Jones. No, I don't know where I can reach him before Tuesday."

Dr. Smith is new to the case and new to the hospital. How does she even know if Sadie is capable (although she seems so) of making this decision, or if the request to go home is just the result of a momentary mental aberration? What is the hospital policy in such matters? Further, Dr.

Smith suspects that Sadie is in a lot more pain than she will admit. She should no doubt be started on an intravenous morphine drip. Could the family manage this at home? Of course not—not without more home support, and there is no time to arrange it.

When Dr. Smith tries to discuss this with Sadie, the dear lady smiles quietly and says, "You let me worry about my pain. I have my reasons, and I'm just fine."

Sadie, for her part, had never thought to sign an Advance Health Care Directive. Her family knows what she wants and so does her own doctor. How could she anticipate that Dr. Jones would be away, or that this would be the time she wants to go home? What does she know about home care and social workers' hours and all that stuff?

In the end, Sadie signed herself out of hospital. At home with a noisy brood of adults and children around her is the way to die in Sadie's eyes.

There are dozens of reasons why each person suffers differently. Some can be resolved and some, try as we may, cannot be remedied. I believe, however, that with good, attentive listening, we can meet most of the challenges terminal illness brings.

In very simple terms, one of the best ways to be assured you will die as you choose is to spell those directions out very carefully and precisely for your family, doctor and anyone who might be involved in your care (see Chapter 7).

DOES "LET ME DIE" ALWAYS MEAN "LET ME DIE"?

The first time people say these words out loud is usually just that—the first time they have said them aloud. I have found that these people have almost always been practising them silently for some time. This is especially true for those who have chronic debilitating illnesses or for those who feel that all sense of dignity has been denied them.

Often they will say to me, "Even if I thought there was a chance it might be a little better tomorrow," or "Even if I thought there might be a cure in six months' time," or "Even if I could get out of this bed tomorrow and walk to the bathroom by myself ... I would ask this. I would ask to die."

It is a myth that only those suffering severe intractable pain ask to die—that if we could resolve the problem of pain for every person, no one would ask to die.

It is also a myth that those who have the opportunity to receive palliative care never ask to die. These are MYTHS.

It is true that sometimes a person will say to me they wish to die when they are really expressing something else. There was a dear old man, a friend of long standing, who, when his companion was diagnosed with terminal illness, said to me, "Marilynne, if you really value our friendship, please do me a favour. Please help me to die now. I cannot bear to live any longer."

My answer was not given in an hour or even a week. I told him I would need some time to think about this. Finally, and at first much to his anger, I told him I could not help him. Not because of any fear of the law. Not because we did not have the means to end his life. And not because of any moral pressure. My answer grew out of my knowledge and understanding of him as a human being whom I had been honoured to call "friend" for many years. Our love and respect for each other had given us the right and privilege to share a great deal over the years, and I felt his suffering within my own spirit.

When he asked me to help him to die I knew that what he was really saying to me was, "Please don't let this happen to me. I cannot bear the idea of the loneliness when my dear companion dies and I am left alone. His pain is my pain—I do not think I have the strength to witness this agony. Indignity to him is my pain also. It is all too much. Please help me by sparing me this unbearable suffering. I too have endured enough."

I understood and felt his agony. But also, I believed in our friendship. I trusted that together we could survive the death of our mutual friend and that the benefit of helping him to endure a little longer would outweigh the possible gratification death might bring at that time. By resisting the strong temptation of an easy death for the well companion, we both found the joy of helping another to a peaceful end. The weeks during which our friend was dying were a strange mixture of sadness, renewal, emotional anguish, comfort and exhilarating happiness.

In this particular instance, "let me die" was a plea for help to get through one of the most difficult situations it is possible to imagine. Others might have expressed it differently, but the meaning would be there for those who would listen.

Far from discounting pleas to die, I take them very seriously. Usually by the time someone has found the courage to say the words, they are most devoutly meant.

So, are we trying hard enough? No. Are we listening enough? No. But there are legitimate cases where physician-assisted dying is a fitting response. If we believe that rational, capable, human beings have a right to self-determination, then I believe that right must include a choice for assisted death under carefully regulated circumstances.

Physician-assisted dying must be a legitimate option for what I believe would be the very few persons in Canada who would choose accordingly. To allow less is to impose a sentence of suffering on the individual that is inhumane and hypocritical in a free, democratic society.

I would qualify the above by stating that the practice of physician-assisted dying could only be acceptable under the guidance of a protocol that would include regulations to safeguard the vulnerable and disenfranchised in our society. It would not be acceptable if such persons felt their existence to be so burdensome that euthanasia was their only choice.

CHAPTER FOUR

How to Put Dignity in Dying

W hat do you mean by dignity? How do your spouse or friend, your mother and father perceive dignity? For this is the essence of dying with dignity. You must first establish guidelines defining the circumstances you can accept, and then use these to steer by on your journey to a gentle death.

Most people find it helpful to seek some assistance in establishing, defining or just confirming their values in this regard. There are knowledgeable, informed persons—able and willing counsellors or advocates—available to assist you in making decisions about the end of life. If, however, you choose to work it through alone (if, for example, complete independence is one of your guideposts for dignity), it is still crucial for you to let those around you know how they can help you achieve a dignified dying. Even if you wish to retain all the power and manage your own death, others must understand that this is the decision you have made so that they will respect your wishes. After exploring all of the alternatives, you must decide what criteria best suit your own wishes, values and beliefs.

To say that we prepare for our death with our birth may at first sound contrived. But if we think about it, it begins to make sense. As Dr. Buckman says, "We die as we have lived." The truth of this statement is manifold.

When we are born, there is at least one other human being who is intensely involved in that event—the mother who gives us life. In most instances, this person continues to hold us, touch and stroke our body, stimulate our senses, succour and nourish us, both physically and psychologically. Some mothers and children bond better than others, and some infants are cared for by someone other than their birth parents. Yet, as humans we still are conditioned from the instant of birth to relate, be dependent and learn the trust in others that allows us eventually to achieve independence. Without human nurturing, we do not thrive.

In the normal course of events, at different stages of life different people have the role of the most significant person in our life, but there is almost always at least one other individual with whom we have a helpful, caring relationship—a relationship that teaches us that we are personally enriched by helping to meet the needs of someone else. Those who do not experience or benefit from this knowledge frequently live and die in solitude and isolation.

The Case of Jim

Jim was a cranky old man. He called me one day in 1981 to introduce himself. Jim had listened to a radio interview I had given the previous day and had thought about it overnight. He had been told he had cancer and would die in a few months. Jim had decided he "could take anything", but he did not want to die alone. Yet he knew this was the most likely scenario for him. He would be in some spotless, white hospital bed, warm, reasonably pain-free (his doctors had promised this), but alone.

Jim had long since alienated his children and even his drinking buddies. In fact there were no significant friends left in his life that he could think of. Jim was tormented by the fear that he seemed destined to die anonymously, alone and in the (emotional) dark.

"Truthfully, you don't owe me nothin', but I liked your

voice and what you had to say. Could you come and be with me when I die?" After further conversation it was clear that he did not need, or even want, anything else from me. His medical care was under control, and he did not choose to have any support beyond what he had stated. We talked, and I agreed that when he called, I would be there.

For four or five months I did not hear from him again. In fact I had more or less put him out of my mind, thinking that perhaps he had changed his mind, or found someone else he would prefer to have with him. He had not even left me a phone number that I could call to find out how he was doing. Then, just as I was leaving the office on a cold winter evening, the phone rang and it was Jim. "Marilynne," the voice croaked, "it's Jim. Remember you promised to come when I call?" I did not question him further but went to the hospital to meet this person who had until now been just a voice on the telephone.

He was quite comfortable, slightly drowsy but relatively calm. I introduced myself and sat near his bed, and he began to talk—slowly and hesitatingly at first, as though it was something he was not accustomed to doing. Then, as his confidence grew, with deliberate and matter-of-fact determination, Jim told me the story of his life. It was not a life he was proud of—surely he was not boasting about driving his children away, or "dumping" his wife? He spoke plainly about "the wasted years—just an ordinary working stiff, satisfied with a paycheque, a glass of beer and an occasional steak.... I did my job and couldn't be bothered with the wife and kids—to hell with all that stuff. In fact I could never be bothered about anyone. So, here I am. Still a miserable old bastard with no time or inclination to change anything."

As we talked—it was mainly Jim talking, with me listening, nodding and touching his hand occasionally—a peace and gentleness grew in the room; but in me there was an intense sense of loneliness. Time passed, and a few hours later

Jim died, with only a stranger to notice his passing.

While Jim did have "someone" there for him in the last hours, we cannot pretend this was a satisfactory achievement. Jim had focused his whole life on himself and his own needs. Truly he died as he had lived—alone.

It is almost always family and friends who must be relied upon for the emotional, social, spiritual, and sometimes even the physical support and care each person needs at the end of life. Such a network must be built from a firm foundation of trusting friendship throughout a lifetime.

The end of life is our last chance to reach success in a number of areas. It is a time for making it right with our families and friends, trying to resolve any difficulties between us and the people around us for whom we care. It is also a time for tying up loose ends, and (if it fits within your criteria) for reaching out to share the second greatest event in *your* life.

We will examine just a few of the more obvious choices you may wish to consider before beginning your planning, if you have not already done so. Keep in mind that the circumstances of your dying, when it occurs, may force you to re-evaluate some of these choices at that time and make some adjustments to your plan.

MAKING IT RIGHT WITH FAMILY AND FRIENDS

We will wish, each in our own way, to say goodbye to those who have played an important role in our lives. But it is almost impossible to do this until we have put to rest any hurts or dissatisfactions that may lie between us and those people. Within a family, angry sometimes even hurtful things *need* to be spoken aloud. In some situations it is necessary to purge past long-standing hurts in order to make room for healing and new beginnings ... even at the end of life.

The Elderly Couple

I recall the case of two elderly people who had been together for more than fifty-five years of married life. When the wife was diagnosed with terminal cancer she became enraged, but not because of the disease or the thought of dying. Her intense anger was directly linked to the style of the relationship—a style that had made the marriage a strong one for many years but that she suddenly realized had become burdensome.

Her husband's health had been slowly deteriorating for the last three years. His condition was not immediately life-threatening, but serious enough to make him feel uncertain and somewhat lethargic. For the past three winters he had said, "No, dear, I just do not feel well enough to take our usual trip to Florida. Let's stay home this year, and I promise we will definitely go next year."

The anger that erupted within her had little to do with the loss of a trip to Florida, but a lot to do with the pattern of behaviour she had allowed to control their relationship over the years. She felt rage both at her husband, who had denied her the pleasure of leaving behind the heavy winter chills for sunnier, warmer climes, and also, far more importantly, at herself for permitting his manipulation and submitting so placidly to his decision. For three years she had rationalized behaviour that really made her very unhappy, either without question, or with excuses such as "I can go next year," and, "Perhaps it would be unfair to push him when he doesn't really feel secure at this time." All the while she honestly knew that the trip would do them both good and that she too deserved this little "perk" they had both worked so hard for over the years.

It took many months of "working it out" before this obedient, faithful, and now dying wife was able to come to terms with the reality of her life and the style of marriage she had accepted. How often had she given in to her husband and denied herself, adhering to this pattern of compliance rather than engage in a confrontation with reality—hers and his?

And there are those, sometimes the very people who are closest, who love so deeply and privately that they cannot allow the dying person to express him or herself. Even family members sometimes forbid discussion of the truth. One little girl whom I shall never forget sought and found her own solution—an answer to an unbearable situation that had been forced upon her.

The Case of Angela

Upon entering the room I thought fleetingly how appropriate the name "Angela" was for this beautiful, blue-eyed child, sitting patiently propped up with pillows in her bed just beside the window. She had been reading, but she politely put aside her book and looked eagerly up as her mother introduced us.

It was 1980 and I was preparing for a TV debate on the philosophical issues of death and dying. My research included visits with persons who were dying or who had faced the spectre of death, and meetings with health-care professionals who worked in fields where death was a frequent occurrence, hospital chaplains, philosophers, religious advisers from many faiths, and ethicists.

A physician of my acquaintance who was deeply committed to the "pro-life" movement had decided that a meeting with Angela would convince me beyond all question that "life at any cost" was the only possible response for almost every human condition. He did believe in the "rightness" of capital punishment and the inevitability of wars, but was convinced that abortion and euthanasia were the devil's work. Suicide was a mortal sin for which there was no redemption, and all persons who died by their own hand were doomed to burn in hell-fire forever.

And so I came to meet nine-year-old Angela. We spent a long afternoon together talking and *"listening"* to each other. First she introduced me to "the real Angela", the one her mother and father really remembered. And with this she showed me a photograph of a chubby younger version of herself with long golden curly hair and a twinkle in her eye. The girl who had invited me to sit beside her on the bed was still beautiful in my eyes—perhaps more so, in a way, because of the courage in the midst of suffering that I read in her face, her bald head and her wasted, mutilated body.

She proceeded to tell me how she had been diagnosed with cancer more than two years ago and that she knew she would die. Angela was heartbroken that her mother and father could not talk with her about her death. She had tried to discuss it with her doctor, but he had rebuked her abruptly for such talk. She told me the story of the treatments she had undergone—surgery, radiation, chemotherapy—"the works", as she put it. In between playing her favourite tapes—mostly peaceful sounds of water and birds singing—Angela described the weeks she had spent in hospital and the time that had been "stolen" (to use Angela's word) from her family. "Mom and Dad are so worried taking care of me, they do not have time for my older brother and baby sister. Sometimes I think they, my brother and sister, must surely hate me, but they don't act like they do. They just seem very sad and lonesome. They seldom go out to play. Suzie is getting so thin and pale. Her arms and legs are just like sticks. I'm really worried about her. John gave up playing baseball, which he used to love, and sneaks in my room often, whenever Mom is not watching, to just sit and listen to the music with me, or once in a while when I'm too tired to read to myself, John reads to me. Mom thinks seeing me like this is bad for the others so she doesn't like them to visit."

Tomorrow Angela was to go back into hospital for yet another operation. She was not afraid, but she was tired. Most of all she was exhausted from trying to explain to her doctor and her parents that she did not want any more treatment. She begged me to explain this to her parents and to see the doctor to "make him listen. Maybe if you tell him he will understand."

Before I left their home, I spent a long time talking with her mother and father. Angela was right—her parents could not deal with her illness and its inevitable prognosis. As for death—they could not even mention the word. "But what about this surgery tomorrow?" I asked, in an attempt to move the conversation in a more specific direction. "What has the doctor told you it will accomplish? After all, Angela has told you often that she does not want it. What do you expect it will give her?" "Angela is just a child," her father abruptly replied. "What do kids know? No, we must decide what's best for her and what is best is whatever Dr. G says is best. That's that. End of discussion."

I continued, quietly, to explain to them that often people, even very young children, have a knowledge beyond their years or education about their own condition and that experience of the kind Angela had been exposed to has a maturing effect on most people. We ought to listen very carefully to what they have to say. I felt that Angela had a remarkable insight into her own situation. I told them of her concern for her brother and sister, that she wanted to spend her time with the family and not in a hospital. That Angela had an acute feeling for the value of time and how it should best serve their family. I begged them just to *listen* and really hear what their precious daughter was saying to them.

After a while I realized that these two adults were incapable of absorbing or even hearing such words. So immersed were they in their own pain that nothing could penetrate the wall of suffering that had cut them off from the voice of

75

reason and caring. They could not even bear to care about their other children or each other.

From this sad house I went back to meet with Dr. G to explain to him the experience of this day. He said he understood the severe trauma but that he could see no alternative but to proceed with the plans for Angela's surgery tomorrow. He was out of options and this was a last-ditch effort to save her life. Drastic as it was (and probably futile, to be perfectly honest), he could not just let her die.

It was with a very heavy heart that I returned to my hotel that night. Many miles from home, frustrated and sad beyond belief over Angela's plight, I dawdled over a cup of tea and a sandwich. I had been so impressed with this spunky, smart, gentle and patient little person—wise beyond her years. I thought about her father and mother and John and Suzie, all traumatized by what life had dealt them. What if they had found another doctor, one who did not impose his own philosophical imperative on his patients? What if Angela's parents had received proper counselling two years ago? Would this family have a better chance of survival now, even with the death of Angela? I thought so. The death of a child is disastrous and does tear many families apart, but others it bonds together and makes stronger, if they have the will and the support to make it happen.

I slept restlessly that night. Even knowing I had to catch an early flight back to Toronto, I was haunted by a child's tears in my dreams. At six o'clock, just as I was about to leave for the airport, Angela's mother phoned my hotel to tell me that her daughter had died during the night. At age nine Angela had hanged herself from the shower-curtain rod in the bathroom. I believe this nine-year-old child, matured by illness and suffering, had made a rational, considered choice to die. All options had been stolen from her. She could endure no more. For her own sake, and that of her family, it had to end.

TYING UP LOOSE ENDS

You have started a project that obviously means a great deal to you. This could be a large or small enterprise. Perhaps you are writing a book on a major event in history that you know you are best able to record. Or you are helping a granddaughter prepare for her new life in Vancouver. After all, you lived there for twenty-five years, only recently moving to New Hampshire to be closer to your roots.

Whatever the project, it is obviously important to you and therefore a matter of significance. Will you have time to complete it? If not, is it important enough for you to seek some help in completing it? Do you even know if you will have the time to meet your goals?

Of course, you cannot expect every physician to be precise within days or even weeks about the probable course of your illness, but you can and should demand some reasonable estimate of the pattern of the disease. "I do not ask for exact percentages or demand infallibility—just an informed, reasonable estimate. Between three and six months, you say? Fine, now I know what I have to deal with and can plan accordingly." And let me suggest that you "tune out" if the same doctor then starts to say, "But I know someone who lived eight years with the same type of ovarian cancer that you have." Such comments suggest either a doctor who does not have confidence in his diagnosis, or an attempt to give you "hope". I suggest that neither is appropriate to your situation.

The best hope comes from knowing the truth, and most people can and do choose to deal with it. Unreality, denial and euphemisms waste the time and energy of the dying. Both time and energy are increasingly precious at the end of life. If your instincts tell you the physician is not confident of his diagnosis, get another opinion and perhaps even another doctor. You do not have the time to spend upgrading her or his education. Neither should you accept any guilt that you might appear selfish if you do so. The doctor will have time to learn in the future. Your own future many be very limited indeed.

Now, more than ever before, you need to know the truth so you can get on with tidying up the "business" of your life. Focus on projects that are unfinished. Do not waste precious time in starting new ones. You may have the time to take on something more later, but for now you will find greater satisfaction in completing one thing at a time.

It may be necessary to re-evaluate your goals as time and illness dictate, but if you anticipate that possibility, adjustments will come easily.

Perhaps you want to read, or reread, some favourite authors. Maybe you wish to explore some new species of wildlife. For the former you can easily create a setting that is comfortable and manageable within the limits of most illnesses. The latter may require more detailed negotiation.

Travelling can present particular difficulties unless you are prepared to make some compromises and sometimes do some extra homework. Things like treatment for your particular illness may not be readily transportable or available in other areas of the world. For example, I found that my decision to live 300 miles north of Toronto during a recovery period following serious illness meant I would not have access to some medications unless I arranged for their weekly transport. When I researched how this could be done, I was told that the usual courier services would not carry such drugs. It took great ingenuity and considerable effort to arrange the care I needed, but as I believed my recovery depended as much on where I was as on the treatment prescribed by my doctors, I was determined to make these two goals converge.

Perhaps one of your "loose ends" is a piece of work you had started in your job. After all, much of our sense of ourselves is knitted into the fabric of our working life. Your boss, however, may see you as too disabled, or as "depressing" to have around, and may discourage you from remaining in your usual work environment. Do not allow yourself to be treated unfairly. Discrimination takes many forms, and sometimes when people cannot deal with their own feelings they act wrongly.

Passive acceptance is seldom helpful. If you need someone to help you fight this battle, find them and pursue your goals. You have a right to end your life as you choose. Usually, however, a quiet non-confrontational interview with an employer can resolve differences. It may be only an unfounded fear of the other party and not a real problem at all. If it does not appear you will be permitted to function comfortably in your workplace, however, arrange to complete your project at home or in a setting mutually acceptable to you and the employer.

Keep in mind the popular phrase of self-help literature, "be good to yourself". If ever the phrase is appropriate, it is now.

SHARING THE SECOND-GREATEST EVENT IN YOUR LIFE

The most important aspect of preparing for death is the way you live. We live with and through those around us and in doing so expand our own sense of being. Moments that are shared make our own joy and sorrow more meaningful. Surely there are few moments more significant than those used in preparing for our death.

You may fear that others do not want to be involved in your dying. Perhaps so. But why not give them the freedom to choose—the opportunity to decide for themselves? Do not just presume you must struggle alone. Of course we would like to have others offer to help us—we do not always wish to be put into the position of having to ask for that help. But when others are too embarrassed to ask what they can do, or do so in a way that seems insincere, it is usually because they do not know what to say or are worried about appearing awkward or pushy.

Allow others to enter your experience of dying. It is a most generous gift that will pay off for both of you. You will have someone with whom to share past and present experiences, and the person will have a memory to call upon at the completion of her or his own journey. The benefits may surprise you both in quite a remarkable way.

Whether you are preparing far in advance (a subject I will explore in Chapter 5), or have just learned that you will soon die, recognizing and internalizing the fact that you will die is an enriching experience. When you truly realize that some day all of "this" is going to come to an end, you have a need to make the "this" better, more significant and more satisfying.

The Young Man with Rheumatic Fever

A young man I know of developed rheumatic fever at age twenty-one. The year was 1958. The accepted treatment was enormous doses of aspirin and months of complete bed rest. At the end of this time he was told he would probably live for five to ten years, if he took very good care of himself. For the next five years, he was so careful he was virtually an invalid. During the next five years he ventured into the world a little farther, practising a profession he really liked—but gently. Each year that passed after his supposed sentence was over, he became more and more assertive, knowing his life was of value and that his work was of vital importance to society. He is now fifty-five years old, his physical fitness has improved and he is enormously productive in his chosen career. In fact, he calculates that he has had three great careers already, and he speculates with eager anticipation about what the next one might be.

I recall the afternoon I was told I had cancer. In a daze, feeling like a zombie, unable to focus on anything except that dreaded word "cancer", I found myself walking through the streets of Toronto, bypassing all subways and buses, to the home of a fairly new friend. This was someone with whom I had almost instantly felt a great rapport and who I sensed had a great ability to comfort. As I reached Jean's door I had to wait to be processed through the security system of her apartment. In my panic I could think only,

"Why is it taking so long? What if she is not home? What if she can-not see me now?" And then, "She has to be there. I cannot go home right now and face this alone." Of course, in only a few minutes there she was. After one look at my face she held out her arms and I was enfolded into the caring presence I so needed. I began to sob, and sob, and sob some more, as we somehow got from the lobby to her apartment. Speech was impossible, but Jean was patient and just held me quietly until the first wave of shock passed and allowed me to explain my behaviour.

How long our shared ordeal went on I cannot recall. It later seemed I had been there for hours. I recalled Gordon, her husband, coming home and Jean gently telling him the news; I recall seeing a cup of tea, but I can't for the life of me remember if I drank it; and then, eventually, I remember insisting on getting myself home. It seemed to me that if I could manage this—the walk to the subway, the subway and bus ride, and the walk home—I would find the strength to face whatever the next days held for me.

With that special sensitivity that drew me to her in the first place, Jean recognized my need to take the next step alone. She let me go, but I suspect that she was never far behind me. "Jean's place" was my haven while I assimilated the language of disaster. From here I moved to share it with my family, who I knew would provide the foundation and support to help me through whatever would come later. And so they did, as did many other compassionate people.

Not everyone has built a foundation of supporters. Nor can we start at a time of crisis to do so, especially if we are ill and feeling frail or vulnerable. In fact, the very confirmation that a person has a life-threatening illness is cause for many to withdraw from those closest to them, for a while at least. Each person responds differ-ently to trauma. Some need time to assimilate the information, to come to terms with it, however well or inadequately, before they share it or seek interaction with others.

Many people find it easier to talk the situation over with a com-parative stranger—a social worker, counsellor, or some other pro-fessional or trained volunteer—than to face their family directly.

The Case of Ian

As I strolled along the Bow River in Calgary during one of my many visits to that lovely mid-western city, part of me was enjoying the serenity of the morning, the enthusiasm of the joggers, the sounds of the river and the joy of seeing a few species of birds that, while not new to my list, were first sightings for me in this part of the world. The other part of me was focusing on what my next appointment might bring.

All I knew at this point was that a young man had phoned me at my hotel to ask me to visit him. His name was Ian, he had AIDS and he needed help. As I would be in town for a week, would I have time to visit and help him work out some problems?

Ian was tall, very lean and quite handsome. He was about to turn thirty, but he seriously doubted if he would make it. The fairly rapid wasting was taking its toll. The tumours in the lining of his stomach meant he could tolerate very little solid food, and even the consumption of most liquids gave him severe pain.

"The worst part of all of this for me, however, is the feeling of isolation and separateness. I would like to talk to my mother. In fact, I would really like to go home to Nova Scotia and be with my mother when I die. But that's not possible."

"Why not, Ian? Please explain a little more to me," I answered. And so he told me the story of his family.

"Well, my mother lives back home in Halifax. I left there four years ago and have never returned. My brother came here to Calgary, too. In fact he lives only a couple of blocks from me—he is gay, too, but we have never said these words to each other. I have a feeling my mother suspects the truth about us, but it has never been spoken out loud. She lives at home with my granny and one of my sisters. My father, such as he was, certainly knew about Fred and me, because before he left the house for the last time six years ago he beat the hell out of both of us, just like he used to beat my mom. We're a strange lot in my family. We *never* discuss anything personal. It's like we're a group of strangers that just happen to be plunked down in the same house together.

"Oh, I think my mom used to be different, but Dad beat the joy and speakin' out of her a long time ago in his drunken rages. What can I do, Marilynne? I can't phone my mom now and say, 'Hey, guess what, Mom, I'm gay and I have AIDS and I'm dying. Can I come home so you can clean up after me when I throw up, give me the pain injections when I need them, and change my diapers, when it comes to that? She's been through enough. No, the best and kindest thing I can do is to leave her alone. But God, I miss her. I really miss her."

I made us a cup of twig tea. He seemed to be able to keep that down without too much pain. I insisted he go back to bed to rest because we had a lot of work to do and it would be easier for us both if he conserved his energy. We would deal with this in stages, I suggested. For the moment we would talk only about Ian—about his physical needs and how they were or were not being addressed, his emotional, social and financial situation, what support systems he had in place and all the routine details of caring for this very ill young man. In the evening I would visit again and, with his permission, would ask his brother to join us. Tomorrow we would deal with finding remedies for problems.

Ian agreed to this schedule but said he very much doubted that Fred would come. I asked for Fred's phone number and suggested he let me worry about getting him there. With this I left to speak at a meeting of seniors at the Kerby Centre.

Seven o'clock saw Ian, Fred and Jean, Ian's evening nurse, sitting in Ian's living-room with our host ensconced on the sofa. By nine-fifteen Ian and Fred were hugging each other. Fred told us, "I never thought Ian cared about me, and the agony of our early years together had taught us to just bottle up the fear and anger our dad had beat into us all. When Ian moved here to Calgary, I came shortly after, thinking maybe now we could make our own family, but each of us was too reserved to even try to express ourselves. Then, when I realized Ian had active AIDS, I'm ashamed to say it but I was too scared to come and visit. Even in the gay community, you hear so much crap about the disease I just decided it was better to leave things as they were—rotten as that was. Ian, I've been so lonesome and feeling so guilty about things—I'm really sorry."

At this point I reminded Ian that I always request a fee for my services. Fred and Jean looked at me warily, but Ian laughed. "Come on," he said, "come and get your hug." Then he explained to the others that the payment I was talking about was my need for lots of hugs—these were my river of life, my source of renewal, without which I would dry up from all the tears I shed, outwardly and quietly within my spirit, for the Ians of the world.

Both Ian and Fred were leery of the response we would receive from their mother but decided to put it off no longer. Fred said that, as the eldest, he should take the responsibility of making the telephone call.

I cannot say that they received an outpouring of welcome at first, but as Fred slowly, and with as much composure as he could muster, talked to his mom and explained their situation, I could see the tension fall away. Finally he said, "Ian, Mom wants to talk to you."

We all left the room, but the apartment was so small Ian's outpouring of sobs could be clearly heard. Not tears of rejection as he had anticipated, but absolute wonder and ecstasy at the acceptance his mother offered. After about ten minutes, Ian asked us to join him again. He had been too emotional to discuss any details with his mother, but she asked if I could be at his side at nine the following morning so that we could meet on the phone and talk together. Jean and Fred helped Ian get settled for the night after we all said our good-byes. Then to work off some of the stress of the day's many activities, including those of the last couple of hours, I walked back to the hotel.

With a little help from a lot of friends, Fred took Ian home before the end of the week. Meanwhile, we had been in touch with a family doctor who had gained a reputation for compassionate treatment of persons with AIDS. Ian's care became a real family affair, with three generations, many extended family—the doctor, a visiting nurse, a couple of cousins, the family minister and who knows how many others—all playing their part. After Ian left Calgary, I did not hear from him, apart from a brief call to say hello and thank you, and to tell me he was "safe at home".

About six weeks later Fred dropped by my office. He hugged me and told me how the end had been. He put two envelopes into my hands. The first was from Ian's mom, and I saved that to read at home later. The second was from the family doctor who had cared for Ian. He was sending in a membership application and fee to Dying With Dignity, but also a letter to explain how pleased he was to know there were people available to counsel those in life-threatening and terminal situations. "I've always believed that death is not a defeat," he wrote, "except when it happens badly. When we do not listen to our patients; when we force unwanted treatment on them; when we insist that the hospital is the only place for proper care; when we deny them the right to choose—this is when we fail." Bravo doctor.

IT IS A MATTER OF CHOICE

Some people wish to have all the information possible and digest it privately. Then they carefully choose to whom, if anyone, they will disclose the news of an illness—life-threatening or not. To these people it is just too personal a matter to discuss widely.

Others will not be able to wait to start calling family and friends to talk about their tragedy. Such people can also be difficult to accept, because they need to share their problems time and time again. Perhaps they feel that by repeatedly talking about the pain, they can make the misery and fear go away, or dissipate it into smaller burdens for each friend to help carry.

All points of view must be respected, all strategies accepted, no matter how difficult it is for those waiting for the signal that tells them where they may fit into the situation. There are times when spouses, children and friends alike feel rejected or cheated because they have not been included in a person's suffering. Each of these will have time to recover—while you may not have the time or inclination to change your style of coping with illness. Whatever your circumstances, do not accept guilt or be anguished about it. You are doing the very best you can!

The Case of Alfred

After a public meeting held at the Royal York Hotel a few years ago, an obviously distressed man approached me. He was having some difficulty breathing and his steps were unsteady. I invited him to sit on a nearby chair, and I moved another close so we could talk privately.

He introduced himself as Alfred F, and told me he was eighty-six years of age. He had travelled the 150 kilometres to Toronto to hear what we had to say. "Did I really believe a person had the right to choose the time and manner of his death?" he asked. "Yes," I replied, "I do, as long as you do not seriously damage another person in the process."

We went down to the lounge, where I thought he might be more comfortable, and he proceeded to tell me his story. He suffered from many health problems and realized he would soon have to sell the farm where he had lived and had earned his living for more than fifty years or make an arrangement with one of his children to run it for him. His doctor had been telling him for years to take it easier. (Considering the shape this man was in now, I heartily concurred.)

Alfred felt very strongly about the right to die. He had seen a number of friends linger on in nursing homes or acute-care hospitals in a condition he thought nothing less than barbarous. This was not for him. The problem was, as he expressed it, "I have nine children and they can never agree on anything. Three of them have joined one of those fundamentalist groups and have visited only once in the last four years and then only to preach to me to mend my ways or I was on my way to hell. Well," said Alfred, "I don't believe in all that stuff, never have and doubt I will change now. Can they interfere in my right to decide for myself if my choice is to die naturally—or even with some help, should it come to that?"

"If they succeed in having you declared mentally incompetent, yes, they can impose their choice of health care on you," I replied. "But, although Living Wills have not been given legal status in Ontario yet, I suggest you complete and sign such a document and a Durable Power of Attorney for Health Care. By the time you need them, the law may be in place to enforce these directives. But please, Alfred, do it now, while you are still comparatively well and there is no doubt about your mental competence."

At that time Norm Sterling (PC), MPP (member of the provincial Parliament) for Carleton, had just introduced Bills 7 and 8 into the Ontario Legislature. They had already passed first reading, and no problems were anticipated for passage of second reading. I had had discussions with various party members and the attorney general, and the matter of Living Wills was seen by most to be a non-partisan issue. After all, death is universal and we should all be able to pursue our own choice of health care. As it turned out, Mr.

Sterling's bills were overtaken by events; the basic principles were incorporated in the *Consent to Treatment Act* later passed by the government.

It was two years later when I heard from Alfred again—or, rather, from his social worker. Alfred's health had deteriorated considerably and he was now a patient in a hospital's intensive care unit. He was asking for me, and the social worker told me she was desperate for some assistance to help "sort out a mess". I said that certainly I would come, but that before I spoke with anyone else I wanted to meet with Alfred privately. She set it up for that evening.

I was not particularly surprised at his poor physical health. Among many other problems, he suffered from chronic emphysema, had been in and out of congestive heart failure, and had suffered a fractured hip in a fall on the farm more than two years ago. (As a result, his oldest son had taken over the farm by obtaining a power of attorney when his father was too weak to resist.) But what was more shocking than his physical condition was the state of Alfred's emotional health.

He felt persecuted, abandoned and disliked by most of his family and very much a victim of an uncaring, unreceptive, overly powerful and paternalistic doctor. After his fall, he explained to me, his eldest son had pushed him into signing away his legal right to control his own financial affairs. From this time on, the only communication he had with Alfred, Jr., was third-hand messages through his other children. Not once in the two years had his son visited him. Nor had he allowed the father to come home to the farm, even for a weekend.

Oh, the seniors' home Alfred had eventually been transferred to when the hip injury had healed was a nice place, and he quite enjoyed the friends he had made there, but it still was not his own place. "I wouldn't have got in the way or been a nuisance, Marilynne. Nor would I have insisted on staying at the farm as my son feared," Alfred said plaintively.

"I liked having people my own age around and the security of the home until I became too sick to stay there. First I got a bout of the flu and that turned into pneumonia. With these weak lungs of mine I just could not seem to fight it off, and things went from bad to worse. I've been in the hospital now for months, and they tell me there is nothing more they can do for me. I'm not in a lot of pain, but there are times when it gets pretty bad. I've been in the intensive care unit now three or four times and on the ventilator periodically. Right now it's okay again for a while, but I know that sooner or later I'll be tied to that damn machine forever. This is no kind of life, and to be perfectly honest I'm ready to go. When I told that to Dr. McD, though, he got real mad and said I had nothing to say about that. My life was in God's hands and I should appreciate the 'good things' and pray more—that would make me feel better. Marilynne, he talked to me like I was a naughty child, and he has been brusque and sometimes downright rude ever since."

I asked him about the rest of the family. "Well they are all busy people, you know, with kids and grandkids and worries of their own. I don't like to bother them, but Frank and Elsa and Erik come by quite often. See the lovely flowers they brought yesterday? They're from Elsa's garden—she takes after her mother for gardening. The rest of the kids? There's the three that live in Windsor. I have not seen them except for once a year for some time now. They are deep into their religion and seldom leave home. Annie and Martha drop in once in a while, and we talk on the telephone when I feel up to it. It's hard, you know, because I get so short of breath. It's probably just as well I don't have the whole gang around anyway."

He told me about the friends he had made at the hospital. There were a couple of nurses he really liked and talked to a lot. There was the social worker, of course. She had become a real friend—someone who would listen and whom he felt he could trust to understand and express his concerns.

Finally he told me what he had in mind. He was not really hungry any more. If he just stopped eating he could probably starve himself to death pretty soon. "I've lost so much weight now, as you can see, that I'm not much more than skin and bone. I've come to the conclusion it is the only free choice I have left."

I asked him how he would feel about having a psychological assessment done, explaining that I thought it important to prove he was not just suffering from depression but was fully competent and capable of making sound decisions. Once that was determined, it should be easier to negotiate other health-care decisions. He understood and said he thought it probably was a real good idea.

The next morning I met with the social worker, and we discussed Alfred's case. She confirmed his impression of the physician in charge of the intensive care unit and agreed it might be less threatening if she approached the doctor regarding the assessment. We also discussed the limited family support, but she assured me that those who did not visit regularly were inclined to upset Alfred on the rare occasions when they did come, since they insisted on praying and preaching to him against his express wishes.

Shortly thereafter, the assessment was completed. I asked the physician for a meeting with the three children Alfred had named and the nursing-team leader and the social worker. While he was quite hesitant, he agreed. From the moment we entered the conference room, however, he was belligerent and uncooperative about listening to any possible change in Alfred's care. In fact, he said without hesitation, since Alfred had recently verbalized that he intended to starve himself to death, he had just ordered him to be put in restraints and to have a nasogastric tube inserted to force-feed him. I told him we were all aware of the very positive report attesting to Alfred's mental competence and that such treatment would constitute a battery. With this he left the room and told us that for his patient's own good we would all be forbidden access to Alfred.

The next step was to approach the hospital administrator. He was somewhat sympathetic, but told me it was hard to get doctors to work in some of the more remote hospitals, and that at present Dr. McD was the only doctor qualified to attend to patients in intensive care. I pointed out the possible legal consequences of treating a competent patient contrary to his wishes. The administrator waffled on this point and said he had better confer with the hospital's lawyers. Perhaps we should all meet the next day. I agreed, but suggested strongly that in the interim he would be wise to advise Dr. McD to rescind the order to restrain and force-feed Alfred.

At this point I called Elsa, Frank and Erik and explained the situation to them. They said they would get in touch with the rest of the family but warned me we might have a fight on our hands. Soon after, they called me back to say that the three siblings from Windsor would come to a meeting on the upcoming weekend, as would Annie and Martha. Alfred, Jr., however, had told them he "couldn't care less what happened to the old man just as long as you keep him out of my hair. All I ever wanted from him was the farm and I got that now, so do what you want and leave me alone."

Dr. McD was intransigent. He would continue to order such treatment for Alfred as he saw fit, and that included force-feeding and any type of restraint necessary to achieve that goal—either physical restraints or chemical ones. The hospital staff and lawyers tried in vain to reason with him.

The family meeting was not a pleasant one. Three of the children agreed that their father should be restrained and force-fed. Two were ambivalent—one minute having one opinion and changing it the next. Alfred, Jr., was out of the picture, and the other three were devastated that their father was being treated so callously with no regard for his wishes.

Finally, Elsa stated with great determination, "That's it, I will bring Father home and take care of him myself." "It won't be easy," I suggested, all the while full of admiration for this strong, determined woman. After further talk we asked the social worker to join us and began working out the details of a care plan.

She was very sorry, she told us, "but things are much worse now. Probably it was all the aggravation, but Alfred has suffered a bad spell and is now almost totally ventilator-dependent." She seriously doubted that he could be weaned off the equipment without risking his life. Elsa held firm. Her father wanted to die in peace, without that machine. If he died, it would be his wish. Clearly, to her, and to us, this was the most humane decision.

"The Windsor three", as their siblings called them, left in a great huff after stating we were all damned to hell and it was no longer any of their responsibility. The others asked the social worker and me to start putting the procedures in motion to have their father moved home to Elsa's place. It took a couple of days, but by Wednesday Alfred was in an ambulance and soon ensconced in a comfortable hospital bed in the living-room of Elsa's home. Many of his children and grandchildren were present to celebrate his arrival—all very quietly, of course, because of his critically frail condition.

Everyone seemed to understand that this would not be a long visit—Alfred probably better than most. He was proud and joyous, but also very quiet and in great physical distress. The doctor had been extremely angry when Alfred signed himself out of the hospital and had refused to order any medications to ease his suffering. I had called every other physician within a fifty-mile distance. All had refused to come or to be involved in the case. The standard response was to the effect that X hospital was the only one within a reasonable distance that had an intensive care unit and that their patients needed that service. They couldn't help it if Dr. McD was difficult, pompous and opinionated. He was all they had until they could find someone else. "We cannot afford to intervene and jeopardize our relationship with him" was the standard, if regretful reply.

"That's okay," said Alfred, slowly and with great heaving breaths. "I'm going to die free and with those who love me most by my side."

And Alfred did die, after forty-eight hours of extreme suffering—choking and gasping each step of the way. But there was joy, too. He was doing it his way, and he was never alone for one second. His children and grandchildren and I took turns, sometimes singly, sometimes in twos and threes, helping him through our love and support to leave the world on his own terms.

In the language of the choice-of-dying movement, we frequently speak in terms of a "good death" or a "bad death". Alfred's story, along with many others in this book, illustrates the distinction between the two quite precisely. In the words of a renowned medical doctor, Dr. Howard Brody: "medicine produces a good death when it uses life-prolonging interventions as long as they produce a reasonable quality of life and a reasonable level of function (defined in terms of the patient's own goals) and when it then employs the highest quality of hospice-style [or palliative-style] terminal care."

Dr. Brody goes on to explain the wrong-headedness of thinking that death itself is a medical failure. Rather, medical failure occurs when the ravages of disease have done their worst yet inappropriate and futile medical treatments continue, either contrary to the patient's expressed wishes or because the patient is insufficiently informed that he or she has other options. Such a situation makes a "bad death" inevitable. It also guarantees extreme grief and bitterness that may never be resolved for those who are left behind.

What patients fear (and we know we will be "the patient" some day) is that we may be "over-treated with death-prolonging technology long after any return to meaningful functioning is possible";

or that our caregivers will *abandon* us just when the need for symptom management, including emotional support, is most critical. As Dr. Brody further states: "walking away, denying that medicine can do anything to help the patient's plight, is an immoral abrogation of medical power."*

In preparing to close a life, each person should be encouraged to seek out the moments, small or large, that are satisfying for that person. Most individuals wish to have their family and friends nearby when they are dying. Many choose to have a spiritual adviser visit them or stay with them when the end of life approaches. However, whenever and in whatever style it happens, if you chose it, then it is right and "fitting" for you. Some find satisfaction in making their own plans for the time and manner of their death. If this is your goal, seek out the information and expertise to make it achievable. In our present legal climate, this is no small task.

---

*Dr. Howard Brody, "Assisted Death—A Compassionate Response to a Medical Failure", *New England Journal of Medicine* (Nov. 1992) 327:19, p. 1384.

CHAPTER FIVE

Planning Ahead

We are all at risk, every day. We could, for example, be in an accident that would render us incapable of communicating how we wish to be medically treated.

Millions of people have seen or read the excellent play and film *Whose Life Is It Anyway?* In this fictitious story, a young man, a sculptor just entering his most productive years, is involved in an automobile accident. In a split second the entire course of his life is altered in a tragic, agonizing way. He is permanently paralysed from the neck down, unable to scratch his nose, wipe away a tear, feed himself or—more importantly, for him—control the medical treatments imposed on him. He cannot prevent the doctor or nurse from tranquillizing him when he questions the value of continuing to exist. They believe him to be depressed and seek to make him accept his condition and their treatment by restraining him with chemical pacifiers. In writing this excellent play, Brian Clark put a face to one of our worst nightmares.

The Case of Dax

In a real-life catastrophe in 1973, another young man, Dax Cowart (a name he assumed along with the different body that had become his legacy after all the medical interventions), was severely burned in a freak gas-line explosion and the ensuing fire. He too could not exercise his own choice to prevent medical teams from imposing agonizing treatments on his body for more than a year. Over 65 per cent of his body was covered with second- and third-degree burns, including his face and hands. He lost his eyes, his ears and most of his nose, and nearly all his fingers had to be amputated. He could speak but did not have the means to exercise his will. He begged, pleaded and demanded to be allowed to die.

Dax was an active, virile, physically and emotionally strong air-force pilot recently released from his term of service when the accident happened. The explosion killed his father and maimed Dax beyond belief. For many months he fought the medical profession for the right to die with dignity. He lost every battle, even though it was recognized that he was lucid, articulate, rational and fully competent. Dax was finally rehabilitated to what is now a "new" person, forceful, informed and courageous as a spokesperson and advocate of patients' rights.

Some might ask is this not a life properly saved? Look what he has accomplished that he would not have done if that same medical intervention had not been imposed upon him. But surely that argument is a red herring. The most precious possession a human being can claim is that of his own person, and that must include the right to self-determination. Dax and everyone else deserves the right to choose for him or herself whether or not to go on with life. The right to decide how, and even if, we will live must be a part of our ownership of our person or it is surely a hollow possession.

Without written directions expressed in advance of catastrophic situations, no one could accurately predict what treatment the young sculptor in *Whose Life Is It Anyway?* would choose or refuse in the long term. Dax, although he certainly expressed himself clearly to his physicians after the explosion, was considered too traumatized to be considered competent. Was this evaluation entirely honest? Or did the medical world see Dax more as a challenge than a human being, so that his wishes were obscured by mumbo-jumbo?

We will never know. Both cases underline, however, how important it is for us to plan ahead and make sure our wishes are known far in advance of when any such decision needs to be made.

Is it honest or fair for another person to decide how much pain we must endure? Should other people determine what physical, emotional and social scars we can tolerate? Or is much of what passes as a concern to preserve life simply blatant paternalism cloaked in rationalizations?

About one year ago a friend of mine, aged twenty-six, suffered a severe heart attack. After a heroic effort by the medical profession and much suffering on his part, his life was saved. After a year of re-habilitation, both physical and psychological, he can begin again to think of the future. His career as a professional athlete is ended. He can, and must, choose another lifestyle, another career in which to find fulfilment. But he will never have the rich sense of security and invincibility he had prior to his "cardiovascular incident" (as the doctors call it).

Can he fully recover and build a new life? Does he have the inner resources to do so? As much as we, his friends, can try to help, only he can decide, knowing all the time it will be hard and for the most part very lonely work. When I asked him recently if he thought life is worth the price, he answered, "I do not know. Per-haps when I find out, I can consider myself healed. I know that for now I have signed a Living Will stating that should my heart stop again, I refuse to be resuscitated." My young friend needs to know that he has that right to refuse heroic measures; but he also knows that he may change his mind at any time.

But what if you are eighty-six years old and you have a severe stroke? You survive it in the purely clinical sense. Your lungs still move in and out by themselves. But you cannot walk or talk or feed yourself. You cannot even eat or taste "normal" food, for everything must be liquefied and fed into your system through a tube in your stomach. You can however, think. Even though you are imprisoned within the silent, locked world of your mind, you know precisely what is being done to you without your permission, without any hope of being able to consent to or refuse these invasions of your person.

You cannot prevent such diseases or accidents from happening to you. But you can determine the course events will take in terms of the treatment you wish to receive. Just as thoughtful individuals plan other important experiences in their lives, so too must you consider preparations for the end of life long before you are likely to face it. It is prudent and entirely realistic to prepare to direct the quality of death while you are healthy, relaxed and in an optimistic frame of mind. DO IT NOW is a wise policy. As long as you are of legal age and competent and mature in your thinking you cannot begin too early to define the criteria that you think are crucial to the "quality of life" you want for yourself. We all understand that other unanticipated events may alter such plans or even change the course of our lives entirely. All the more reason for planning and making rational, reasonable decisions immediately. If your circumstances alter, you can always change your mind.

ADVANCE HEALTH CARE DIRECTIVES

Without planning, our life and our death will proceed by pure happenstance, a gamble few individuals really wish to accept. There are two types of advance health care directives. The most commonly known is the instructional type, the Living Will. The other is a proxy directive, frequently called a Durable Power of Attorney for Health Care. By completing and signing a Living Will or a Durable Power of Attorney for Health Care now, you will be taking the first step toward having some control over your own person at the end of life.

BACKGROUND TO THE
DEVELOPMENT OF LIVING WILLS

In 1967 a lawyer, Luis Kutner, introduced the concept of a Living

Will at a conference of the Right to Die Society in New York.* It was his contention that it is a patient's right to consent to or refuse treatment, and thereby the law recognizes the inviolability of the human body. He proposed that, while still healthy and mentally competent, a person could specify to what extent he would consent to treatment in the future. In recognizing the principle that a patient also has the right to refuse treatment, even if such treatment would prolong his life, this could be indicated in a written document prior to the actual event.

The New York–based Euthanasia Education Council was the primary mover behind the spread of the Living Will concept. (The Euthanasia Education Council later split into Concern for Dying and Society for the Right to Die; these two societies have since rejoined and become Choice in Dying.) The Living Will was brought to Canada by Dying With Dignity in 1982. The first document distributed by this organization was essentially that designed by Concern for Dying in the United States. The increased sophistication of both the medical and legal aspects of the right-to-choose-to-die movement then led to development of a greatly revised document, which Dying With Dignity began distributing in 1992.

In 1987, Dying With Dignity also developed the first type of Durable Power of Attorney for Health Care used in Canada, and this document has since become used nation-wide, by lawyers and ordinary people alike.

Currently many other versions of a Living Will or an Advance Health Care Directive are available. Two of the most effective and popular are the "Let Me Decide" directive developed by Dr. William Molloy, MB, FRCP(C), and Virginia Mepham. Dr. Peter Singer, MD, MPH, FRCP(C), FACP, of the Centre for Bioethics, University of Toronto, has also done considerable research into the

---

*Reported by Sidney Rosoff, "Participants' Lectures" of the World Federation of Right to Die Societies Conference, Japan Society for Dying With Dignity, 1990.

use and design of effective advance directives and in 1993 introduced a revised version.

Living Wills of various types are now recognized in many countries around the world. In 1992 Denmark reported at the World Federation Meeting of the Right to Die Societies in Japan that the Danish government had passed legislation giving them legal status. Citizens of that country may register their document officially with the government and it will be honoured.

A LIVING WILL

A Living Will governs what happens to your body before death (as opposed to a Last Will and Testament, which governs the disposition of property after death). A Living Will sets out in writing your specific wishes about consent to, or refusal of, medical treatment. The Living Will allows you to direct your family, physician and others about your health-care choices based on your own values, wishes and beliefs. An excellent form of Living Will is published by Dying With Dignity, a registered charitable organization listed in Appendix D. The text of the Living Will document may be found in Appendix C.

There are some fundamental elements that should be incorporated in a Living Will.

1. It should state, in terms that reflect your own philosophy, your understanding of the value of life and your wish for a dignified dying.

2. Every advance directive must contain positive, specific statements about what type of health care you do wish under life-threatening situations, as well as treatments or interventions you would refuse to authorize. If you state only, "I do not want any treatment in the event I become terminally ill," you may deny yourself comfort measures such as adequate pain control and

sufficient hydration to keep your mouth moist. You also risk having it interpreted by health-care workers as a demand to be abandoned when you most need their professional expertise and supportive care.

3. A Living Will should be witnessed when it is signed. Witnesses should be persons who have reached the age of majority, and some authorities suggest that it is unwise to have as a witness either someone who is a major beneficiary of your estate or your physician. This point is hotly debated, but remember that all the witnesses are affirming is that the person signing the document is the person whose name is indicated as the subject referred to in the Living Will. They are not required to agree with the directions that have been stipulated, nor are they required to be legally qualified to testify to the mental competence of the person signing the document. They should be reasonably confident that the subject signing is fit to do so, but to go further would require special capabilities that family or friends acting as witnesses would not usually possess.

4. The document must be dated on the day it is signed and witnessed. It is also advisable to redate and initial your expressed wish annually.

5. Should your health status change dramatically, or should you change your mind about what treatments you would accept or reject, the document should be amended, initialled and dated as described for the original draft. If major changes are considered, it is wise to obtain a new document and carry out the full procedure again, making sure to destroy all copies of the now out-of-date Living Will.

6. After the Living Will is properly completed, keep the original in a secure but accessible place and give a photocopy both to your physician and to your family or the friend who is most likely to

be consulted about your health-care decisions. You may also choose to leave a photocopy on file with your lawyer, but this is a matter of personal preference.

7. If you change your mind about the stipulations in your Living Will, it is your responsibility to revoke the original document and advise anyone who has a copy that you have done so. At any time, however, even in the last moments of life, you may change your mind about any previously written directive. An oral indication to any care provider is all that is required.

8. Some organizations, including Dying With Dignity, provide a wallet-sized version of the Living Will that you may carry with you at all times. This is an excellent idea in case of accident or some other event that might prevent you from expressing your wishes directly.

9. It is not usually necessary to involve a lawyer in the preparation of this document. This could be an unnecessary expense that does not contribute significantly to the validity of the document. On the other hand, you may wish to inquire if your province or state requires a lawyer to be involved (in Canada, so far, this is not the case). For information on such issues in your province or territory you can contact one of the provincial agencies listed in Appendix E.

DURABLE POWER OF ATTORNEY FOR HEALTH CARE

While some Living Wills also include a Durable Power of Attorney for Health Care component, most do not. (*It is called a Durable Power of Attorney because the document endures even after you have lost competency.*) The Durable Power of Attorney for Health Care empowers someone else to make health-care decisions for you when you can no longer do so yourself. The person you choose must be well informed about your criteria with respect to the quality of life, so that he or she may properly make the decisions that you would make if you were capable of doing so. This is not an easy task to perform. Those holding such powers are frequently expected to make very difficult decisions. Such a decision might include giving directions to withhold medical treatments (such as forced feeding or cardiopulmonary resuscitation) that could further prolong your life (or your dying, depending on how one looks at it). You must make absolutely sure, through detailed discussions before you appoint the person as your attorney, that he or she is fully prepared to act accordingly and accept what may be an onerous responsibility.

The Durable Power of Attorney for Health Care must be properly completed, witnessed and dated. In most provinces the services of a lawyer are required to execute it. There are several types of "proxy" directive to choose from. Ideally, you may wish to have the specifics of your health-care directives detailed in a Living Will, and *also* have, in case it is needed, a Durable Power of Attorney for Health Care in case you lose the ability to communicate and need someone to speak for you. You may choose to bring one of the standard forms of this document to your lawyer, thus eliminating the additional cost of having a separate form drafted. A Durable Power of Attorney for Health Care is essential if your next of kin do not or are unlikely to agree with your views on dying with dignity, or are not prepared to support the instructions in a Living Will. A proxy type of directive is also a good idea if, for example, you have a family history of strokes or severe heart attacks or other ailments that could render you incapable of communicating your wishes.

With a signed, witnessed, Advance Health Care Directive, there should be no confusion or ambiguity for either the physician or the family about what kind of care you want and how far they may proceed in prolonging your life. With a properly drafted and executed document, the lines are clear, both for you and for the health-care providers.

Although it may sound a little cynical, after your death your relatives may be sufficiently disrespectful of your wishes to harass a physician for failing to prolong your life even though it would also have prolonged your dying. For your own protection and that of your health-care providers, a written, signed Advance Health Care Directive can save everyone a great deal of anxiety and potential problems.

I cannot emphasize too strongly that you must discuss your beliefs, opinions, feelings and wishes about your health-care choices with your family, friends and health-care providers. The medical care you receive is contingent on good communication with your physician, nurse, hospital and any person whom you expect to care for you.

In jurisdictions where there is a statute governing these issues, the law is clear. Where such statutes do not exist, you must rely on the discretion and goodwill of care providers. If you encounter any problems in this regard, contact someone to advocate on your behalf, as your wishes deserve to be respected.

While it has happened that a physician has ignored a person's Advance Health Care Directive, the physician does so at his or her peril, as the following case demonstrates.

Malette v. Shulman

Mrs. Malette was involved in a devastating automobile accident one evening. Her husband was killed outright, and Mrs. Malette received serious injuries to her face. When she was brought to the emergency department of Kirkland Lake and District Hospital it was determined that she had severe facial injuries and was semi-conscious and in shock. The nurse on duty informed the physician on duty, Dr. Shulman, that she had found a card in Mrs. Malette's purse. Across the top of the card was the notice "No Blood Transfusion". The card went on to declare that the holder was a Jehovah's Witness and stipulated: "no blood or any blood products [are to] be administered to me under any circumstances."

Even with this very clear directive as to the patient's wishes, values and beliefs, Dr. Shulman decided to transfuse Mrs. Malette.

To summarize the case briefly, Mrs. Malette was so emotionally traumatized by Dr. Shulman's intervention that she filed a lawsuit against him for a battery. A battery is defined as the non-consensual invasion of a person's bodily integrity. While the treatment imposed on this patient may, of itself, have been beneficial, Mrs. Malette and her attorneys believed that the "advance directive" she carried with her was clear and that, in fact, other options of treatment were available had the physician chosen to use them. Certainly Dr. Shulman had no malicious intent to harm the patient. Far from it. But he did ignore her specified wishes, and he did so at his peril. The courts agreed with Mrs. Malette that Dr. Shulman had acted in a way that violated her legal right to accept or refuse any and all treatment, even if such a decision might have led to her death.

The Supreme Court of Ontario awarded Mrs. Malette damages against Dr. Shulman. The Ontario Court of Appeal confirmed the judgement.*

YOUR RIGHTS UNDER THE LAW

In Canada, as in most democratic countries, individuals must consent to be treated before any medical treatment may be imposed upon them. The only exception to this principle is in the case of a true emergency when the injured or sick individual is unable to express his or her refusal of treatment and would otherwise perish or be seriously afflicted by lack of treatment. In such a case it would be

---

*Reported by Prof. Barney Sneiderman in "The Shulman Case and the Right to Refuse Treatment", *Humane Medicine* 7, no. 1 (Winter 1991).

considered imprudent not to act to save someone's life, unless the person carries an instruction to the contrary stating that he or she has signed a written advance directive. Of course, a proper advance directive should indicate not only that a person refuses treatment in certain situations, but—equally important—what treatment the person does wish to receive under specific conditions.

When you visit your health-care provider, if you feel you require assistance in stating and insisting on this right, take a friend along for support. In times of stress it is helpful to have a second person to listen to any instructions your health-care provider may give. If you need an advocate, seek one out. This may be a social worker, a nurse, a chaplain or a family friend. Some health-care facilities, nursing homes, community centres and social-service groups such as Dying With Dignity have advocates who would be able and willing to act on your behalf. It is YOUR responsibility, however, to recognize when you need assistance and to seek it out.

THE FAMILY AND ADVANCE HEALTH CARE DIRECTIVES

An additional and not inconsiderable consequence of having signed an Advance Health Care Directive is that it relieves your family and friends of the burden of decision making when both you and they would far rather they concentrate all of their energy on supporting you during your illness.

All too often at such a time your energies are dissipated by fruitless and frustrating debates. Would Mom want me to bring her home? Should I encourage the doctors to try another course of chemotherapy? Would Dad want resuscitation to be attempted if his heart stops, or would he prefer to be allowed to die in his natural time? On and on the questions revolve in our heads until we would like to cry out, "Help! Somebody! Anybody! Tell me what I should do!"

The two cases that follow illustrate the difference it can make to family members when a person has or has not signed an Advance Health Care Directive.

The Case of Fred

Fred is forty-five years old. He has Lou Gehrig's disease (ALS) and will die some time within the next six months. Three and a half years ago Fred was vice-president of a large Canadian manufacturing firm, owner and operator of a forty-acre hobby farm, and an avid golfer. He was an active, vibrant, virile man—one of the movers and shakers of the community he lived in just one and a half hours' drive north of Ottawa.

Fred is a husband and the father of an active, independent son and a beautiful teenage daughter. He is competent, alert, imaginative, funny and very intelligent. He is now also completely paralysed except for the index finger on his left hand and the ability to move his head about thirty degrees to left and right. His only comprehensible words, which he utters with great difficulty and expenditure of energy, are "yes", "no" (which he often yells in a whisper of distress or alarm), "water" and "shit". The last is not used in the sense of a physical need to evacuate his bowels. Such feelings and instincts have long since been taken from him. Rather he uses the word "shit" out of acute anger, frustration or fear.

Consider, for example, the time the hydrotherapist said, "Don't worry, I'll be right back. I just have to answer the cellular phone beside the pool. It might be my service calling," as he let go of the inner tube that was holding Fred above water. Some time later, after Fred had been dragged off the bottom of the pool and had the water pumped from his stomach, he said "shit, shit, shit" quite a few times. Needless to say this was the last time Fred trusted anyone to give him hydrotherapy or any other "therapy".

After many discussions, Fred, his wife, Frances, his physician and I have drafted his Durable Power of Attorney for Health Care. It has been properly witnessed and is on file in the doctor's office. It is also on Fred's hospital record (in case he is inadvertently taken to hospital again), and copies are taped in many prominent locations to the walls of his house.

Fred has been very specific in his advance directive. He does not choose to have his life terminated by anyone. Neither, however, does he choose to have it prolonged. Fred will die in his own home. When he starts to choke from the build-up of secretions in his throat and lungs, he has refused the use of a suction machine. Prolonging his life with a ventilator is out of the question. He will, however, accept morphine or other medications that will ease his suffering from the feelings of suffocation, choking and pain.

In exercising his right to self-determination, Fred is fortunate that his choice fits neatly with his family's wishes, his physician's sense of "fitness", and the law.

The Case of Eva

Eva has lived in a home for the aged since she suffered a stroke six years ago. At that time, her son (her only family) had her admitted to the home, then promptly moved to Detroit. When I try to talk to Stephen about his mother, he interrupts and replies, "My mother? She died six years ago."

Stephen holds Eva's power of attorney, which gives him control over her property. Under the law, as her only living kin and in the absence of written instructions to the contrary, he also has the authority to make decisions about her health care.

Eva's friend Mary has been visiting her every week for as

many years as they can both remember. They experienced much in life together, as only long-time friends can. They both survived a concentration camp and came to Canada to enjoy the freedom and quality of life denied them in their native Hungary.

Now, Eva is half paralysed, eighty-two years of age and speaks only with difficulty and preferably in her childhood language. She has little money and, most importantly, is denied the right to live and die where and how she chooses.

She is not experiencing severe pain, but her quality of life has deteriorated and she wishes to have no aggressive measures used to keep her alive. Last week, Eva developed pneumonia. She asked, through an interpreter, not to be treated with antibiotics or oxygen and requested that resuscitation not be attempted if she suffers cardiac or respiratory arrest. Eva refuses to eat and pulls out the intravenous line unless the nurses restrain her with leather straps attached to the sides of the bed.

The doctor supervising her care telephoned the son, who has not even visited his mother in the intervening years, and asked for directions. The son's succinct instructions to the doctor were: "Do everything you can to keep her alive. Just don't bother me about it."

Mary called Dying With Dignity to ask if we could intervene on Eva's behalf. She was desolate that her friend was dying in such conditions. As Eva has been evaluated as no longer mentally competent, she cannot any longer enact an advance directive naming someone other than her family to direct her care. The son's instructions, as legal next of kin, will be followed by the hospital staff unless we can successfully negotiate this much-wanted death.

(Postscript: With the help of Dying With Dignity's counselling and advocacy service, Eva was allowed to die, in comfort, without restraints or further force-feeding, forty-eight hours after Mary's call.)

THE PHYSICIAN AND ADVANCE HEALTH CARE DIRECTIVES

Advance Health Care Directives are welcomed by the majority of physicians in Canada. Thoughtful, concerned and caring doctors enjoy working with an equally thoughtful and caring patient. People who show that they have given serious consideration to their present and future health, quality of life and dying, and have articulated their choices accordingly, relieve the physician of an unwanted decision-making burden.

In an article entitled "Family Physicians' Attitudes toward Advance Directives," Drs. David L. Hughes and Peter A. Singer reported that 86 per cent of physicians favoured the use of advance directives.* While many physicians are still not very familiar with these documents, and many have not been presented with one by their patients, most doctors are pleased to see them introduced into the health-care system. The above-mentioned study was done in the province of Ontario, but in 1991 the Canadian Medical Association also came out in strong support of Advance Health Care Directives with a position statement directed to all doctors in Canada.

A physician must be protected from prosecution or harassment when providing the best medical care in accordance with the wishes and directions of his or her patient.

The Case of Joseph

At 5:00 a.m. one day in October 1992, a physician phoned me in considerable distress. Joseph, his patient of only recent acquaintance, was dying. I knew Joseph for a year, ever since he had been told he was dying of cancer and asked for my

---

Canadian Medical Association Journal 11 (1992), p. 146.

assistance in drafting a Living Will. He told me he was eighty-four years old and had lived a full life. Joseph never married and had only one brother, whom he had not seen or heard from for more than five years—"Not even a Christmas card," he would say, "and good riddance. We never did have much in common other than our parents, and obviously they died a long time ago."

Joseph and I kept in touch every few weeks just to talk and, as he said, "to keep you posted". The lung cancer had at first progressed gradually, but metastasized (spread) to other vital organs and was now moving very rapidly. I had already been to say my goodbyes to Joseph, for he wanted to say our farewells while he was still able to converse and enjoy a little humour with me. In fact, on my last visit I had taken him a full five-course meal from his favourite Greek restaurant. He had consumed the whole thing—every morsel—even though he knew he would pay the price in later discomfort. "What's a little pain," he would say, "for such a treat?"

I was rather surprised to receive the doctor's call, because I knew that both the patient and the doctor were in full accord about the choice of care. They had covered every contingency (we thought) in his advance directive.

What could not be foreseen, however, was that, suddenly and without invitation, Joseph's brother would arrive on the scene. He very aggressively presumed to instruct the doctor that "everything is to be done to prolong Joseph's life. I'm not ready for him to die yet. We have business to discuss and family matters to be settled. If you let him die now, there is going to be big trouble. I'll sue you for neglect or whatever else I can drum up. I'm tired now from my flight from South America, so I'm going to my hotel for some sleep. I'll expect Joseph to be alert and ready to talk to me when I come back later in the morning when I'm rested."

Both the physician and Joseph knew his condition was unpredictable—no one knew from one hour to the next if

Joseph would ever waken again. Joseph had asked to be kept sedated "even if this means I will die sooner. I've finished my business and am ready any time."

To the physician his duty was clear. His responsibility was to respect his patient's wishes and allow him to die in peace and comfort as soon as possible. But the peace they both sought was shattered by the interference of the only member of Joseph's family. Inevitably Joseph would die very soon. If the brother tried to pursue his threat of a lawsuit, it would probably be thrown out of court, if it even made it that far. But in the interim, the brother could make the doctor's life miserable and greatly disturb his medical practice.

Joseph did not believe he required a Durable Power of Attorney for Health Care. The only person who could even remotely challenge his wishes was a brother he had not seen for five years.

(Postscript: Joseph died with dignity at 7:15 that same morning. The doctor and I—Joseph's friends—were present.) The brother had left strict instructions at the hotel desk that he was not on any condition to be disturbed.

When advance directives are fully recognized in every province and territory as well as in federal law in Canada, there can be no reason for qualms or need for hesitancy on the part of a doctor about following the patient's stated directions for care. I believe this will happen in the foreseeable future. In the interim, if it came to a court of law, there is no doubt in my mind that the physician would be exonerated of any wrongdoing. Simple justice demands that a person's professional and personal life must not be placed in jeopardy for following the directions of a competent patient.

CHAPTER SIX

Is There a Choice?

When we examine end-of-life issues, particularly as they relate to ourselves or our families, the questions that come to mind may include:

- What did the doctor really say?
- How long do I have to live?
- Will I have to stay in hospital?
- Who will take care of me?
- Will I be in pain?
- What if the pain gets worse? Will a doctor be there to help me?
- How is my family going to react?
- Should I tell them?
- Should I put myself through chemotherapy?
- What is chemotherapy anyway?

Some of these and hundreds of other questions have answers. Some do not—not at present, anyway. First, however, we must be sure that the information we have received is correct.

All too often the message an ill person hears is incomplete. The alternatives offered appear to be so limited that only one course of action seems possible. Even though health-care providers may have supplied information about a range of choices, the message does not always get through. There can be as many reasons for this gap in communication as there are people (see Chapter 2).

PALLIATIVE CARE

One style of care for the terminally ill that has come into wide acceptance in recent decades is palliative or hospice care. Palliative care is defined by Harry van Bommel, author of *Dying for Care: Hospice Care or Euthanasia*, as "the physical, emotional, spiritual and informational support given to someone who has a terminal or life-threatening illness and to their families."*

The terms "palliative care" and "hospice" are essentially interchangeable. Hospice care is an interdisciplinary program of palliative care and supportive services that may be provided either in the home or at a hospice centre. Such centres may be free-standing settings such as Casey House in Toronto; hospital wards that have been specifically redesigned and converted into units more conducive to the "care versus cure" philosophy; scattered beds within an acute-care or chronic-care facility designated for terminally ill patients; or a system of community-oriented home-care services for palliative-care patients and their families.

Palliative care is a philosophy of caring for a person, and the person's family and friends, with the goal of alleviating suffering and providing support rather than curing the disease. Palliation deals with physical symptoms, stresses, anxieties, feelings—the total situation and circumstances of the dying person and the person's family and caregivers.

While it may be necessary to continue with such things as some diagnostic tests, the aim of these procedures is to make the end of life more comfortable rather than to prolong the dying process or cure the disease.

Experts caring for those at the end of life are called palliative-care specialists.

---

*(Toronto: NC Press, 1992), p. 15.

BACKGROUND TO
THE DEVELOPMENT
OF PALLIATIVE CARE

The primary model of palliative care was developed in England, by Dame Cicely Saunders. Cicely Saunders designed a "hospice" unit specifically to meet the needs of terminally ill patients. From this facility, hundreds of other specialists have been trained and have carried her philosophy of care throughout numerous countries.

In Canada, the first such service was opened at the Royal Victoria Hospital in Montreal, where a section of the hospital was redesigned to meet the needs of dying patients and their families, friends and care providers. (At this and many other such facilities even the family pet is welcomed for visits.) When the need outgrew the number of beds available, trained personnel were assigned to attend patients in general hospital wards who could not be, or preferred not to be, accommodated in the palliative-care unit itself. Dr. Balfour Mount has become internationally famous for his work as founder and director of the Royal Victoria Palliative Care Unit. Under his direction the service to patients and their families and friends is compassionate, administratively exemplary and innovative. The Montreal unit has become a sort of Mecca visited by the many Canadians who wish to learn about palliative care.

Free-standing hospices have not gained as much popularity in Canada as they did in the United States, under the guidance of Dr. Kübler-Ross. There are only a few free-standing institutions in Canada. Those that do exist may specialize in a particular disease; for example, Casey House in Toronto accepts only persons suffering from AIDS. While this organization and project has been an extremely worthwhile model, I believe that in the near future we may see a revision of policy that will recommend a different, or perhaps expanded concept of care more in keeping with the home-care model. Some individuals, among them Dennis Norton in Winnipeg, have undertaken to provide one-on-one care of persons at the terminal stage of AIDS in their own homes. This is difficult and may be personally taxing for the caregiver, but it can also be rewarding for both patient and caregiver.

Every dying person and the person's family should have access to palliative-style care. It ought to be a fundamental part of routine health care in Canada. Unfortunately, however, this is not yet the case.

SOME PROBLEMS— REAL AND PERCEIVED— WITH PALLIATIVE CARE

1. A lack of personnel and financial resources. Some opponents of other choices, such as physician-assisted dying, will tell you that if there were adequate financial resources for every person who needs hospice care, no one would ever choose suicide or a physician-assisted death. I do not agree, for reasons that will become clear.

2. Insufficient beds and services allocated to specialized care of the dying. Harry van Bommel, author of *Dying for Care*, has stated in public interviews and speeches that palliative care is actually available to only 5 per cent of those who need it in Canada.

3. Inflexibility within the existing hospice services.

4. Overemphasis on "specialty" training for those who wish to work in the field of palliative care. We already know the value and reliability of volunteer palliative-care programs and services, but some medical professionals do not recognize as legitimate the independent work of unofficial experts, even those trained within other areas of the health professions.

5. Overemphasis on research at the expense of patient care. Specialists in this field, as in many others, become so concerned

with research and testing of their theories that the primary goal of caring for the terminally ill individual gets lost.

6. Differences in personal preference. Some people do not find the concept of palliative care acceptable to their personal goal of quality of living and dying. These persons choose a different death for themselves.

Overall, I strongly believe that the primary roadblock to providing hospice care to persons in need is a matter of history repeating itself. Medicine has a tradition of turning concepts of care into "specialties", making all sorts of conditions for the practice of each specialty that unnecessarily limit its application and usefulness.

The Case of Maryann and Martha

At 8:45 a.m., Maryann walked into the Dying With Dignity office. She had just passed another sleepless night and decided she would come to the office early on the chance that someone would be there to help her. We shared hot chocolate and some emotional moments together, as Maryann slowly told her story.

Maryann's mother, Martha, is a resident in a large convalescent nursing home. She is eighty-eight years old and is suffering terribly from emphysema, angina, osteoporosis and, most recently, a compression fracture of the spine. Mentally, however, she is and always has been fully competent and capable. Martha had been in an acute-care hospital for a short time for treatment of the spinal condition, but her age and general frailty deterred the doctors from attempting surgery, so she has now been transferred to "rehab".

The rehabilitation hospital has said to Maryann, "Confidentially, Martha is not a likely candidate for total rehabilitation. We'll keep her as long as we can, but, you know, beds are scarce." So there she lies until the allotted time for such stays is up. At that point she will be transferred to yet another institution, until fate intervenes to grant her the merciful death she so desires.

Meanwhile, hospital policy and her assigned physician deny her even a modicum of comfort. I asked Martha and Maryann's permission to arrange a conference with the institution's primary-care physician and head nurse to inquire about and advocate on a number of quite routine comfort-care measures.

Could she have oxygen to assist her breathing? I asked. The response was, "No. You see it won't really do her much good physically considering the condition her lungs are in, and she would just become psychologically dependent on it."

Could she be given food that she could swallow, instead of tough meat that choked her? The head nurse's reply was, "It's better to keep her on as routine a diet as possible. Don't baby her so."

What about small doses of morphine to give her some relief from her constant, agonizing pain? The answer was yet another no. "This is a rehabilitation hospital. We do not encourage the use of narcotics. After all, the patient might then not be a candidate for the nursing home when her time is up here, and where would that leave us all?"

My involvement in this case lasted just a little over three weeks. Yet for many months, if not years, Maryann and Martha had been frustrated by these and other restrictive attitudes and policies that are so prevalent in the health-care community. I was determined to find some remedy for their situation. After receiving permission from Martha, we had a lengthy conference with her family physician. It was agreed that we would try to have her moved home.

It was fully understood by all that Martha did not want to have her existence prolonged, for it had long ceased to be a life in which she could find pleasure to balance the constant suffering. Even the time she had with Maryann was coloured by her unremitting pain and by worry over her daughter's lack of rest. She told me privately in one of our many conversations that her life had been rich in the love of her family and friends and that she was ready to go to God.

The home-care team and the VON (Victorian Order of Nurses) nurse were most helpful in setting up regular visits. They taught Maryann how to give her mother the medication she required and what food to prepare to try to support her dwindling appetite. A homemaker was scheduled to come in twice a week to help with the cleaning, shopping and any errands that needed attention.

We also met with a few close friends, who were grateful to be asked to help. One was a recently retired registered nurse, and she and another friend were adamant that they could manage as a team to sleep over every third night to allow Maryann a respite. Maryann was to sleep at the nurse/friend's house and take care of her two new kittens. Both experienced the healing powers of being relieved of some responsibility without burdening the other person.

A volunteer from the church welcomed the opportunity to come and help Maryann with Martha's evening care—turning and bathing her and helping to make her comfortable for the night.

I encouraged these gracious ladies to read June Callwood's book *Twelve Weeks in Spring*, which provides helpful insights into a team approach toward providing hospice care in the home.

At this point, Maryann and I had a talk with Martha. We had wanted to make sure all the services she would need could be put in place before we got her hopes up about returning home. Martha was thrilled and said quietly to her daughter, "and it won't be for too long, dear, for God is going to take me to His home soon."

During many telephone calls and personal visits, I was

reassured to find mother and daughter relaxed and peaceful. The friends and professionals alike had faithfully respected the wishes of these two loving people.

The parish priest happened to drop by during my visit one day, and we had a long talk about setting up a "caring committee" within the church community. I promised to help him get such a program started.

At home, pain was not a problem, for the family doctor had ordered an infusion pump whereby a small needle is inserted into the tissues just under the skin to routinely inject morphine. This way Martha received a steady, continuous small dosage, and Maryann and the other caregivers did not have to worry about finding a spot in which to inject her, or about the correct dose to be administered, or about making sure someone experienced in giving injections was always present. Nor did Martha need to be stuck with a needle every three or four hours. Of course, a pain pump could also have been ordered by the hospital physician, if he had been so inclined, but that would have contravened this particular hospital's policy of denying morphine to "chronic" patients. All other needs seemed to be met with equal ease, through the superb cooperation of this customized home-care team.

Two weeks after coming home, Martha died peacefully in her sleep, with Maryann stroking her face, dry-eyed and grateful for the final end to her mother's suffering.

Maryann has adjusted to her grief and is now a volunteer helping others to assist their loved ones to die at home.

Martha's experience of dying is a prime example of good palliative care in action, without the need of formally qualified palliative-care specialists. All the members of Martha's team became part of her group of experts, learning and contributing as they went along. Martha was denied nothing and was content. Her home-care setting became a classroom in which many others learned about and benefited from participating in the hospice experience, without adding to the demand for scarce hospital resources or increasing the drain on the public purse.

Another, somewhat different experience evolved for me some fifteen years ago, before the founding of Dying With Dignity.

The Case of Mrs. W

Shortly after I moved into a new neighbourhood in Toronto, I became aware of a particular high-pitched cry emanating from a house a few doors up the street. After making a discreet inquiry I paid a call on my new neighbour. The lady answering the door was about the same age as myself, warm and friendly. She invited me in for tea and welcomed me to the block.

After a few moments of idle chat I broached the subject that had brought me to her door. Telling her of my background as a nurse, I mentioned that I had noticed the cries and recognized them as the sort of sound frequently associated with Alzheimer's disease. The main purpose of my call was, I explained, to offer, if she ever needed any help, to be available to her.

She was so relieved and grateful that she began to weep softly, explaining the all-too-common dilemma of people with chronically ill family members. Her mother had developed Alzheimer's disease some six years ago and had become progressively more disabled, both physically and mentally. For the last three years Dorothy, the daughter, had not been able to leave the house, except for the occasional visit to a dentist or doctor for her own needs. At these times a neighbour living between our two houses would come in and stay with her mother. All her groceries and other necessities were delivered to her.

When I suggested she might like to get out to go to a movie, do her own shopping occasionally, or just go for a walk in the crisp fall air, her initial reaction was so hopeful and happy she seemed to glow. Then, just as quickly, her smile left her, and she explained that she felt her mother might be too panicked if she was not there.

After further discussion and after I had paid a visit to Mrs. W's room, we decided to give it a try. I promised to come by early the next evening when I returned home from work so that she could go out for an hour to do just as she pleased. Much to her amazement, and my gratitude, for I had not really known what kind of difficulties I might encounter, Mrs. W was most cooperative as I sat near her bed and read to her.

Mrs. W was quite content as long as the story was always the same—*Alice's Adventures in Wonderland*. After a few such visits I tried to find out how much Mrs. W understood of the story, but all she wanted was to hear the familiar words again and again. The tale of Alice had lost itself in the comfort of the sounds. But that didn't matter, for it made Mrs. W happy.

The next time I visited I brought my large Persian cat, Mr. Oliver, to join our small reading group, and Mrs. W was delighted to have him lie quietly on her lap or beside her on the bed as she absent-mindedly stroked his long, blond fur. He soon became a regular partner in our time together.

The experiment of giving Dorothy short breaks was so successful we decided to try to expand the idea. I asked a number of neighbours if they would come to visit one evening. We explained that Dorothy's mother was suffering from Alzheimer's disease and could not be left unattended. She was not violent or dangerous in any way. She had a very sweet disposition, and the screams they had no doubt heard were her way of communicating some distress—usually of quite a minor or routine nature. For instance, Mrs. W would scream if she wanted a drink of water, or to have help to travel the short distance to the bathroom, or to be helped back into bed. She was very frail and had little memory, but loved to be read to. On Dorothy's behalf, for she was too shy

IS THERE A CHOICE?

to make such a request, I inquired if there was anyone living close by who had some free time and who would be willing to volunteer to relieve Dorothy occasionally.

The response was quite touching and, to Dorothy, almost overwhelming. Each person, it seemed, had a similar experience to share of a granny or a friend who had been caught in the same sort of trap. Most of the neighbours volunteered immediately for an hour here or there, and almost before Dorothy realized it, she was not only receiving respite from her mother's constant demands but had also acquired new friends who were also learning the real meaning of community.

One of the neighbours took on the responsibility of scheduling with Dorothy; another decided to arrange for "Dot" to take a weekend trip to go to the Stratford Shakespearean Festival. Our local gardening authority undertook to help Dorothy (and some of the rest of us) put our gardens and lawns in "apple-pie order", as he called it. And so the concept of community became a reality, developing from one caring interaction to another. I'm not pretending it was always a perfect system, but generally things worked quite well, and if someone needed help, there were many sources to draw on, including the regular VON nurse, who was gracious and pleased to encounter such cooperation.

In fact, when Mrs. W died a year later, the habit of helping was so much a part of our experience that it continued, benefiting many neighbours, including myself when I became seriously ill a few years later.

INSTITUTIONALIZED
PALLIATIVE CARE

In general, I am a strong proponent of all kinds of palliative care—the formal variety as well as the more casual sort of care provided in many family settings. I do disagree, however, with the tendency of the medical establishment to focus on it as a "specialty" to which more of Canada's already scarce financial and human resources should be allocated. Rather, I believe this type of care would serve all better if it were treated as a part of standard medical practice.

All doctors should be knowledgeable about and capable of providing good pain management to their patients—not just physicians with experience in palliative care. MDs who are not presently so qualified should surely expand their education immediately. When a person is reaching the final stages of life, it is natural and reassuring for them to have their family physician providing the immediate "hands-on" care for both the patient and the family. And yet more and more often the family physician is sidelined by a "specialist" who has known the patient and family only briefly. When the illness is cancer, the oncologist takes over. If it is AIDS, the specialist in that field assumes primary-care responsibilities. And if the patient is dying where there are palliative-care facilities, it is the palliative-care specialist who determines the best treatment modality to be employed. All these very highly qualified doctors are relative strangers to the ill person.

Of course we must also recognize that many people, whether from choice or circumstance, do not have a family doctor. Many people, in fact, do not have families or friends who are in a position to take over or even assist with their care at the end of life. For these persons, acceptance into a palliative-care program is a reasonable and invaluable alternative.

Another group of people choose not to be cared for at home or by family members or friends. For these persons, too, admission to an institutionalized hospice setting can be a blessing.

To summarize: palliation involves a philosophy of care, one that is based on caring and not on attempts to "cure" that are clearly futile. Properly planned palliative care does not include invasive procedures, but focuses on symptom control and pain management and on carrying out the patient's wishes with respect to quality of life and death.

While most persons in palliative care and hospice situations usually receive good symptom management, such is not always the case. Some patients feel that only if they are willing to forfeit their right to make choices do they receive all the help they need. Even then, there are palliative-care physicians who will deny the suffering person sufficient analgesia to control pain.

The Case of Mr. V

Mr. V sought my advice more than a year ago when he first received the diagnosis of a brain tumour. He told me the cancer was too far advanced for surgery and he understood he would live three to eighteen months by the most generous estimate his neurosurgeon could provide.

He was a man in his mid-seventies who had emigrated to Canada from Czechoslovakia about thirty-five years ago. He followed a strict code of conduct, according to which he believed his wife and daughter should not have to make decisions about the acceptance or refusal of life-support treatments should he become incapable of communicating his own wishes. Therefore he wished, while he was competent, to sign an advance directive that he hoped would cover all contingencies.

Mr. V had chosen to remain at home and had been receiving palliative-care service that provided home visits by the physician as well as other members of the team. He had experienced a gradual deterioration up to about three weeks before the final crisis.

By now he was uninterested in food but was able to take enough fluids to keep himself from feeling thirsty. He could no longer walk and had full nursing service to provide him with routine physical care.

Mr. V's wife was grief-stricken and was able to contribute little more than some transient emotional support. It was his daughter, Theresa, who had taken a leave of absence from her work, who now proved to be the primary family caregiver. She took care of both her mother and her dad, consulted with the doctors and nurses and generally managed the household around her father's needs.

On a couple of occasions she called me with concerns about the borderline pain control Mr. V was receiving. I visited and consulted with the nurses and between us negotiated with the doctor in charge to modify his narcotic orders accordingly. However, I sensed that Mr. V, his daughter and the nurses were becoming increasingly worried about the doctor's reluctance to increase the dosage much further.

Finally, Theresa asked outright if she should try to engage another physician for her father. Taking all the ramifications of this into consideration, we agreed to hold off on a decision just a little longer, as Mr. V kept saying, albeit with less and less conviction, that the palliative-care physician had assured him he would not die in pain.

About three o'clock one afternoon I received a call from Theresa at the Dying With Dignity office. I could hear her father screaming in the background. She told me that the pain had been increasing steadily now for some hours, and that although the doctor's service had been notified, he had not yet returned their call. I told her I would come immediately.

As I approached their home (I was still two doors away) I heard almost inhuman screams issuing from the house. Running to Mr. V's door I almost collided with the palliative-care doctor as he was leaving the house. It was the same doctor who had promised his patient he would not die in pain.

I asked him why he was leaving when Mr. V was screaming like this? What did he intend to do to bring the suffering under control? His response was, "This patient is chronically ill and also over-emotional. I can't be responsible for encouraging dependent behaviour. He'll just have to cope with the dosage he is on now."

When I suggested that the pattern of deterioration and the symptoms themselves were sufficient evidence that Mr. V would die soon—that there was little sense in worrying about drug dependence when Mr. V was in such agony and that he, the physician in charge, had an obligation to ask Mr. V about his choice of care—he replied that he had made his decision and would not change his mind.

Theresa asked this doctor to withdraw from the care of her father, and Mr. V agreed with this decision.

Fortunately, we were able to call upon another doctor with more enlightened views, and although the alternative offered Mr. V was a drastic measure, a surgical procedure was performed within a short time and his pain was immediately gone.

Mr. V died less than forty-eight hours later, content, lucid, pain-free and grateful for the quality time he had been able to experience those last two days and nights with his wife and daughter.

PAIN CONTROL

Pain can be managed in a number of ways—some of them quite harmless and non-invasive. I have discussed in an earlier chapter the myths of narcotic dependence and possible "overdose" from large doses of painkilling drugs, such as morphine. It is also worth mentioning that plain aspirin and acetaminophen (e.g., Tylenol) can be quite efficient in dealing with simple to even moderately severe pain and do not cause constipation and other devastating side-effects. In fact, such drugs are more valuable and effective in treating the pain of some physiological conditions than the most powerful narcotic. Another very effective option is to alternate narcotics with non-narcotics, or to use aspirin or Tylenol for the "breakthrough" type of pain that can occur between doses of narcotics. The trick—and it is not such a difficult one with a little bit of careful observation and cooperation between the health-care workers and the patient—is to find the balance that works best for each individual.

Steroids and anti-inflammatory medications, tranquillizers and certain anti-anxiety, hypnotic and other drugs can also be very useful as acceptable methods of controlling pain.

Strange as it may seem to some, chemotherapy that may not be therapeutically valid for curing a cancer or other disease can also be a helpful part of a pain-management plan. One must be sure to have good advice in weighing the potential risks versus the probable benefits with this as with any other treatment.

In addition to chemical means, a number of other methods of pain control are available. Acupuncture is an ancient form of pain management, and more recently even less invasive varieties of this treatment have come into favour, such as acupressure. Whether it be meditation, music therapy, yoga, tai chi, funny films, classical or funky music—if it works for you, GO FOR IT!

OTHER ALTERNATIVES

Many other styles of treatment and approaches to life-threatening illness also deserve attention. All too often traditional medicine scoffs at ideas that do not follow conventional lines of thinking. Of course we must be on the alert for frauds and fakes that merely exploit people's vulnerability. And those facing the threat of terminal illness are frequently in their most vulnerable state.

However, just because an idea is new does not make it bogus. Some individuals find comfort in trying a number of homeopathic remedies, even if they are not altogether convinced the treatments will cure the disease. At times it is good to be proactive, and to search out possible remedies, rather than simply sitting at home (or in a hospital) waiting to die or, for that matter, sticking with the standard approaches just because others before you have accepted them.

Not so many years ago, every woman who was diagnosed with

breast cancer was mutilated with a radical mastectomy. These women were often left devastatingly maimed, physically and psychologically. The medical profession now agrees, however, that only a small percentage of breast cancer cases require such radical surgery. Some accredited studies quote figures indicating that as many as 50 per cent of breast cancers respond as well to very minimal medical intervention as to major treatment and that the majority can be removed with a simple lumpectomy.

It is both a strength and a weakness of traditional medical practice that it tends to be very conservative. It allows for very little flexibility, very little encouragement for those who wish to request or experiment with new concepts and alternatives for the ill.

Innovative thinking has helped many individuals to harness the healing power of their inner strength. I think of such works as Norman Cousins's *Anatomy of an Illness*, which explores the healing powers of humour; Dr. Robert Mendelsohn's *Male (Mal)practice*, an insightful investigation of the effects of the male domination of medicine; and more recently, Dr. Bernie S. Siegel's discussion in *Love, Medicine and Miracles* of the healing power of love.

When I was very ill in the early eighties, Dr. Carl O. Simonton's book *Getting Well Again: A Step-by-Step, Self-Help Guide to Overcoming Cancer for Patients and Their Families* was the current trend. His ideas on how our emotions can affect the body's ability to fight cancer cells were extremely innovative. Over the years he and others have modified their program, and perhaps patients have become more realistic than I was in terms of my personal expectations. I did not find success with the techniques Dr. Simonton described at that time.

And herein lies one of the traps the very ill can easily fall into, often through their own desperation, while in a vulnerable state. I began to blame myself for not trying hard enough, not following the philosophy closely enough; I even finally convinced myself that there was some deficiency in my motivation, that I did not value wellness enough to make the disease disappear. With the help of some strong friends I did come to terms with the reality that for me this particular method of therapy was not right, even though I did and still do believe the principles are helpful and may be appropriate for numerous others.

SERIOUS QUALITY-OF-LIFE
DECISIONS TO BE MADE

Every illness has its own persona, its own face, and its own dilemmas. I cannot possibly cover in this book all the quality-of-life decisions that can and should be made. Such an assessment and evaluation requires one-on-one counselling for each individual and a more expanded, in-depth look at the possibilities. I will try, however, to deal with some of the more obvious points that deserve attention by patients and their families and caregivers.

At least some of these issues should be addressed in your Living Will or Durable Power of Attorney for Health Care (see Chapter 5). Even so, as I have stated earlier, we cannot possibly predict every issue with which a disease will confront the individual.

In general, you may have decided that when you near the end of life you would rather die in your own home than in an institution. If this is feasible, state your preference loud and clear, both in your Living Will and to all those around you. If you are not being heard, call in an advocate to help negotiate your wishes.

The choice of whether or not to consent to various treatments should also be stated in your Advance Health Care Directive. However, it is the physician's responsibility to keep an ill person constantly informed as to changes in her or his condition, so that reasonable decisions may be made or altered according to the patient's preferences.

A very dear friend who was dying of ovarian cancer had completed a Living Will in the early stages of her illness. In it she had stated that she would never permit nasogastric (a plastic tube inserted into the stomach through the nares) or gastrostomy (a tube inserted through an incision in the skin into the stomach) treatments as part of her care. This was written into her Living Will

130

specifically to prevent any type of force-feeding from being attempted should she become incapable of refusing consent to the procedure.

As the disease progressed it became more and more apparent that in fact an opposite situation was developing. The tumours in her abdomen began to grow very quickly and caused a blockage fairly high in the bowel. Rather than a concern to force food into her system, the problem now was how to relieve her distress from the accumulation of fluids within the upper bowel, stomach and oesophagus. A nasogastric tube could not handle all the accumulated fluid, and the only solution was the insertion of a gastrostomy tube located so as to relieve the constant pressure and discomfort. I discussed this with my friend and she immediately amended the Living Will and consented to the surgery. The purpose was, after all, not to prolong the dying process but rather to provide a reasonable level of relief from the suffering.

Similar types of flexibility in decision making may be necessary with many situations. The person suffering from ALS may initially make a decision to refuse to be suctioned if fluids start to build up in the throat and lungs. Many persons also determine in advance that they do not wish to be treated with respiratory assistance such as a ventilator. While this decision may continue for the duration of the illness, there must always be the option to change one's mind. It is the responsibility of health-care providers to reassure their patient of his or her precise health status at all times so that informed choices are possible.

I have met many patients with cancer and other apparently irreversible conditions who, after researching alternative treatments, decide on a course of therapy that many traditional doctors might not approve of. Unfortunately, sometimes if the patient still wishes to proceed with an experimental course of non-traditional treatment, the family practitioner may refuse to continue caring for the patient and family. This seems unnecessarily rigid to me. What is lost if a patient finds comfort—physical, emotional, spiritual—in pursuing an alternative type of treatment?

I recall a friend's account of her husband's situation. This gentle-man believed to the day he died that he had extended his life by a year and a half by sticking to a diet of organically grown fruits and vegetables puréed and supplemented with specific minerals and vit-amins. The diet sounded dreadful to me, but what does that matter? He had faith in it, and in the long run seems to have gained some great quality time with his wife and children.

He and his youngest son spent an entire summer at the cottage taking apart and restoring an old engine. The father found joy in teaching the son some of his special skills, and the son is left with a marvellous memory of a rich, rewarding and very personal time together. The motor will lose its usefulness and value soon enough, but the memory will influence the son's impression of living and dying throughout his life. The greatest loss this family experienced by the father's choice of treatment was that the family doctor abandoned his patient because "to continue to care for you if you persist in this treatment would be to say I approve of it. I cannot do that."

SUICIDE AND PHYSICIAN-ASSISTED DEATH

Finally we come to the ultimate and what I believe is the supreme choice each person is entitled to. There are valid cases where physi-cian-assisted dying is a fitting response. If we believe that rational, capable human beings have a right to self-determination, then I be-lieve that right must include a choice for assisted death under care-fully regulated circumstances.

Physician-assisted dying must be a legitimate and legal option for the very few persons who are likely to choose it. To allow less is to impose a sentence of suffering on a person that is inhumane and hypocritical in a free, democratic society.

I would qualify the above by stating that physician-assisted dying could only be acceptable under the guidance of a protocol that would include regulations to safeguard the vulnerable and disenfranchised in our society. It would not be acceptable for such persons to feel that their existence is so burdensome that euthanasia is their only choice.

Perhaps I need to clarify why I believe this option would be acted upon by only a small percentage of persons. In my experience with those who are initially grappling with the information that they have a terminal condition, many express a sincere wish to "get it over with". These persons state at this time a need either to take their own life quickly, or to find a physician who will agree to provide the means and sometimes be the agent of the person's death "when I decide it is time".

This initial reaction and its expression are quite in keeping with the normal fears and frustrations of trying to cope with information that is very difficult to accept. This is also a time of testing—testing family, friends and caregivers; even testing oneself. All too often, however, there is no one to listen. The family, friends and caregivers are trying to assimilate and cope with their own anticipatory grief, deal with their own fears and confront their own mortality in the mirror of the person in front of them. They also find it too painful at this time to truly listen to such statements. They fear they might say the wrong thing, therefore contributing to a perceived feeling of hopelessness in the ill person, who is talking about what has been, until very recently, a taboo subject.

To find an individual, whether a counsellor, chaplain, social worker or friend, who will not only permit but encourage the ill person to talk about these feelings is a relief and a consolation. It provides a forum in which all subjects are welcome and all feelings are allowed. Sometimes this is all the ill person requires—to express such thoughts openly, without fear of being considered crazy or "clinically depressed". Once this goal has been achieved, whether it takes a short or long time, the person's sense of powerlessness is overcome or at least put into its proper perspective, and the thought that was bursting to "get out" is complete.

Some individuals, however, have a sincere and quite rational need to direct the time and manner of their own death. In these persons one must recognize there is no other dignified or satisfactory option. In Chapter 9 I will discuss the ramifications of such a decision, but for now will deal with this only as a matter of fact.

ANTI-CHOICE FACTIONS

While there are those who are opposed to self-determination at the end of life, there is a large segment of our society (over three-quarters of Canadians) who would vote to legalize euthanasia or physician-assisted suicide according to 1992 and 1993 national polls (see Chapter 7).

The same sort of inflammatory rhetoric that was and is used by the anti-choice movement regarding abortion in Canada is also prevalent on the issue of physician-assisted dying and euthanasia. The words are graphic, dramatic and simplistic. When challenged in public or private debate, however, the so-called right-to-life opposition quickly resorts to name-calling and regurgitation of the same tired old anti-abortion slogans and arguments.

Some anti-choice lobbyists are, of course, people with strong religious convictions who truly believe what they say and who live their own lives accordingly. They believe that life of and for itself must be preserved and prolonged at all costs. I do not quarrel with their personal beliefs or decisions. Far from it; I respect them and whole-heartedly support their right to choose. As long as only they themselves must pay the price of their beliefs, I would support them all the way. As I believe in a competent human being's right to self-determination, I would challenge any attempt to frustrate a patient's wish to live as long as possible, regardless of the circumstances. This is a fundamental principle of freedom and autonomy.

In reality, however, it is my experience that a great many followers of the "right-to-life" movement are ill informed about how much pain and suffering the dying individual is condemned to by such a stance. In televised and radio debates with representatives of groups such as Alliance for Life, Physicians for Life, Nurses for Life and the Christian Medical/Dental Society of Canada, I have found that the standard tactic is to attack me as a person who holds life cheap, places little value on suffering and would encourage suicide and murder as a convenience for weak, cowardly persons. (Paradoxically, these same groups also frequently favour a death penalty, believe war is inevitable, and condone violent acts of self-defence as righteous deeds. I will deal with these contradictions further in Chapter 11 and other portions of this book.)

At the World Federation of Right to Die Societies Biennial meeting in San Francisco in 1988, one of the speakers was the president of the California Medical Association. I recall him standing at the podium saying, "It's easy to die, just don't expect me to do it for you." Wherein he positioned his hand in the shape of a gun, held it to his own head and imitated pulling the trigger.

To die, either by natural causes or through the taking of one's own life, is seldom a simple or "easy" matter. It takes a great deal of determination and strength of purpose (especially in the prevailing legal climate) to plan for one's own death, to ensure that those who might be targets for harassment after the death are protected and to perform the irrevocable act that will end one's own life without placing other people's lives or well-being at risk.

On the plus side, some of the most peaceful, dignified deaths I have witnessed are those by suicide or physician-assisted death. The deaths of Betsy and of Michael (see Chapter 1) and of Mr. and Mrs. T (see Chapter 9) occurred with a deliberation and overwhelming sense of pride and satisfaction in their personal dignity and freedom. I envied them their peacefulness.

That said, I should also emphasize that I adamantly oppose any attempts to coerce or intimidate physicians, nurses or other caregivers into providing assistance to those who wish to end their lives before the normal course of disease dictates. There are enough doctors in Canada who would courageously, though regretfully, assist a patient to die if this was the patient's clearly, freely and repeatedly articulated choice and the only compassionate alternative.

CHAPTER SEVEN

Social Values

A BRIEF HISTORICAL
PERSPECTIVE ON MEDICINE
AND SOCIETY

The last century of medicine has been exciting, confounding and sometimes even miraculous. In the not-too-distant past, devastating illness regularly wiped out large segments of the world's population. Diseases such as plague, smallpox, rubella, scarlet fever, yellow fever, leprosy and tuberculosis killed or maimed hundreds of thousands of people, acting with genocidal force at times to obliterate whole tribes, especially in the more isolated regions.

While many of these diseases are still with us, the discovery of vaccines, other scientific advances and sometimes quite simple methods of prevention have made most of these virulent killers now at least controllable. The discovery of insulin (pioneered by F.G. Banting and H.C. Best, at Toronto) as a treatment for diabetes has not only prolonged lives, but has given persons stricken with the disease a quality of life impossible prior to 1920. Tuberculosis, while still a devastating illness, is not the death sentence of only a few decades past. And so it is with many killing diseases.

We understand better the role of cleanliness and reasonable isolation to prevent contagion. When I was a youngster, I recall, our household was disrupted and my poor mother cut off from the community for weeks when first one child and then another came down with measles, scarlet fever, and other childhood diseases. For long weeks at a time there would be a sign nailed to the front door by public health officials stating that our home was "Under Quarantine". Now, children are often back to school in days, because we better comprehend the ways in which diseases spread.

But while we have seen enormous successes, there are new scourges to remind us we are not so clever after all. At the same time as we are saving numerous lives through more effective treatments of some diseases—certain leukemias, for example—new diseases are being discovered faster than we can imagine. AIDS will probably be known by future medical historians as the most destructive and socially altering disease of the twentieth century. Undiagnosed until June 1981, this disease killed 100,000 persons in the next ten-year period in the United States alone. Untold numbers of persons suffer from contamination by HIV (human immunodeficiency virus), the virus associated with the development of AIDS. And AIDS, although we have only been able to identify it for thirteen years, has been responsible for enormous changes in our attitudes and interactions with each other throughout the world.

INSTITUTIONALIZED MEDICINE

Another drastic change in health care has been our increasing reliance on hospitals, nursing homes and other types of health-care "institutions". Until relatively recently, the majority of families cared for ill members in the home environment, and most doctors, nurses, midwives and other health-care providers travelled to the patient's home. Both these practices have become rare, although economic necessity and changing concepts of health care are now reversing these trends.

A couple of generations ago our grandparents spoke of hospitals as places one was sent to only for very serious illness, surgery (a drastic and much dreaded fate), some difficult births, if one had no family to provide care or if one was suffering from a disease that family members, no matter how loving, could not manage. When I began nursing in the mid-fifties it was not unusual to find a family with no history of hospital use.

Then we went through a period where hospitals became the "chic" place to visit for the wealthy and bored. One went there for a "rest cure" to be pampered and catered to. The poor, however, were left to seek other remedies for the stresses of life.

THE AGE OF
THE SPECIALIST

The second and third quarters of this century were an exciting time in medicine. There were new drugs, new surgical procedures, new treatment modalities of all kinds popping up every day. In fact new specialties in medicine were emerging with great regularity. This was the age when the doctor became not just someone who treated people but an expert in the care (and sometimes the cure) of the heart (cardiology) and shortly after in special surgery related only to the heart, veins and arteries (cardiovascular surgery); the nervous system—incorporating the brain, spinal cord, spinal nerves, autonomic ganglia and all the rest of the complex system that regulates reception and response to stimuli (neurology and neurosurgery); the respiratory system; the digestive system; and all the other systems that make up the human body.

In recent decades we have seen a proliferation of specialization and subspecialization in medicine. When I was training for a nursing career the new heroes were the cardiovascular surgeons and neurosurgeons. A doctor might now hold a live human heart and brain in his or her hands. This was visually recorded and brought to us in *Life* and *Look* magazines. We saw the first real pictures of the human foetus in the womb and were awestruck.

The downside was that men and women started to be as subdivided as the specialists who treated them. We were seen only as female patients by obstetricians/gynaecologists, or only as male patients by urologists, or only as heart patients by cardiologists. I have heard patients referred to only as "the gallbladder", "the hysterectomy", "the diabetic", "the amputee", "the cataract", "the gastric ulcer", "the duodenal ulcer" and so on. Specialists who treated bone problems (orthopaedic surgeons) became surgical subspecialists of the hand or the hip. We've all heard variations on the joke, "Oh no, I can't treat you. I'm a specialist in treatment of the right great toe. Your problem is in the left great toe." It sounds silly, but it also has the ring of unpleasant truth.

Transplants of body organs and parts went from the miraculous two decades ago to the commonplace. We can replace a kidney, a lung, a heart, a bowel, bone and artery segments, and knee and hip joints. Specialists re-attach limbs, a penis, a nose or an ear with great skill. Many of these latter discoveries came about through desperate measures on the battlefield to try to restore lives and bodies literally blown apart.

But all of this has come at a price. Of course we appreciate the restoration of health to many who would otherwise have died or been horribly disabled or maimed. No one wishes to deny the great benefits modern science has brought. But we must now ask whether advances in medical technology have too drastically disrupted the natural life cycle. Just because we can intervene to save or prolong life, does that mean we should always do so?

The miracles these last decades have brought have also created even greater moral dilemmas. Medicine can keep a body functioning for more than thirty years in a "persistent vegetative state". Is that how you would choose to exist? Never to see or hear or think, understand a word spoken to you, feel a hug or a kiss? To lie in bed or be moved to a chair like a piece of protoplasm—neither alive nor dead? And what about your family? Would you choose to have them visit and never know if you are aware of their presence, or not to visit and feel the pangs of guilt?

Do we ask the terminally ill if they wish to have death-prolonging treatments—all the "bells and whistles"—imposed upon them, or do we just avoid "unpleasant" discussions and proceed to do all that can be done to prolong dying just because it's possible? All doctors and nurses can feel like heroes. All families can forget about feeling guilty that they didn't visit Mom or Dad for the last two years. Tough words, maybe, but before you brush them off, ask if there is not a deeper value to consider.

In December 1991, the United States Congress passed a law, "The Patient Self-Determination Act", which requires all hospitals, nursing homes and other health-care facilities that receive government funding to discuss the question of life-prolonging measures with every patient within a reasonable time after admission. Every person (or the family if the patient is unable to communicate) is asked whether or not he or she would choose to have cardiopulmonary resuscitation attempted to prolong the person's life should this become necessary. While the law has some flaws, it is certainly a useful step toward acknowledging the right of patient choice.

We cannot simply blame advanced technology. We must also accept that we, as the consumers of health care, have not been sufficiently involved and vigilant with regard to the decisions that are being made for us. The general public needs more information and more education about the real cost, in personal and economic terms, of high-tech, low-touch medicine.

THE BIRTH OF THE BIOMEDICAL ETHICIST

Biomedical ethics is truly a child of recent developments in medicine. Few doctors are trained to pronounce on such issues as "What is life and where does it begin and end?" New specialists have to be educated to deal with these complex questions. It is an ever-expanding wheel, this matter of life and death. Doctors, nurses and the rest of society cannot expect a few specialists to resolve the problems for us. We can, however, engage their assistance in making our own decisions.

BIRTH AND DEATH
AS ILLNESSES

At times one gets the impression that we are afraid we shall run out of problems so we busy ourselves with fantastically creating new ones. Since when did the natural events of birth and death become a specialty or a disease process? And why?

We are no longer content to treat the living; we must also take over the role of a supreme power (or prove we can at least challenge that power) by creating life. So, too, it seems we must prolong life beyond its natural course.

And to do this we need "palliative-care specialists"—experts in the care of the dying. Terminal care was once the province of family physicians, but in this area, too, the general practitioner has been replaced by yet another specialist. Unfortunately, there are not and never will be enough palliative-care/hospice specialists to care for all the dying. Harry van Bommel, author of *Dying for Care*, estimates that approximately 5 per cent of those in need of terminal care have it available to them. So what is happening to the other 95 per cent of Canadians who are in need? And what about that unknown but significant percentage of persons who do not wish to be treated with palliative care, who would choose an expedited death—choose to die sooner rather than later—no matter how well their symptoms can be managed?

ATTITUDES OF FORMAL
RELIGION TOWARD DEATH

In the past fourteen years of my work with Dying With Dignity I have frequently been invited to "preach" or give an address by many of the religious denominations throughout Canada. Anglican, Presbyterian, Catholic, Unitarian, United Church, Jewish and various other congregations have reached out to discuss the issues of death and dying.

This was not a role I adapted to easily, for I am not a student of religion and am uninformed about what each group is truly looking for. The best I could do, I finally decided, was to share with them my own experiences of the fears, needs, wishes and values of those nearing the end of life as well as the concerns of families and friends. I would also share my ideas about what and how those affected can help each other and what role each person may play in providing a gentle, caring, comfortable and compassionate death for another individual.

Some groups were simply glad of the opportunity to learn about some of the fears of dying and what each of us can do about them. Recognizing what it is we fear is always the first step toward meeting and overcoming the problems. Following some talks, a church or community would establish a "caring committee" to offer support to the dying, and their families.

CHANGES IN FAMILY STRUCTURE

The twentieth century has seen the loss of intergenerational family units. In fact, in many families a single parent is responsible for most if not all the care of the children. Even where there are two parents, these are more often than not two working parents.

I have a number of siblings. Both our parents died this past year. It was a time of great sadness and yet of sensitivity and togetherness for all of us. Even with several of us to share the responsibilities of trying to meet the needs of both ailing parents, and even with the best cooperation and coordination of efforts, it was a demanding time. Like many families, my siblings and I come from various parts of the country and have full-time jobs and family commitments of our own. Even with the best home-care services the community could offer and willing help from relatives and friends, there were times of extreme stress.

I am all too aware of how few families have the resources to pull together a sufficient number of people to assist them in their hours, weeks and sometimes months of need. What is the solution? Is there a solution?

Perhaps if you start now you can find your own answer. Each of us needs to begin now (whatever our age) to build our own caring community. In Chapter 6 I talked about how, for a year, a group of neighbours worked together to provide respite care for the daughter of Mrs. W and how this pattern of involvement continued for others in need. These are the kind of communities our ancestors knew. There will never be enough health-care dollars to take care of each of us in our own homes or in health-care institutions, and we need to accept this fact sooner rather than later. If you and I expect a support system, we need to get busy building it by first offering our help and hands to others.

Statistics Canada tells us that by the year 2030, more than half of Canadians will be sixty-five years of age or more. While issues related to dying are certainly not the exclusive concern of the elderly, we must still consider what this means in terms of the demand for health-care providers.

Daniel Callahan, in his book *Setting Limits**, tells in the opening chapter of spending time in a "tearoom" when he was a child and being impressed by the prevalence of the frail elderly, "most mysterious in their solitude", in this quiet place. "Once in a while two elderly women would be eating together, but most often each was alone, dining delicately and slowly, obviously drawing out as long as possible the ritual of nourishment and life in a public place ... at the restaurant I saw ... old age as isolation and loneliness. Only later was I to visit nursing homes and to learn much more about old age as a time of crushing physical and emotional burden for some, and trouble to be endured until the release of death."

It does not have to be thus.

---

*(New York: Simon &Shuster, 1987) p. 13

THE ECONOMICS
OF HEALTH CARE

Economists all over the world are trying to forecast the future of health care into the next century. In Canada we are proud of our health-care system and accustomed to thinking of it as "the best". It's free, universally accessible and modern! But is it?

Certainly it is not free. Each Canadian pays dearly for the care every other Canadian receives. Doctors have the added perk and security of knowing in advance that their patients' bills will be paid. You have prepaid and will continue to shell out billions of dollars so that medical treatment will be there "when you need it".

It cannot continue. In 1992 and 1993 we have seen enormous cutbacks in services, facilities and treatments. People are waiting longer and longer for life-saving treatments. And yet we continue to spend more than 80 per cent of all health-care dollars on caring for those in the first and last year of life. I am not saying this is wrong. But I am asking when we are going to face some truths and re-evaluate this trend.

Already we are experiencing the results of decisions regarding allocation of health-care resources. If not now, the decisions will very soon be of this variety. "We have one intensive-care bed available. Who gets it? Will it be the seventy-five-year-old in pretty good health but needing an aortic aneurysm repair, or will it be the fifty-five-year-old father of three with an acute heart attack?" Or what about this one: "We have to cut $3 million from our budget this year. Do we let X number of nurses go, or do we forget about the new research project on prevention of cardiovascular disease?"

It sometimes is all too easy to fall into the trap of basing moral (or immoral) decisions on questions of convenience.

"LET THOSE INFECTED WITH AIDS HAVE EUTHANASIA!"

Can you believe that this sort of remark is one which I hear regularly in this civilized country of Canada? Well you had better believe it, because the attitude it reveals is part of the subculture that takes advantage of the vulnerable in our society. It is an aspect of the "me first" philosophy that can take a rational, reasonable argument for physician-assisted dying onto the real slippery slope some like to use as an excuse for prolonging life at all costs.

Slippery slope? Man has been on a slippery slope since we made the first decision to save one life rather than another. Every time we allocate health-care resources to one type of health promotion and not to another, it is the "thin edge of the wedge" (another favourite expression of advocates of life at any cost).

I do not fear these red-herring arguments because I have great faith in our society. Ninety-nine per cent of our health-care workers are highly ethical, caring persons making the very best decisions they can. The fact that they need to learn more about sharing decision making with their patients and with families, nurses, ethicists, clergy, etc., does not make them evil people. Rather, it makes them human and therefore fallible. Why do we try to pretend they are omniscient?

Most people accept right-to-die arguments more readily for some patients than for others. It may seem "easier", for example, to allow an AIDS patient to receive physician-assisted dying, or the person with ALS, or the patient screaming in agony from certain devastating cancers. But the fact that some patients seem more entitled to receive our moral "permission" to anticipate death obscures the real issue—that this is a basic human right.

We must find the time and the will to become better informed and certainly more involved in the debate about the right to a dignified death. Remember—it's only a matter of time. No one gets out alive!

OTHERS EXPRESS
THEIR OPINION

It has been consoling and edifying, in recent years, to see how many other responsible thinkers are entering into this debate. I wish I could invite each of you into my library of books and articles on this subject; but for now I will share only a few thoughtful pieces written and published by members of the clergy, an ethicist and a noted journalist.

"Doctors Should Let Us Go with Grace"

– Rev. Bruce McLeod, minister,
Bellefair United Church, Toronto, Ontario

"Increasing the morphine might embarrass her chances of recovery," said the intern in a Toronto hospital room last week. The older woman before him, unable to speak, had runaway cancer, stroke, a recently amputated leg, and a deep, wet cough. Eyes widening, face contorted, straining to double up, she cried out.

"It may not be the pain," the intern said: "Her agitation may be a function of her stroke." Nurses, providing hands-on care all day, disagreed.

"I can't watch her suffer like this," said one.

Since morning, they had tried to persuade her doctor to change the medication order which allowed for morphine by mouth or injection only. The woman could no longer swallow; a needle, administered with difficulty an hour later, still had no effect. The nurses wanted permission to hook up an intravenous drip to give steady, and adjustable, relief.

Her doctor, warning of the dangers of lowered breathing levels and possible addiction, retired to the operating room.

Hours later, an evening nurse supervisor, irate, sent a message saying the woman's family was outraged.

An intern was dispatched; he told nurses the order was unchanged. "She might die," he explained to visitors in the room. "We'll all die," someone replied. "What victory is a few more breaths?" The intern, neither addressing nor touching the woman, suddenly gave in.

A morphine drip was attached, the dosage just sufficient to cover the pain. Nurses fixed the woman's pillows, speaking to her reassuringly. Five days later, when I last saw her, she was quiet. Gangrene has struck her remaining leg. Her life is subsiding. But she does not cry out; though drugged, she responds to the voice of her closest friend.

"Some doctors have trouble with death," the evening supervisor said. "That's not my problem; it's theirs." She was quick not to include all doctors. Many, motivated by the same desire to alleviate suffering that first took them into their profession, exhibit great kindness to dying patients.

Others, however, are better at treating diseases than persons. Only reluctantly do they give up trying to cure. Once diseases prove resistant to their best efforts, these doctors seem at a loss. Their training, apparently, has not equipped them to help people die.

They should not be blamed too soon. They reflect the priorities of a society which likes people not to look their age, expects all diseases to fall before medical technology, and prefers not to speak of death at all.

It was not always so. Medieval paintings of the Dance Of Death showed kings and peasants dancing with images of their own deaths. Later woodcuts depicted joking Death transforming doctors' medicine bottles into hourglasses. The effect was not depressing. Death's familiar presence, as in some village life today, made the dance's brevity more precious than if it had no end.

Not until the Renaissance was the physician expected to

prolong life unnaturally. Nineteenth century bookplates show doctors battling personified diseases. In a 1930 print, a surgeon at bedside crushes approaching Death with a medical textbook. The doctor, not the patient, combats death; victory, it is implied, will, if not this time, eventually be won.

Yet, for all the wonders of medical progress, human life, as was said millennia ago, still averages out at "three score years and 10"—in privileged parts of the world more than that, in other places considerably less. The price of arrival on this amazing planet remains the same—the necessity to leave it. Those doctors serve best who help us, when the time has come, to go gracefully, not hanging on, and without unnecessary pain.

(This article originally appeared in the *Toronto Star*, July 28, 1989.)

"Euthanasia: Cruel or Merciful?"

– Rev. James Dickey, minister,
St. Andrew's Presbyterian Church, Stratford, Ontario

In 1847 British physician James Simpson pioneered the use of chloroform as an anesthetic. This great boon to suffering humanity was not perceived as such by all segments of society. On the contrary, some very vocal and literal-minded clergymen took it upon themselves to launch a crusade against the use of the anesthetic, most particularly in childbirth. After the Fall, did God not say to Eve (and through her to all women after her) "I will greatly multiply your pain in childbirth, in pain you shall bring forth children ..." (Genesis 3:16). What right had medical science to meddle with the word of God?

Of course, this mean bit of misogynist, fundamentalist thinking found few sympathizers. Fighting fire with fire (or perhaps fire and brimstone with fire and brimstone) one doctor—it may have been Simpson himself—pointed out that in the second account of creation "... the Lord caused a deep sleep to fall upon the man, and so he slept; then He took one of his ribs," (from which Eve was created) "and closed up the flesh of that place" (Genesis 2:21). As neat a justification of the use of chloroform as the proof-text method of abusing the Bible could afford. More effective was the imprimatur placed on the use of chloroform by the supreme arbiter of Christian morals, Queen Victoria. In 1853 she was given chloroform as an anesthetic during the birth of Prince Leopold. With the prince's birth the critics of chloroform ceased to receive even the slight support they might have had.

The debate on the moral propriety of anesthesia has never been revived. We can not, nor would we want to, forbid the amelioration of pain on so flimsy, even ridiculous, grounds.

The debate over the practice of euthanasia, a word adopted from the Greek meaning "easy or good death," not "mercy killing," is by no means as easily understood, or resolved, but some of the anxieties and fears expressed over the issue rest on no more substantial arguments than those raised by the Victorian literalists.

Unless one is an utterly consistent pacifist, unequivocally opposed to abortion, to some forms of birth control, to military or police action leading to death(s), and to capital punishment for any crime, the preservation of life at all cost is not an absolute, ultimate value.

If one is a Christian, the belief in another existence beyond death, though this life is to be lived "abundantly," keeps death from any greater stature than "the last enemy" to be "swallowed up in victory." This belief once led some sects of late 3rd and early 4th-century Christians to court martyr-dom. St. Anthony, during the persecutions of the Emperor Diocletian, journeyed a full 325 kms for the sole purpose of securing his own death. The church put a stop to this. St. Augustine, the pre-eminent theologian of his age, wrote against the practice and condemned suicide.

The church today holds life sacred, especially in the face of those who would throw it away, or take it away, using the promise of eternal life as a consolation prize. Nonetheless, it cannot have absolute ultimate value for the Christian either. It hardly did either for Christ or his disciples who knowingly placed themselves in life-threatening situations, with pre-dictable results.

To place an absolute, ultimate value on this life betrays either fear or superstition.

When the dying process has irrevocably begun, or rather, when it has been irrevocably accelerated—for we all begin the dying process at the moment of birth—I see no ethical or moral compunction to do nothing but let nature unwind what is left of that life until the end, however painful, sad, or even sordid. In these instances we are outside the realm of "suicide."

To assist in the process of dying, either passively, or, with safeguards, actively, is no more "playing God" than the employment of birth control (or restraint) in spacing the births of children. We assist the life process from conception onward, co-operate, through medicine, with God in the timing and shaping of his gift. To refuse to do so when, at the other end of life's journey, God's intentions and the body's deterioration are manifestly clear, is both cruel and unChristian.

Do the blank-minded, lying diapered and staring unre-sponsively at the ceiling, sometimes for years, provide us with a "lesson," a path for spiritual maturity through suffer-ing, or growth in grace? There are enough other lessons to be learned from the many other forms of suffering flesh is heir to. What kind of God would set such a final "lesson?" Not the one made manifest in Christ Jesus.

The 10 per cent or so of cancer patients for whom widespread metastases makes pain relief a hunt and chase, or for those for whom the pain-killing drugs provide no relief (a colleague of mine recently heard his mother die in scream after scream, over days), provide a lesson of sorts to those who watch with them; an unforgettable and totally unnecessary lesson.

Surely a legal process could be established whereby, in full health, a person could leave instructions that would apply in the event of such avenues to death. Surely the doctors could be protected by honoring their rights not to participate in active euthanasia, if they so chose.

Ambiguities will remain. For example, at what point can the suffering be considered terminal? With five days, five months or five years left? Life is never tidy, in the living of it, or in the decisions thrust upon us.

But I sincerely believe, with the late theologian and preacher Leslie Weatherhead, that "… those who come after us will wonder why on earth we kept a human being alive against his own will, when all dignity, beauty and meaning of life had vanished; when any gain to anyone was clearly impossible … I for one would be willing to give the patient the Holy Communion and stay with him while a doctor, whose responsibility I should share, allowed him to lay down his useless body and pass in dignity into the next place of being."

A much more relevant text than the one around which this column began is "Blessed are the merciful; for they shall obtain mercy."

(This article originally appeared in the *Toronto Star Saturday Magazine*, September 22, 1990.)

"Keeping Control Over Life and Death"

– Arthur Schafer, director, Centre for Professional
and Applied Ethics, University of Manitoba

Dying can be a dangerous business, especially for all of us who worry that, when we reach the end of our lives, we will simply lose control of our fate. In most cases, doctors and our families usurp the terminally ill patient's right to decide just what is done when death is at the door.

Not only may this loss of control undermine the patient's autonomy and sense of dignity, but the aggressive use of modern medical technology to prolong life may inflict unnecessary suffering.

These days, most of us seem fated to die in hospital, surrounded by rotating teams of anonymous health-care professionals rather than by family and friends. It may not be easy to die with dignity when you have tubes coming from every orifice and are either crazed with pain or stupefied by drugs to control it.

Scarcely more appealing is the prospect of lingering unconscious for days, weeks or months in a vegetative state. Of course, patients in terminal comas do not suffer pain or discomfort, but does that mean they aren't harmed when their lives are prolonged artificially?

For a great many people, the prospect of hanging on in such a state is worse than death, because it robs them of their dignity and imposes burdens on those they love.

Not surprisingly, there is a growing movement in Canada, and many other countries, to give some measure of control to patients by "de-medicalizing" death. In response, many hospitals have introduced palliative care wards, where the staff try to control pain and reduce discomfort but recognize that it may be better to accept the inevitable.

Given this trend, groups such as Dying With Dignity are lobbying for legal recognition of "living wills," which allow people to make sure they will die the way they want to even if they cease to be mentally competent.

Some people are shocked by the idea, but several provinces now recognize living wills as legally binding.

A leading Canadian cancer specialist has declared, without embarrassment, that these documents are "actually a way of making sure the patient is not assaulted."

Thousands of Canadians have drafted living wills, and many carry a little card in their wallet so that in the event of an accident, doctors will know when to stop treating them.

How disappointing, then, to discover from a study published in The New England Journal of Medicine that many hospital patients who signed living wills received the same treatment as those who had not. Part of the problem seems to be that information is simply not available to those deciding what treatment to give.

To avoid this, those concerned about how they die should do more than simply draft a living will; they should discuss their wishes with family, friends and their doctor. It also may be a good idea to give a trusted friend what is called "durable power of attorney," so he or she can serve as a surrogate decision-maker.

Hospitals can help in the process. For example, it is not uncommon to see DNR—do not resuscitate—written on the hospital chart of a terminally [ill] patient. Studies show, however, that only rarely is the patient actually consulted when this decision is made. (According to one survey, only five of 115 patients made the decision themselves; in most other cases, family members were involved.)

Why is this? Because it [is] usually hospital policy to take such a step only when death is imminent. By waiting until the last moment, they ensure the vast majority of patients won't be able to make the decision themselves.

A way must be found to approach patients about their wishes before they are too sick (or too sedated) to express them. The problem is that no time seems like the "right" time to do this. The solution may be to raise the issue as a matter of routine with everyone who is seriously ill when they are admitted to hospital.

This would certainly take a load off the family's shoulders. Having to choose whether your spouse, parent or sibling lives or dies can be highly stressful and divisive, pitting relatives against each other.

Some stress may be unavoidable, but the situation is seriously aggravated when—and this often happens in hospitals—the family is asked, "Do you want us to keep the patient alive or let him or her die?"

If, instead, people were asked to supply information about the patient's own attitudes and values, no one would have to "play God." The patient's wishes would prevail.

(This article originally appeared in the *Globe and Mail*, May 14, 1991.)

"Right to Die Needs Sanction in Law"

—Rev. John Wesley Oldham, minister,
Donnelly United Church, Winnipeg, Manitoba

I have noticed how your paper has given considerable coverage to the ongoing topic of "Doctor assisted suicide". The Jan. 14 issue ran both a statement by Catholic bishops as well as a letter to the editor.

The story of Sue Rodriguez, a mid-forties woman from B.C. with Lou Gehrig's disease, has caught the heart of compassionate Canadians even more so than did the Nancy B. saga.

I write as a cleric of 23 years, and as a member of the Right To Die Society and Dying With Dignity, two groups advocating the removal of doctor assisted suicide from the Criminal Code.

The recent Gallup poll reveals that 77 per cent of Canadians (up 2 per cent) are in favor of doctor assisted suicide for terminally ill people in ongoing suffering who wish to die.

The *Free Press* Jan. 14 article reveals that the Roman Catholic bishops are strongly opposed to the 77 per cent. Obviously the vast majority of Roman Catholics are ignoring the Pope and the bishops on both matters of birth control as well as doctor assisted suicide. I am very suspicious of a church dictating morality for a pluralistic society or claiming that it has a monopoly on knowing what dying people wish or need. I regret that the Catholic officials are opposing a basic right to self determination and patient autonomy. I have been advised that the Catholic church is facing legal action for apparently preaching lies and circulating false information in the State of Washington during a recent debate and vote on this subject.

Every week I visit people in nursing homes and extended care wards in hospitals. I expect that some of the people are happy there, but the blank faces and distant eyes of the majority reveal to me that the majority do not want to be there or here in the mental and physical condition they experience. Indeed I know of very few, if any, who want to exist in a drugged state or otherwise locked up as captives in a prison known as a residence or a nursing home, which is not home at all but a jail. At least car accidents or massive heart attacks kill you quickly instead of this slow dying under the so called best medical care.

I know of many people who are in a vegetative state and where treatment is futile, but they are kept from dying naturally, the way God intended, by being force fed with a tube. What an insult to one's dignity!

More and more ethicists are regarding this kind of so called treatment as a clear invasion of one's body. The quality of life for some can be improved, but for many, death is but being postponed while life is not enhanced. Until recently pneumonia was seen as a friend and as God's way.

Many people are asking me for advice as to how they can be assured they can die with dignity and not be kept captive to a doctor's fear of legal action. Certainly The Treatment Directive (Living Will) legislation is a small step in the caring direction. But research reveals that most people will never fill out living wills and many doctors ignore them. Besides, what you define as "heroic or aggressive measures" may be seen as routine treatment by the medical officials.

I realize that it is against the law of the land for me to give counsel or advice to a person asking about suicide. However, the law of Christian and humanitarian compassion, the law of the heart, takes priority over the criminal code.

I support the work of hospice and palliative care and am an advocate of a person's right to live. However, I am also called to speak out for those who wish to die before the law allows them to.

Currently many doctors in North America and in Manitoba are not recording the complete truth on death certificates because of the threat of legal action. There is an increasing example of cases across Canada where doctors have risked being honest about the actual cause of death, without losing their position in the medical community or facing legal action.

The time has come for Parliament to catch up to the 77 per cent of Canadians on this matter and give doctors the legal protection and give patients the right to doctor assisted suicide.

(This article originally appeared in the *Winnipeg Free Press*, Saturday, January 23, 1993.)

"Some Further Thoughts on Dying With Dignity"

– Tom Harpur, Toronto author and broadcaster

As most of you know, Sue Rodriguez, a 42-year-old British Columbia woman in the last stages of Lou Gehrig's disease, is seeking the right to a doctor-assisted suicide once her pain and helplessness render her unable to take her own life. Her lawyer will be presenting her arguments before the Supreme Court in Ottawa on May 20.

On March 21, in a column, *The right to die with dignity*, I argued that hers is a profoundly "pro-life" position and that Rodriguez is using her last hours in a heroic fight not just for herself—to avoid a hideous, terrifying death by choking and suffocation—but on behalf of all Canadians who don't want to spend their final hours as medical hostages, hooked to machines and drugged out of their minds. As one writer in The Star's editorial section said, the terminally ill are not simply in the hands of God, as many opponents of a merciful intervention insist, but, in most cases, "in the hands of the pharmaceutical companies."

My article, together with others on the same topic in *God Help Us*, has provoked a large number of letters, some abusive and ill-tempered, many supportive and "sound" in the sense that they agreed with my position! Seriously, I have learned much from all of them. One in particular was both moving and extremely articulate. I want to share some of it here.

The writer, a middle-aged woman who has been challenged by "moderate cerebral palsy" all her adult life, says the current pressure for some form of legal euthanasia and/or assisted suicide in extreme cases "frightens me." She says it has never been her physical limitations that have bothered her the most: "I have long since come to terms with the fact that I have to use a keyboard instead of writing; I have periodic pain and need to use crutches (both hips are dislocated as a result of an abusive physiotherapist); and eventually I did come to terms with being slow. What I have not been able to accept is the way people treat me and the internalized oppression of feeling that I am a burden to my family and myself."

Like many other disabled members of society, this woman has experienced a lifetime of being made to feel worthless, or at any rate less human and less valuable than those who—to all outsiders—seem "normal" and whole. Her parents, she says, treated her as a burden and as responsible in some undefined way for her limitations. She was constantly told she wasn't trying hard enough and, eventually, she became a sort of scapegoat for the family's emotional dysfunction. Both a brother and a sister were hospitalized for manic depression.

She writes: "To this day, it's not my physical limitations that stop me from working; it's my lack of confidence and self-esteem. I never feel good enough. Perfection seemed the way to compensate for my disability; instead, perfection has paralyzed me emotionally...." She was constantly warned to avoid being a problem and "not to bother" other people. She finds it all too easy to appreciate why so many people with disabilities are abused physically, sexually and emotionally. There's an unconscious sense out there that such people are unwanted anyway.

Given all of that, it's not difficult to understand this woman's apprehension that the disabled, especially if they are lonely, unsupported and poor, might feel societal and/or internal compulsion to have a doctor-assisted suicide or to seek some form of euthanasia (by direct, active medical intervention) to end their lives. Feeling themselves to be a burden, or at best marginal to mainstream society, they might feel it a kind of duty to either "off" themselves or to seek out a doctor to do it for them.

Since this woman's plea is honest and also represents an argument used by those who shout the slogan of "the slippery slope" whenever euthanasia is discussed, it deserves a reply. Euthanasia *could* be used by a Nazi-like society to get rid of the unwanted and to avoid the responsibility of compassionate caring for the weaker in our midst. We must be grateful for her cautionary note. But while giving it full weight, it's important not to overestimate its cogency.

Nobody in the current debate is talking about giving doctors or anyone else carte blanche to start killing people. To suggest this is either to miss the point or to fog the issue deliberately because of a hidden agenda. As with the recent legislation in the Netherlands, any move to a more loving and democratic approach to dying with dignity will be guarded by the tightest of preconditions and controls.

I have confidence in our doctors and I have confidence in the vast majority of Canadians who want significant changes made soon on this vital matter. Ours is a society that keenly wants to be more accepting of the disabled on one hand and more truly human in its approach to dying in our complex, high-tech world on the other.

Under any new legislation permitting doctor-assisted suicide or direct euthanasia for those who are terminally ill and in chronic pain (far more people than the critics care to admit) nobody, disabled or not, would be able to get a doctor to act on frivolous or socially engendered grounds. The proper medical criteria would have to be present, including corroboration of these by a second doctor and possibly a judge as well.

I have great respect for the lady whose letter I have quoted from here. I have little or none for those healthy people opposed to euthanasia who keep trotting out the line that because it might be abused it ought not to be permitted. If you follow that kind of logic to its conclusion, none of us would be allowed any freedom at all. Much too risky by far!

(This article originally appeared in the *Toronto Star*, May 9, 1993.)

"The Rodriguez Decision"

– The Venerable John Lawrence Moore,
clergy staff member, St. Patrick and St. Jude
Anglican Church, Winnipeg, Manitoba

The decision of the Supreme Court of Canada that refused to grant Sue Rodriguez's request for doctor-assisted suicide was distressing. My wife who died earlier this year at the age of 44 from complications arising from multiple sclerosis had desired assisted suicide five years ago. Being a member of the clergy for over 21 years I have too often witnessed the agony of the terminally ill who wanted to die and with them have entered into conversations regarding death and suicide. I support the right of terminally ill people who voluntarily desire death to receive what they want in the most preferred setting surrounded by family and friends and with competent counselling.

The 4–5 decision by the Supreme Court of Canada hopefully will generate momentum for Parliament to tackle this issue within the year on behalf of thousands throughout Canada who are in a similar situation to Sue. In the October 1 article entitled *Rodriguez faces final weeks*, Sue is quoted saying 'It has been worth it, far more than I ever anticipated'. We as Canadians will benefit from the courage, determination and leadership of this modern Canadian heroine.

The law needs to be changed allowing for assisted suicide and to permit counselling to commit suicide. According to the recent polls of Canadian opinion almost 80% of Canadian people support humane death provided there are safeguards for the terminally ill who voluntarily request assistance. Action by Parliament within the year as Chief Justice Lamer hopes could prevent unnecessary suffering for thousands of Canadians and their families who find themselves in this situation because of modern medical advances.

The danger of inaction is that individuals will prematurely end their lives or cause themselves grave injury and increased suffering from fear that they will eventually lose all control over their life.

My own wife lived for five more years after she repeatedly expressed a desire for assistance in dying. While palliative care could do many things it could not prevent the loss of dignity or the emotional, spiritual, physical and psychological suffering that occurred. It is difficult to fully appreciate the absolute terror involved as one's body slowly ceases to function, even including the loss of memory.

Individuals want and deserve to die with dignity in a place of their choice and in the presence of loved ones or friends. It is time to put into action humanitarian values and compassion.

(This letter originally appeared in the *Globe and Mail*, October 14, 1993.)

CANADIANS HAVE VOTED!

Polls have been conducted over a period of twenty-five years on the issues of euthanasia and physician-assisted suicide. The dramatic rise in the number of those who support such action under some circumstances reflects that Canadians believe the time has come for government to listen and legislate physician-assisted dying.

GALLUP POLL

The general public have been asked the following question by Gallup for twenty-five years. "When a person has an incurable disease that causes great suffering, do you, or do you not think that competent doctors should be allowed by law to end the patient's life through mercy killing, if the patient has made a formal request in writing?" Here are the results.

	Yes	No	Qualified Don't Know
1993	77%	17%	6%
1991	75	17	9
1990	78	14	8
1984	66	24	10
1974	55	35	10
1968	45	43	12

(Results accurate within a 3.1 percentage point margin of error, nineteen times out of twenty. From Gallup Canada, the *Toronto Star*, November 23, 1992.)

ANGUS REID POLL 1993

In the National Angus Reid Inc. poll, "Euthanasia in Canada: Public Opinion on the 'Right to Die' and Doctor Assisted Suicides", released March 30, 1993, the questions posed were worded somewhat differently. The first question was: "One issue that's received attention lately concerns the 'right to die'—that is, whether a person who is terminally ill and wants to die before enduring the full course of the disease, should have the right to take their own life. As a moral question, do you personally support or oppose the concept of people having the 'right to die'?" The response, in Canada as a whole, was as follows:

Support	Oppose	Unsure
76%	17%	7%

The second questions was: "A related issue is 'doctor-assisted suicide' which refers to a medical doctor assisting a terminally ill patient in ending their life if they want to. Do you think doctors who are willing to do this should be legally permitted to assist the death of a terminally ill patient who wants to die, or should 'doctor-assisted suicide' be prohibited by law?" The response was as follows:

Yes, Legally Permitted	*No, Prohibited*	*Unsure*
70%	24%	6%

(With a sample of 1,500, one can say with 95 per cent certainty that the results are within plus or minus 2.5 percentage points.)

What do *you* think?

How Does the Law Stand in Canada?

I n Canada, the primary legal obstruction to assisting another human being to improve the quality of his or her dying by determining how and when it will take place is a century-old passage in the Criminal Code, section 241. The section reads as follows:

Every one who
(a) counsels a person to commit suicide, or
(b) aids or abets a person to commit suicide,
whether suicide ensues or not, is guilty of an indictable offence and liable to imprisonment for a term not exceeding fourteen years.

The original law making suicide a crime was changed in 1974 to decriminalize the act of suicide itself. However, section 241 of the Criminal Code still stands, and it is this section that needs amendment today. The problem is that section 241 is too broad. It protects the vulnerable, but is also interferes with others who might have a valid medical reason for assisted death. It is not the intention of Dying With Dignity and most others in the right-to-choose-to-die movement to have the section struck completely; rather they seek to have the wording amended in such a way that it will continue to ensure the protection of vulnerable persons. We do wish, however, that those who for medical reasons fall within particular criteria or guidelines should be eligible for physician assistance in dying.

No one denies that there are many vulnerable persons who require the protection of the law. Take, for example, those in a temporary state of clinical depression, perhaps caused by a traumatic event in their lives. These persons will recover and go on to lead productive, happy lives, and it would be unconscionable to encourage or support them in a transitory wish to die.

There are also many unemployed and unemployable, many disabled of all ages, and many senior citizens whose families might, for selfish or downright malicious reasons, encourage them to seek assisted suicide. All kinds of people in difficult situations could be at risk of being intimidated or coerced into feeling their early death would be a convenience to society.

But does section 241 really protect such people? Perhaps it does serve as a mild deterrent, but how useful is it against someone who has a strong malicious or selfish reason to bring about the death of another? Surely other sections of the law, such as those dealing with conspiracy, manslaughter and murder, are more effective in this regard.

Section 241 is doubly flawed. It is not an especially effective deterrent against those who seek to prey on the vulnerable, but at the same time it forces persons enduring intolerable suffering to exist in that state against their own wishes, thus denying them their right of self-determination as citizens in a free democracy. Competent, rational human beings must have the right to determine their own health care according to their personal wishes, values and beliefs, as long as such a determination does not jeopardize the safety or well-being of any other person.

I do not believe, for instance, that people have the right to kill themselves by driving recklessly and in so doing jeopardize the safety of others. To kill oneself by causing an explosion that will inevitably put others at risk is an abomination. It is also reprehensible to end one's own life without regard to the trauma it might inflict on the vulnerable. I shall never forget the horror suffered by two young children who arrived home after school to find their mother hanging from the hall chandelier, or by a teen-age boy who found his father with his head blown apart from a self-inflicted shotgun wound in the kitchen of their home.

But this book is not directed to those who have irrational or transitory thoughts of suicide, but sufferers for whom the end of life is near but who are being denied relief. We also need to consider the anguish of family members, friends and even health-care professionals who must continue to witness, day after day, the suffering of people they love and wish to help. If a remedy for such suffering does not exist within the law, people will have recourse to the unwritten law of simple justice.

RECENT COURT DECISIONS

In the last few years a number of court cases have shown the quandary the legal system is in about this issue. In its argument before the Supreme Court of Canada in the Sue Rodriguez case, Dying With Dignity outlined some of these problems.

Developments in the medical sciences and in the protection of human dignity have created expectations in Canadians that they will be able to exercise greater control over fundamental issues respecting personal autonomy and human dignity, bodily integrity and issues of life and death.... The advances in medical science, and in particular the capacity of medical science to intervene in the natural cycle of life and death, have led also to a re-examination of many fundamental issues, including the protection Canadian society should accord to the values of sanctity of life. Of particular importance ... is the circumstances under which a person may determine the manner and time of his or her own death.*

The Case of Dr. de la Rocha

In Timmins, Ontario, the forty-nine-year-old chief of surgery at St. Mary's General Hospital, Dr. Alberto de la Rocha, administered an injection of morphine and potassium chloride to his seventy-year-old patient in 1991. Mrs. Mary Graham was suffering from terminal cancer of the cheek, mouth and lung. It was clear that during much of her remaining time she would have to endure great agony. As Nicholas Ionides reported in the *Globe and Mail* of April 5, 1993, her forty-six-year-old son, George, testified at the trial of his mother's doctor that he and his brothers regarded his mother's death as being "very peaceful, very dignified, and very humane," and that it was "a beautiful experience".

The doctor's motives were clear—to save his patient the pain, suffering and humiliation of protracted illness. His community recognized this when they rallied to his support, as did many of the hospital staff and Dr. de la Rocha's other patients. Initially, the doctor was charged with second-degree murder, but the charge was later reduced and he pleaded guilty to a much lesser charge, of administering a noxious substance. He received a three-year suspended sentence and was not banned from practising medicine.

The case of R. *v.* de la Rocha was presided over by Honourable Mr. Justice S. Loukidelis, Ontario Court (General Division), April 2, 1993.

---

*Extract from written argument submitted to the Supreme Court of Canada in the Sue Rodriguez case by Dying With Dignity, in its intervention.

In a case in Toronto in 1992, a young nurse was brought up on similar charges.

The Case of Mr. Mataya

Joseph Sauder, aged seventy-seven, suffering from profound and terminal side-effects following surgery at Queensway General Hospital, died in Wellesley Hospital intensive-care unit after receiving a lethal dose of potassium chloride. Most of his major organs—kidneys, lungs and liver—had stopped functioning and life was no longer sustainable for more than a brief period. His condition worsened to the point where his family (on behalf of the irreversibly comatose patient) and doctors agreed that all life-support systems, including a respirator, should be discontinued.

Mr. Sauder was given two injections of morphine and Valium and then disconnected from a ventilator. It was expected he would die within the hour. Mr. Mataya was then left alone to watch Mr. Sauder slowly choke to death. In an acute state of distress, the nurse administered his patient a dose of potassium chloride.

Mr. Mataya told other staff of his actions when he learned that an autopsy was to be performed, in the belief that the lethal injection would be detected upon examination. He was subsequently charged with first-degree murder in November of 1991.

Members of the patient's family consistently requested that Mr. Mataya not be severely punished for his actions. Everyone, including the court, realized that it was technically impossible to determine the precise cause of death—it could have been the morphine and Valium, the potassium chloride or natural causes following removal from the ventilator. Further, it was recognized that a nurse is placed in an intolerable situation when left alone, without support of colleagues or other caregivers in such a situation.

Scott Mataya received a suspended sentence after pleading guilty to a charge of administering a noxious substance. He is further prohibited from practising as a nurse in the future.

Questions that continue to plague me about this case are, "Where were the other nurses and the doctor who ordered and administered the morphine and Valium and also disconnected the ventilator during the time between the removal of life support and the patient's death? Why was no one there to support Mr. Mataya in this distressing vigil?"

Many times in my own nursing career, and more often in recent years of counselling and advocating in such situations, I have been present during the often distressing experience of a patient's death by suffocation.

Once, during my long stay as a patient in hospital, my roommate, Mrs. O, pleaded with her doctor time and again to assist her in her death. One quiet Saturday morning, when few staff and even fewer medical colleagues were on duty to observe his actions, he agreed. This gentle, dignified lady was not suffering severe physical pain, but as she said to him and also to me, "My sister makes this trip every day and sits here for hours—waiting, just waiting. We have never had much in common and it is such a chore for us to sit and stare at each other every day. I know this situation could go on for some while yet, but the end is inevitable. I cannot convince my sister to stay at home, even for a day. It is time to call an end to the ordeal for both of us. I've made my peace with God, and He will care for me now."

Dr. M returned to the room a short while later and started a morphine drip. Mrs. O gradually became more and more relaxed, and before she fell asleep she rang the call bell and asked the nurses to push our beds together. "Marilynne is going to help me with my prayers." And so I did. Together we said the rosary and, as she became more drowsy and slipped gently into a coma, I continued on with the Hail Mary, the Our Father and finally an Act of Contrition. I knew she did not hear these words and it was a strange feeling to recall them so easily and precisely from my younger years, but somehow it seemed fitting. Mrs. O died about twelve hours later.

The day nurse had visited only once or twice and then only to check that the intravenous was running at the prescribed rate of flow. She did not examine or even touch Mrs. O, but rather seemed to pretend the patient was not really here. That nurse, in my opinion, abandoned Mrs. O and abrogated her responsibility in doing so.

At the change of shift, however, a newly graduated nurse was assigned to Mrs. O's care. As soon as she came to visit on her first rounds shortly after four o'clock, she heard the gasping sounds that often accompany approaching death and finally louder more difficult gurgling sounds of mucous building up in the throat and of stertorous, irregular breathing. (These specific symptoms do not accompany all deaths.) She knew I had taught nursing and asked me, with panic in her voice, "Should I get equipment to suction her with? What should I do?" I reassured her that Mrs. O was quite unaware of this natural physical process. While we who were acting as her companions through these hours were bound to be somewhat distressed, Mrs. O was not experiencing any discomfort, and I was there to help comfort them both. "The sounds of death are much harder on you," I assured her, "than they are a difficulty for Mrs. O. Come here and sit with us and pray as Mrs. O asked us to." The nurse was a Mennonite, I recall, and together we held each other, stroked Mrs. O's face and brow and softly repeated the prayers we both knew. Following this, the nurse went to the waiting-room to comfort Mrs. O's sister with a cup of tea and kind words.

While I knew the young afternoon nurse was distressed by witnessing this death, I also knew she had learned more about real caring for a patient in these few hours of gentle, non-interventionist vigil than the older, more experienced day nurse would ever allow herself to understand. As the evening wore on Mrs. O's body gradually became more peaceful, the sounds less dramatic, and with graceful dignity she gave up her spirit to the God she loved.

I have felt deep within me the anxiety Mr. Mataya and every nurse experiences in these situations. One needs strength, companionship and support to "wait it out." To leave either family members or health-care professionals alone at this time (unless it is their wish) is a cruel and thoughtless deed. I honestly wish every doctor and every nurse to have such an experience as part of his or her compulsory medical education. Every professional needs to be this close to the actual experience of death to fully appreciate its trials and its blessings.

Another case that did not receive as much media attention as those of either Dr. de la Rocha or Scott Mataya involved a young man, also in Ontario. Since his name has not been widely circulated, and out of respect for his right to privacy, I shall use a pseudonym and call him Mr. J.

The Case of Mr. J

In this case the defendant, Mr. J, begged the nurses to increase the morphine his dying mother was receiving by IV drip. They told him she was receiving the maximum dose ordered by her doctor. When the nurses left the room, however, he increased the morphine himself. A while later, when the nurses made a routine check they discovered the change and reset the dose to that ordered by the physician. The patient died the next day. The nurses debated the issue and one month later, in consultation with the physician and hospital administrators, decided to report the case.

I have discussed this case with the coroner who led the investigation. He told me that two other members of the young man's family were also in life-threatening situations, and the investigators recognized that he was under such stress that leniency was called for. There was nothing to be gained for him or for society through severe punishment. That he had already experienced in horrific abundance.

While initially he was charged with attempted murder, after a preliminary hearing the charge was reduced to "mischief likely to endanger life". Finally this was changed to "administration of a noxious substance", and he was given a probationary discharge and no criminal record.

On many occasions and in most of our provinces coroners have said to me in an undertone, "We respect each other and appreciate each other's position and goals." The message is: "If you do not tell me anything that would cause me to force an investigation that will certainly cause this family yet more grief, I will not feel the need to proceed further."

We are playing games with the law. We all recognize that there is a problem. If the legal authorities in Canada feel that such cases are acts of mercy and not ill-intentioned criminal acts, why does Parliament not recognize its responsibility to amend the law?

Two other cases illustrate further the scope of the dilemma the law puts us in.

The Case of Otto G

A sixty-five-year-old comatose man was the subject of a potential civil suit between the Jewish General Hospital in Montreal and his family. The patient had been in a persistent vegetative state after suffering a severe stroke. While he did breathe sometimes on his own, he required some assistance by a respirator.

The medical staff in charge of his care had determined that any further treatment was futile and that Otto G should be allowed to die without further intervention. His family disagreed and were prepared to fight the case in court.

Both parties eventually agreed to an out-of-court settlement.

In one recent highly publicized case, the patient in question, a young woman, was asking to have her right to refuse treatment confirmed in law.

The Case of "Nancy B"

Nancy B was a patient in Hôtel Dieu de Québec Hospital. This case is not considered an assisted suicide, but rather deals with a person's right to refuse treatment. It is important in the examination of the issues surrounding assisted dying in that many of the legal and medical authorities, mistakenly or otherwise, include it in their list of current indicators of change in the attitude of Canadian courts toward patient rights and autonomy. In this particular case, Justice Jacques Dufour of the Quebec Superior Court said the patient, "Nancy B" (a pseudonym), who suffered from a neurological disease called Guillain-Barré syndrome, had the right to decide to have life-sustaining equipment disconnected. Death would be the result of the underlying disease and not the result of self-inflicted injury. Going one step further, Justice Dufour stated that no doctor should be held liable and accused of careless conduct and criminal negligence for respecting the patient's right to self-determination, and her wish for life-support treatment to be discontinued. According to transcripts of the hearing (as reported in the *Globe and Mail* by Rheal Séguin, January 7, 1992), Judge Dufour went on to state to Nancy B, "I can tell you that it will be more difficult for me to render my decision after having met you, but I wish you good luck. And if you change your mind the court will be very happy, but I understand. I want to say goodbye and I will think a lot about you …"

Nancy B suffered from an irremediable condition and had been existing as a totally helpless and physically dependent patient for two and a half years with no possible expectation that her condition would improve. The judge had allowed for a thirty-day appeal period between the time Nancy B won her case and the time when the life support could be withdrawn. Nancy B enjoyed the month's hiatus, but during that time she did not change her mind. She and her family demanded privacy from the media, the curious and those who wished to interfere with her decision. Without fanfare, and with the support of her doctor, her nurses and her family, Nancy B at last ended her life peacefully, as she wished.

Nancy B's doctor later spoke about the case at a seminar moderated by Dr. Peter Singer and sponsored by the University of Toronto's Centre for Bioethics. I was very moved by Dr. Daniele Marceau's description of the difficulty experienced by the health-care team who had cared for Nancy for so long when they first heard of her wish to die. As Dr. Marceau described her patient's life (never breaking confidentiality by revealing her real name), one could hear the ache in her voice. The doctors and nurses who had cared for Nancy over the two and a half years thought of themselves as part of her extended family. And so they were. They had organized and participated in social events together with their delightful charge; they had laughed and cried with her and held Nancy and her family in times of stress—just as all caring families do for each other.

At this same seminar, Professor Bernard Dickens of the Faculty of Law, University of Toronto, and Anne Lapointe (lawyer for Nancy B) discussed the fine points of the law. Both reiterated that this case itself was not a request for assisted suicide or for euthanasia, but rather one that referred only to a patient's right to refuse treatment at any time. Prof. Dickens also spoke, however, of the need for a change in the legislation to address the more complex issues of physician-assisted suicide and euthanasia.

The Case of Sue Rodriguez

Canada's most important (to date) dramatic and high-profile court case with respect to the issue of physician-assisted suicide took place in 1992-93.

Sue Rodriguez, a young woman aged forty when she was first diagnosed with ALS, was an intelligent, aware person. She had done her research and knew full well the death that was in store for her. Mrs. Rodriguez, mother of a small child, knew that the disease would gradually rob her of the ability to walk, move her body at will, eat and finally breathe without mechanical assistance. Her mind would remain alert, however, trapped in the shell of her body. Sue Rodriguez did not find dignity in the prospect of such a life and wished instead to circumvent such an end by requesting physician-assisted suicide at a time and in a manner of her own choosing. She determined that she would like to activate a machine that would facilitate her death, but would also like to have a physician present, in case, through some unpredictable eventuality, something went awry and she needed further aid in dying.

Christopher M. Considine, lawyer for Mrs. Rodriguez, took her case to a lower court, to the Supreme Court of British Columbia, which denied her request, and then to the B.C. Court of Appeal. In the judgment on appeal, the decision was lost by a vote of two to one. Justice McEachern in his dissenting opinion, based mostly on arguments relating to the Canadian Charter of Rights and Freedoms presented by Mrs. Rodriguez's counsel, outlined a set of guidelines by which he felt Mrs. Rodriguez could be granted her wish.

The matter then proceeded with unusual speed to the Supreme Court of Canada. On May 20, 1993, the Supreme Court of Canada heard the Appeal of Sue Rodriguez *v.*

Attorney General of British Columbia and Attorney General of Canada.

Parties who intervened were:

- the British Columbia Coalition of People With Disabilities;
- Dying With Dignity: A Canadian Society Concerned With the Quality of Dying;
- the Coalition of Provincial Organizations of the Handicapped;
- the Right to Die Society of Canada;
- the Pro-Life Society of British Columbia and the Pacific Physicians for Life Society;
- the Canadian Conference of Catholic Bishops and the Evangelical Christian Fellowship;
- People in Equal Participation Inc.

I can elaborate on the rationale of Dying With Dignity's intervention, since as executive director of the organization, I played a significant role in this action. The reasons why Dying With Dignity felt it was essential to intervene in Sue Rodriguez's appeals were as follows:

1. Each person suffering terminal or irreversible illness should have the access to assistance, under proper circumstances, to exercise free choice in the time and manner of his or her death. However, proper legal safeguards are needed to ensure protection for vulnerable persons.

2. We recognize the necessity to balance the sanctity of life principle with the need for human justice.

3. By virtue of our expertise, Dying With Dignity believed that it could present a unique perspective and an approach which would enable the Court to respond

favourably to the Appellant's request, through specific procedural safeguards.

Dying With Dignity presented the Supreme Court with alternative arguments to the Charter remedies requested by the counsel of Sue Rodriguez and others who supported her. We argued, first, that because of the complexity of the issue, its importance to our society as a whole and the need for safeguards and procedures, Parliament and not the courts should deal with the issue. The courts can remove section 241(b), but to do so would leave a vacuum. Only Parliament can legislate a comprehensive scheme that will protect the vulnerable and safeguard those who want to exercise their choice. This has been a long-standing objective of the society.

But, if the court were to accept this first argument, it still would not have been any help to Sue Rodriguez. So we made a second argument. In cases where the letter of the law leads to an unjust or unfair result, the justice system as a whole usually responds to ensure that justice is done. For example, someone may be convicted of an offence but be given a nominal fine or a suspended sentence. In this spirit, we asked the Supreme Court to recommend to the attorney general of British Columbia that any physician who helped Sue Rodriguez should not be prosecuted. The court could do no more than recommend, so the result would not be wholly satisfactory to Sue Rodriguez. While the court did not accept these arguments, the effect of the majority decision is to clearly leave it to Parliament to amend section 241(b).

In a narrow five-to-four decision, the Supreme Court of Canada dismissed the appeal of Sue Rodriguez in its decision announced September 30, 1993. The majority decision, written by the Honourable Mr. Justice Sopinka, concluded that, given the concerns about potential abuse and the great difficulty of creating appropriate safeguards, the blanket prohibition on assisted suicide is "not arbitrary or unfair" and should therefore be upheld.

But consider this: four dissenting judges, in the highest court of the country, including Chief Justice Lamer, concluded, in separate decisions, that the prohibition against suicide is invalid because it violates certain rights protected by the Canadian Charter of Rights and Freedoms: the right to security of the person, which protects the dignity and privacy of individuals with respect to decisions concerning their own body; and the right to equal treatment under the law, because the prohibition prevents persons physically unable to end their lives without assistance from choosing an option that is available to other members of the public.

Chief Justice Lamer recommended that the declaration of invalidity be suspended for one year to allow Parliament to address this issue and that, during this one-year period, Sue Rodriguez and other persons who are physically unable to commit unassisted suicide, be granted a constitutional exemption that would allow them assistance under court-approved conditions and safeguards.

Sue Rodriguez lost her legal battle to die with dignity. But in the hearts and minds of millions of Canadians the legal fight of this courageous lady was not in vain. Nor will the fight for freedom of choice in the time and manner of one's own death stop here. And while the Supreme Court did not grant her petition, Sue Rodriguez knew that she had benefited all Canadians by raising awareness of this critical issue concerning free choice in dying. Her fight may inspire Parliament to make necessary changes in the Criminal Code.

PARLIAMENT AND THE RIGHT-TO-CHOOSE-TO-DIE DEBATE

On no fewer than six occasions between 1991 and the present, the

Canadian Parliament has had a chance to listen to the voice of a significant majority of Canadians. But our MPs have failed to measure up to the task of full, reasoned, rational debate and have bent to the will of a small, vocal minority who do not accept or trust the principle of free choice of individuals.

BILL C-203: MR. ROBERT WENMAN

On May 16, 1991, Mr. Robert Wenman, a Progressive Conservative member of Parliament for Fraser Valley West, British Columbia, introduced Bill C-203, an act to amend the Criminal Code (terminally ill persons).

The purpose of the bill was to protect a physician from criminal liability where the physician does not initiate or continue treatment at the request of the patient or where the physician does not prolong life, except at the patient's request. It would also protect a physician who administers pain-killing treatment to a patient, even though the effect of that treatment would be to hasten death.

Bill C-203 passed second reading on September 24, 1991, and was referred to a legislative committee. Testimony was heard from twenty-five witnesses between September 24, 1991, and February 18, 1992, when abruptly the proceedings were adjourned with no date set for resumption of the hearings.

While any private member's bill has little likelihood of becoming law, especially when there is questionable support from the majority government, a few very significant factors played a major role in the demise of this particular bill.

1. The Canadian Medical Association refused to testify at the hearings. On November 28, 1991, a letter from the CAM was read to the committee stating that: "The issues addressed by the Bill are currently the subject of intensive review by the CAM's Committee on Ethics and a Joint Committee comprised by the CAM, the Canadian Nurses Association, and the Canadian Hospital

Association. We believe that to appear before your Committee at a time when our own review of the issues is not yet complete would be to do both your Committee and our members a disservice.*

According to a *Globe and Mail* report of February 27, 1992, the CMA's decision not to comment on the bill prompted one committee member to say, "Doctors aren't concerned about this bill—why should we [be]?"

2. The Department of Justice, whose minister at the time was Kim Campbell, refused to comment on the text of the bill and focused instead on the argument that more consultation was needed.

3. Finally, as was reported in the *Globe and Mail's* February 27 article, "three Liberal members [of the committee] who seem to see no separation between the church and the state" and a Conservative member of Parliament who was not a committee member but "was parachuted in to join the Liberals' 'God Squad'" successfully buried this noble initiative.

BILL C-261: MR. CHRIS AXWORTHY

On June 19, 1991, Mr. Chris Axworthy, a New Democratic Party member of Parliament representing Saskatoon–Clark's Crossing, introduced Bill C-261, "An Act to legalize the administration of euthanasia under certain conditions to persons who request it and who are suffering from an irremediable condition and respecting the withholding and cessation of treatment and to amend the Criminal Code" ("The Euthanasia and Cessation of Treatment Act", for short).

---

*See Minutes of Proceedings and Evidence of Legislative Committee H on Bill C-203.

The explanatory note continues: "It would also protect doctors involved in euthanasia-like situations by providing that a doctor acts legally where the doctor administers pain-killing treatment to a terminally ill patient even though the effect of that treatment will hasten death. It also makes clear that a doctor acts legally where the doctor does not initiate or continue treatment at the request of the patient or where the doctor does not prolong death, except at the request of the patient."

The bill would have allowed someone "suffering from an irremediable condition" to apply for the right to euthanasia using a specific form, to be witnessed by two people not related to the applicant, and to be accompanied by a medical certificate signed by the attending physician. This document would then be presented to a "referee" appointed by the attorney general. A decision would be made not later than five days after receipt. Successful applicants would receive a euthanasia certificate, a copy of which would go to the patient's doctor. In the case of a refusal, the patient could apply in writing to the attorney general. Again a decision would have to be given within five days.

The euthanasia certificate would remain in effect for three months from the date of issue and could be revoked at any time by the patient. Only a qualified medical practitioner would be allowed to administer euthanasia, except in accordance with the act.

With regard to this bill, Dying With Dignity had some reservations about the bureaucratic nature of the proposed procedures. We felt the process added an unnecessary layer of decision making that could ultimately create additional stress for patients already enduring a great deal. We did, however, respect the courage of Mr. Axworthy in his attempt to sensitize Parliament about this serious crisis in the care of those at the end of life. (He has continued to inform the public on the need for legislative action through his many appearances at DWD forums.)

Although Bill C-261 was placed on the order paper on September 24, 1991, it was declared not to be a votable bill and was therefore granted only limited time in the House of Commons. It was debated briefly at second reading on October 24, 1991, and then dropped from the order paper.

HOUSE OF COMMONS STANDING COMMITTEE ON JUSTICE AND THE SOLICITOR GENERAL RESPECTING THE FRAMEWORK DOCUMENT ENTITLED "TOWARD A NEW GENERAL PART OF THE CRIMINAL CODE OF CANADA"

On March 25, 1992, a subcommittee was struck to study proposals for changes to the Criminal Code. Although many groups testified, including Dying With Dignity, the results were most unsatisfactory.

Dying With Dignity's position is that health-care matters should not be and need not be a part of the Criminal Code, provided such health-care delivery is performed by licensed health-care providers as regulated in their specific provinces. Further, we hold that:

1. The criminal law should be used only in circumstances where other means of social control are inadequate or inappropriate;

2. The criminal law should be used in a manner which interferes no more than necessary with individual rights and freedoms;

3. The criminal law should set out clearly and understandably
   a) what conduct is declared criminal, and
   b) what culpability is required for a finding of criminal liability.

We argued strongly for amendment of section 241(b) of the Criminal Code. The White Paper that followed the six months of hearings, *100 Years of Criminal Code*, stated that: "While the proposals contained in the white paper address most of the principle recommendations of the Parliamentary Sub-Committee, some areas, such as physician-assisted suicide, are not covered by the proposals. Such issues require further study and need careful review of the legal and ethical issues involved."

Other bills that have been put to the government but not yet debated include the following.

BILL C-385:
MR. SVEND ROBINSON

On December 9, 1992, Mr. Svend Robinson, a New Democratic Party MP representing Burnaby–Kingsway, British Columbia, introduced a private member's bill C-385 entitled "An Act to amend the Criminal Code (aiding suicide)". In the explanatory notes Mr. Robinson stated that the bill's purpose is "to allow for physician-assisted suicide upon the request of a terminally ill person".

Mr. Robinson is a strong supporter of patient autonomy in general and was a friend of Sue Rodriguez in particular. The closing of the 34th session of Parliament prevented this bill from coming forward for debate, so that, as the expression goes, it "died on the order paper". To receive further consideration, it will now have to be reintroduced as a new bill.

MOTION:
MR. IAN WADDELL

On February 17, 1993, Mr. Ian Waddell, New Democratic Party MP from Port Moody–Coquitlam, British Columbia, presented the following motion to the House of Commons: "That, in the opinion of this House, the government should consider the advisability of introducing legislation on the subject of euthanasia, in particular, of ensuring that those assisting terminally ill patients who wish to die not be subject to criminal liability."

For discussion of the bill at a later stage, there were relatively few MPs in the House, and debate was closed after about an hour. What does Parliament so fear that it cannot even allow debate of the subject? In arguing his motion, Mr. Waddell quoted David Suzuki, a noted Canadian author from Vancouver, as follows: "politicians in the future will be measured in terms of their ability to deal with the more complex questions and the public wants us to do that. That is why it should ultimately be done here and not ultimately in the courts."*

MOTION:
MR. RAYMOND SKELLY

On June 7, 1993, under Private Member's Business, Mr. Raymond Skelly, a New Democratic Party MP representing North Island–Powell River, British Columbia, proposed in the House of Commons, the motion: "That, in the opinion of this House, the government should urgently consider amending the Criminal Code to permit physician-assisted suicide when:

(a) it is requested by the patient;
(b) the patient is terminally ill and will experience a painful death;
(c) two independent physicians certify that the patient's condition is terminal; and
(d) the office of the Attorney General for the province has reviewed the case."

Mr. Skelly's motion received minimal attention in the House because of a ruling that the time provided for such business was finished.

---

*House of Commons, *Debates*, February 17, 1993, p. 16095.

HON. JOAN B. NEIMAN—
SENATE PROPOSAL

On January 20, 1994 Senator Joan B. Neiman (L), gave notice that she would ask the Senate to appoint a special committee to study the legal, social and ethical issues relating to euthanasia and assisted death.

There was a general agreement that the subject required careful, non-partisan study, and the hearing of evidence from people with personal experiences to share, as well as from health-care professionals.

The special committee expects to complete its study and report to the Senate before the end of 1994. If it concludes that the evidence it has heard warrants it, it will recommend changes to the current law.

In closing this chapter on the state of the law in Canada, I must emphasize that the issue is now out in the open. As the proliferation of media items attests, it will not disappear from the Canadian scene just because it makes some people uncomfortable. Simple humanity demands a resolution to this debate, either in the courts or in legislation.

CHAPTER NINE

When Is the End, the End?

This question is one of the great mysteries that still fills me with awe and wonder. It is when I sit beside or rest on the bed holding close to me a person who is near death that I feel most strongly the glory of creation. A human being, dying in peace and dignity, is the essence of the power of life and fortifies my belief in the value of living. To come full circle and to do so in comfort and companionship reflects, like an image in a still clear pond, the spiritual side of ourselves.

Even very young children who recognize that the end of their life is near take on a glow of tranquillity that spreads around the room to those who need their strength. Parents, deep in their sorrow at their impending loss, become gentle and calm at this moment.

But it is in the elderly where I have most often seen the greatest gratitude and peace. Not peace as in passivity, but rather as in the sharing of a secret of what life is all about. These people have succeeded in fulfilling an important goal of life, achieving the satisfying conviction of a life completed—a circle joined.

The Case of Margaret

Margaret was an elegant, quiet gentlewoman of eighty-six

years. She lived in a large, beautifully appointed home in Toronto's Rosedale district. Margaret's situation was "comfortable" and materially she wanted for very little. Yet in her estimation her life now lacked "quality" and she was ready to die. Margaret had outlived all her family and friends. Her husband had died ten years earlier and her one son had followed him a couple of years later. Both of their deaths had been preceded by illness and had been natural and expected. Neither had suffered unduly, and Margaret, possessing both practicality and "good common sense", as she put it, had got on with her grieving and continued with her life.

The live-in housekeeper had been in Margaret's employ for many years and they got on very well. Each respected the other's needs and abilities. Her friends from the busy days of university, marriage, child-rearing, work and energetic volunteerism were, for the most part, gone now.

Margaret requested that I come to her home one day for a visit and to discuss a matter of deep personal concern. She had heard me being interviewed on CBC's *Radio Noon* that day and said she recognized a kindred spirit, someone who, she felt, might help her to deliberate on an important issue. "I do not want you to make any decisions for me. Please understand that. But I do need someone to help me make sure I have reached the right decision for myself."

We met about ten days later, for she had said this was not urgent, and I was occupied with a couple of pressing cases. During our first encounter, on a beautiful, crisp autumn morning, we strolled about the grounds of her home, examining the garden and talking about her life. We agreed the fall was our favourite time of year with the brilliant colour of the chrysanthemums, the crisp sounds of fallen leaves beneath our feet and the energetic scurrying of the squirrels preparing for their winter needs. Margaret had a simple but aesthetically satisfying garden—neat and understated, like its owner.

Suddenly she smiled and said, with a twinkle in her eye, "Now I recollect what has been nudging the back of my mind since you arrived. Some years ago you lived quite nearby. Although we never met formally, I definitely recall 'Marilynne and Mr. Oliver'. My husband and I used to speculate about who was going to win, you or 'Mr. O', as Mark called him. Is your lovely cat still with you and did you ever convince him he should walk sedately on the leash?"

I laughed with her and told her that "Mr. Oliver" had quietly but firmly informed me that cats, especially thirty-five-pound Persian aristocrats (as I know he considered himself), do not travel at the end of a piece of rope, no matter how elegant the merchandise. And yes, though he was by now quite elderly, he was still a dear companion.

Margaret had decided it was warm enough to enjoy a cup of coffee on the terrace as she broached the subject of her "plan" as she called it.

She wanted to die, Margaret told me plainly and without any evasion or emotional outburst. But first she wanted to know if her wish was rational, sensible and proper. Of course she also needed to know if her plan would be foolproof, not hurtful to whoever found her (probably her housekeeper) and, most of all, dignified.

I explained to her it was my practice to spend some time with people who made such a request before I would discuss in detail the matter she had raised. It was essential to me to get to know something of the "person"—his or her state of health physically and emotionally, social perspective and, without equivocation, reason for wishing to die.

Margaret accepted this, and in fact seemed comforted by it. "I'm pleased to know you're not just some fanatic who takes life and death casually. If all I wanted was to find out what drugs to take and how to do a proper job of it," she said, "there are books I can read for that. In fact I attended the public forum Dying With Dignity put on some years ago with that lovely lady Betty Rollin. Now there is a brave and noble woman dedicated to her mother in a way few can imagine. No, you are right," she confirmed, "you must become better acquainted with me before we discuss any of this further."

The second occasion we met was over dinner and an evening at the Toronto Symphony. We both had season tickets and worked out an exchange with friends so we could attend a concert together. It was an especially good performance that night with a Brahms selection we each admitted was one of our favourites.

Our last meeting was one of my choosing. I had told Margaret that for "therapy", to help me stay calm despite my rather stressful life, I would often go bird-watching on Sunday mornings. This particular Sunday, I selected a ravine where I knew many interesting species were likely to be found. We were not disappointed. It was as though the birds knew we needed their gentle presence that day and did their best to accommodate us.

We walked almost five miles in the course of the morning. Margaret, for all her four score and six, was healthy, alert and eager to learn a little about something she had not studied previously. Before long she was spotting as many birds as I and recognizing them by their uniquely distinctive calls, even when we could not see the bird itself.

Eventually we found a comfortable place to rest and began to discuss the questions Margaret had initially called me about. After observing her and noting the richness and clarity of her day-to-day life; learning more about the unassuming but generous contributions she had made to the world around her; enjoying her good humour, quick intelligence, gentleness and joy of life, I had come to the conclusion that Margaret was making a truly rational, thoughtful decision.

To some it may seem a contradiction that, with all her

blessings, Margaret chose to die now, while in the fullness of her capacities, but to me it did not. I understood her need to control her own destiny and to die as she had lived. You see, Margaret was fully alive and alert but she had accomplished all the "business" of her life.

One week after this last visit I received a brief note, a message from the housekeeper. "Dear Marilynne," it read: "Both Brahms and I are at peace. Thank you for your friendship and understanding. My blessings to you in this noble work. Margaret."

In thinking about Margaret I cannot help but remember the dying weeks of another wonderful woman, slightly younger than she and, unlike Margaret, unable to make a choice to live or to die. My friend was in the terminal stages of ovarian cancer, a monster that more frequently than not is discovered too late in the progress of the disease to be cured. She too was very much in charge of her care decisions, however, and chose to live every second given her. To accomplish this my friend had to make many compromises in terms of pain control and other treatment options but, just as with Margaret, she too had her objectives. I recall lying beside her on the bed, cradling her in my arms the last nights of her life. We also shared a love of Brahms, but for a different reason. It was the longest-running tape in our collection and therefore could play quite some time before I had to stir, let go of my friend for a moment and change the tape.

Each of these people recognized the end of life approaching and each made plans. The plans were very different, but each was "right" for the person who chose it.

Some people believe that humans can will themselves to die. In some cultures and under certain circumstances it may be true that they can. From my own experience I know, without a shred of doubt, that my grandmother accomplished this deed.

Grandma was not particularly old in terms of years, but her early life had been hard and in later life she was plagued by chronic pain.

She was a stubborn, outspoken, hard-nosed, demanding lady. She also had a heart of pure mush. When I was a child I did not understand her. I loved her, yes, but as for understanding her—definitely not. Yet it was always comfortable to be near her, for I sensed that with Grandma there nothing too terrible could happen to us. She was a take-charge, at times rather bossy lady, whose resourcefulness had helped her through some difficult years. (I can just hear some of my colleagues murmuring, Aha! so that's where it comes from. But I know they wear the same forgiving, tender smile that I do when I think of Grandma.)

One February evening many years ago, I was sitting at home marking papers from a test I had given to the student nurses in a course I taught. The students were waiting for their results the next day. It was also my birthday, but I had been out for a lovely meal with a special "beau" the night before, so the lack of a celebration didn't bother me. Grandma telephoned and we chatted for almost an hour. This was unusual, for Granny was very aware of the cost of long-distance calls, and we usually only talked for ten minutes. I would tease her about having her egg timer handy to make sure we did not run over the allotted time.

This call was different in other ways too. She was reminiscing about both the good and the difficult years we had known together. It was an hour of "Remember when ..." and "You know I was always sorry for the nickname I gave you as a young 'un—'the rat'—what a thing to call a young kid even if you were the scrawniest thing I ever saw." We laughed together, and I assured her I had forgiven her a long time ago. Finally, when I sensed her getting tired, we said the usual things and then she spoke words I had not heard from her before. She said, "Goodbye, my Marilynne." Grandma had always avoided saying goodbye, choosing instead to end a conversation with some brusque remark, half in rebuke and half coaxing, asking how soon I would visit her in Stratford again.

The unusual quality and tone of this call did not register with me until the telephone rang quite early the following morning. It was my mother calling to tell me Grandma had died that morning.

Suddenly it struck me. She did it again. Grandma did it her way—
she refused to die on my birthday, but die she did, when she chose.
Although she suffered severely from scoliosis and its many dreadful
side-effects, there was no physiological reason for her death. She
had just decided that this was her time and willed herself to die.
The ambulance had been quick to arrive to give emergency care,
the doctors had continued with the efforts at cardiopulmonary
resuscitation begun by paramedics and every other life-prolonging
measure had been undertaken. My mother later told me how hard
it was for her to hear their heroic but violent activity, when all the
time she wanted only to be with her mother. If it had been in her
nature she would have screamed for it all to stop. In the end, the
doctor's efforts made no difference, for Grandma was through with
life.

AGE IS ONLY ONE PART
OF THE DYING EQUATION

At seventeen one does not usually think it is time to die, especially
if one is competent and comforted by a loving family. But most
teens do not have to face dealing with terminal and mutilating disease.

The Case of Danny

Danny was just turning sixteen when he felt the first sharp
pains in his knee. He was playing hockey and thought he
had twisted the leg somehow while scrimmaging for the
puck. The coach had sensed something was not quite right
with him and signalled him off the ice. Danny put the incident out of his mind until later that night. This time the pain
wakened him from a sound sleep. Down in the kitchen he
had a drink of orange juice, fixed an ice pack and then went
back upstairs to bed. The pain lasted a little longer this time,

but eventually he fell asleep, still convinced he had injured his leg during the game.

A few days later he finally told his mom he had done "something dumb" and his knee was hurting him quite a bit—sharp pains that seemed to come at any old time. An appointment was set up immediately with the family doctor, who referred him to an orthopaedic specialist.

After innumerable tests and a barrage of consultations Danny was told they strongly suspected a tumour and he would need surgery immediately. Danny's parents were shocked, but they insisted Danny be told the truth—that the probable cause of his pain was cancer and that Danny's leg might have to be amputated.

Within twenty-four hours, this threat became a reality. For more than a year after that first operation Danny underwent treatment after treatment to try to cure the disease.

In the spring of Danny's seventeenth year, he phoned me to ask if I could visit him in the hospital. Two days earlier he had been readmitted to undergo amputation of his other leg. But he had known long before, he later revealed to me, that the cancer was spreading. Some patients become very knowledgeable in an instinctual as well as a clinical way about their disease. Also, Danny had talked to others during his many visits to the clinic for treatment. He was "educated" in a way only the person suffering the illness can be.

Danny explained to me that he did not wish to consent to the removal of his second leg. In fact, he stated very definitely, "I have had enough treatment, Marilynne. It is time to go home, spend some quality time with my family, and let go. I'm ready to die now and I do not want this to happen by bits and pieces. My brother and sister as well as my parents need time to adjust to my dying, and it would be easier for us all in our own home. There are some buddies I'd like to see, some music I would like to listen to, and just some quiet time I need that I cannot get here in the hospital. Will you help me explain this to my family? I'm worried they might not understand or may even be over-impressed by the doctor's arguments in favour of more treatment. It is not that I have given up hope. It's just that I see things from a different perspective, and that includes making my own choice about how I want to live the time that is left."

I visited with Danny for quite a while. He was a truly remarkable young man, mature beyond his years. But then critical illness has a way of maturing people. Far from being depressed or hopeless about his situation, he had developed a very realistic attitude to his condition. Danny had done a great deal of research during his long stints of inactivity. He questioned the doctors and nurses and listened to and assimilated their answers, "separating the wheat from the chaff", as he politely put it.

That evening I was present for a family meeting, first with Danny and his parents. Then he asked if his siblings could come to the TV room down the hall from his own room, where there would be room for us all to be together. It was a tearful session for everyone, Danny included, but at the end of it we agreed to go home and think over all the things that had been said. Tomorrow we would ask for a meeting with the specialist and Danny's family doctor to discuss the situation.

Danny died almost six weeks later, sitting in a chaise lounge on the backyard patio, with his parents, his sister and brother, his grandparents, an uncle, two school chums and myself, all gathered around him. The family dog, Rags, was curled up on his lap, and the simple jazz he loved echoed from the kitchen. This was Danny's time to die, and he blessed the family that helped him to "do it right".

While almost all the people with whom I come into contact as a counsellor and advocate are special, there is one very dear couple whom I shall never forget. They too, after many months of deliberation, decided to die at a time and in circumstances of their own choosing.

A Case of Double Suicide

I first met this elegant, dignified couple at an annual meeting of Dying With Dignity in 1982. A group of more than seventy people had gathered at Friends' House in Toronto, a meeting-house run by the Quakers that we liked to rent for special occasions. For Mr. and Mrs. T this was their first meeting with the society, although they had been members for a year.

It did not take the executive committee long to realize that these people had a great deal to offer the organization, and soon they were deeply immersed in the society's work. They were particularly supportive of its participation in the World Federation of the Right to Die Societies and held a grand dinner for me and a few mutual friends the first year I was elected to the federation's board of directors.

Between this couple and myself a great mutual respect and deep fondness soon developed. Mr. T would come and visit the office and share with me his pride in and the worries about his daughters and his fear and concern when Mrs. T had a small stroke. When she became well enough, we had quiet lunches together, with Mr. T always being concerned he did not take too much of my "valuable time".

A number of years after Mrs. T's stroke, Mr. T called me to ask for a confidential appointment. I recognized immediately from his tone of voice that this was to be somehow different from our past meetings. He asked me to meet him at a park nearby (a place he knew I often went to have some quiet time to grieve for friends lost or simply to mull over a particularly difficult case), and then to go with him to his favourite restaurant for lunch. During the meeting he told me that he and his wife were considering a double suicide and needed to discuss this with me. He was very concerned to avoid making any difficulties for me or the society. I reassured him that, as this was a simple "what if" discussion, we were free to speak openly and candidly to each other.

After reassuring myself that the proposal was being made with equal competence and rationality by both husband and wife, that they were in fact considering a choice that was "fitting" for them, I began the difficult task of helping them to prepare their family for this decision. I have always believed that every competent person has the right to determine the time and circumstance of his or her own death, as long as the person does not cause irreparable harm to others by doing so. At first Mr. T was adamant that he could not tell his children and grandchildren. We had many discussions on this point, and finally he came to realize that they did have a unique relationship. Yes, they did truly respect Mr. and Mrs. T's wishes, values and beliefs, and, if given the opportunity, would continue to do so.

A few members of the family came to me at various times. Some were very angry at first, but as we discussed the source of their anger, they came to realize it was their own loneliness, fears and feelings of rejection and failure that were making them angry. Some came simply to talk about the impending deaths, confirm that it was a rational decision and reassure themselves that Mr. and Mrs. T would not suffer. Whatever their reasons I welcomed the opportunity to explore the issues with them, partly to reassure myself that all was in order, and partly to help them resolve their personal problems with this decision.

About six months after the first meeting in the park Mr. and Mrs. T announced to me that they had completed all their preparations and had set the time and date for their death. Everything had been planned to the last detail. The drugs they would take, who would find their bodies, which person would be called to verify the deaths, and so on.

The day arrived, and although I had previously planned to be away on holiday during that time, I returned to Toronto early to be available in case they or their family needed me. Mr. and Mrs. T were, however, determined to manage all the details by themselves so that no one would suffer any legal repercussions from their deaths.

Mr. T came to have a cup of coffee with me that morning. We spoke of many things, but mainly about family matters—how this one would manage fine while that one might need more support. I assured him I would be available to comfort and care for them if they wished it. In Mr. T's mind, he was comfortable that all matters had been resolved. He returned home to his wife to enjoy the rest of their day in quiet solitude.

Mr. and Mrs. T ended their own lives, as they had so carefully and considerately planned. The family was understandably saddened by their death, but all agreed that "they were proud of" their parents and grandparents. When I attended a celebration of the lives of these two wonderful people, that was the expression I heard again and again—"I am so proud of them. They died as they had lived, with careful thoughtfulness and most of all, with dignity."

I miss these dear friends as if they were my own family, and I also applaud their strength, determination and courage to live and die as they saw fit.

ENOUGH IS ENOUGH

There are those who endure decades of disease and illness with a courage and forbearance that few of us can even imagine. Most severely disabled persons find life at least acceptable, and many have satisfying and productive lives. Consider Stephen Hawking, the British scientist who has had Lou Gehrig's disease for twenty years.

Sometimes however, a person who lives with severe disability decides life is no longer worth the cost.

The Case of Don

Don is a fifty-three-year-old man who has spent most of his adult life confined to a wheelchair or a bed in a small room in an institution. He suffers from multiple sclerosis. For the last four years a nursing assistant has provided most of the primary care for Don on a volunteer basis. When she replaced her car a year ago she decided to invest considerably more money and bought a specially designed van that allows her to take Don for outings in his lounge chair. They especially enjoy going to the movies.

When Sylvia, his nurse friend, brought me to meet Don, he had just asked that his case be transferred to another physician. His rationale was that he wished to be allowed to die and knew his present doctor would not support him in this objective.

Dr. Brown was a good, attentive physician and Don had no complaints about her care except in this one area. From conversations he had had with her, he knew that her religious beliefs would conflict with his own. Don believed that another physician would increase his doses of pain medication to a level that would depress his systems sufficiently to allow him to die reasonably soon. Knowledgeable about his disease, he understood that his lungs were fragile and would not recover from a severe bout of pneumonia. He had indicated some time ago that he would refuse both antibiotics and any form of mechanical intervention to prolong his life.

Don was not depressed. His family—his mother and two siblings—had signed a letter stating they supported his wishes. Just that week a competency board had stipulated that Don was rational and fully competent to make decisions on his own behalf regarding his health care.

However, without a change of doctor, he knew he would not be allowed to die soon. In fact, when Dr. Brown discovered his intentions she immediately demanded that the competency board reconvene to re-evaluate Don's state of mind. Since it had been only five days since the last hearing and nothing that had occurred in the interim suggested that his mental state had changed, her demand was refused.

Suddenly, early one evening, Don's nurse, Sylvia, called me and asked if I would come immediately. It was a holiday weekend and she had been visiting her family earlier in the day. At five-thirty in the evening when she arrived to give Don his evening care, he was noticeably short of breath. She had sat by him while he slept and upon waking Don had smiled at her. "You see," he said, "one can die by wishing it. Enough is enough, Sylvia. Don't let them do anything to prolong my dying."

By now it was the change of shift, and Sylvia did not know the staff on duty. One thing worried her. What if a nurse called Dr. Brown? (We had not been able to arrange for a new physician yet.) When I walked into the room Don gave me a weak grin and an attempt at a wink and told Sylvia it would all be okay. "Between the two of you, I know I'm in safe hands." The nurses did come by and we had a private consultation together. They had all known this patient for a long time. They listened with their hearts and went on with their work, leaving Don in our hands. At about nine o'clock I called Don's parents and told them that he was rapidly growing weaker. They were themselves both very frail and to travel to Toronto now would be a great burden. They had visited Don the day before, and he had told them he was praying very hard to die. They all cried and prayed together that his wish would be granted.

I put the telephone close to Don's ear and saw the smile and tears of joy as first his mother and then his dad had their private words with him. Then he gradually fell asleep. At precisely midnight Don passed from a gentle coma to a dignified, quiet death. There were no bells or whistles to announce his passing. It was as Don had willed.

For some people there is a will to die stronger than any medicine or treatment invented to keep them alive. Others, who wish they could die, do not have this unusual gift.

Many in this latter group have made a rational decision that the end of life has arrived, but are forced by archaic laws, by all-too-understandable fear of these laws and by other circumstances to continue a life that they regard as well and truly finished. It is my strong belief that to deny them the right to choose in this matter is cruel and unusual punishment.

Is it really civilized to insist on prolonging the suffering of an individual dying slowly with ALS or imprisoned in a paralysed body? Frequently we are fortunate enough to be able to negotiate a path to death through the kindness and courage of a physician, or inventive friends and colleagues. Their ability to recognize that the right to die with dignity is as important as the right to live with dignity makes them true heroes of medicine.

CHAPTER TEN

How to Survive
as a Caregiver

I hear the question so often: How do people who are in constant contact with suffering and death cope emotionally? Many times the question is asked by the spouse or other family members of the sick person. Frequently someone in an audience I am addressing will ask it. I can tell from the person's face or voice that some personal anguish is behind the question, and I wish I could leave the podium immediately to put my arms around the person and talk it through. In small, intimate groups I have been known to do this; but in larger groups I know such behaviour would cause the questioner more embarrassment than benefit. So—the healing must be put aside for the moment, and I try to find the person at the end of the meeting to arrange some time together.

I get many calls from health-care workers about how to handle a specific case. All too often, however, it becomes clear that behind any individual problem is a whole complex set of problems faced by anyone in a caring role.

The Case of Susan

Susan is a social worker in a large metropolitan hospital. Her job is to minister to the needs of patients (and their families) in intensive care units—particularly surgical and neurological units. Two years ago there were three social workers to handle the workload, but as a result of budget cuts only Susan is left.

Her problems are many and complex.

The sheer number of patients is too great for one person to handle effectively. Susan is caught up in managing one crisis after another and cannot give patients the full attention she feels they deserve.

All of the patients in these units are in life-threatening situations. For many there is no hope of recovery, and some are in a "persistent vegetative state". These patients do not get the most appropriate care for their needs, but no other unit on the regular wards has sufficient staff or is set up to provide safe nursing care.

Caring for patients in a persistently vegetative state is as stressful as caring for persons in the intensive neurosurgical unit, where the incidence of severe trauma or death is extremely high. Few nurses can cope for long with the pressure of an assignment with high mortality rates. Susan is expected to absorb such stresses routinely.

The families of patients in these units are under enormous stress day and night, sometimes for weeks, perhaps even for months. For good reasons, patience and tempers run short. The waiting, the worrying, the uncertainties, all take their toll. The waiting is the largest part of the problem for many. Patients who are in intensive care units usually require careful and frequent monitoring of one kind or another. The staff of such units need time and a calm atmosphere to perform these tasks properly and efficiently. Also, the patients are usually very sick, and need all their energy to recover. Thus, visiting must be limited to very brief periods by very few persons. Time becomes a heavy burden for those waiting for news or for a five-minute visit with someone they love. Susan has to try to help the families deal with the inevitable anxiety that results.

Susan feels that she has been left without a support system

of her own. With whom can she share her own pain, or her concern about the ethics of keeping someone alive who clearly is asking to die? How does she begin to conduct a proper negotiation to resolve differences among family members who disagree about the kind of care that "Mother" or "Grandfather" would want when no advance directive has been provided?

Susan hasn't time to investigate tertiary-care facilities that might provide more appropriate placements for certain patients. One such patient, whom we may call "Granny", requires too much care for transfer to a nursing home. She is not a candidate for a rehabilitation centre, for everyone recognizes that rehabilitation is no longer a possibility for her. Granny's own family consists of one daughter who is quite disabled with arthritis and cannot care for her kin at home even with a generous amount of home-care support.

When Susan called me, she was on the verge of resigning or requesting another assignment, though she was reluctant to do so. It was a challenge and a pleasure to assist her in establishing a support group within her own institution. It just takes one person to get the ball rolling, and Susan became that catalyst. Within a short period of time this group established a schedule of meetings, some formal, some informal, during coffee breaks, or within regular business hours. A program was organized and guest speakers were brought in to talk about some of the more complex ethical, legal and administrative issues. An informal system of emotional support was always available, as soon as others recognized they were not alone in their feelings and frustrations.

"I JUST NEED TIME TO CRY!"

For the non-institutional or independent patient advocate, the difficulties can be more complicated. You have been sitting at the bedside of someone who has just died. Your latest vigil may have lasted only a few hours, or at most a few days, but your relationship might have developed over a period of months or even years. The person has become a friend, but you must now let go. And there is no time to grieve because three more people need your attention. One case may involve a lengthy dispute with a hospital many miles away. Negotiations are reaching the crisis stage and you know you must be there for two days next week.

Family life and other work pressures also cry out for your presence, and each deserves a full commitment. Life does not go into a holding pattern just because it is five in the morning and you have not slept for many hours. So what do you do? How do you keep your own physical and mental health in the midst of unresolved grief and a pressure-cooker lifestyle?

Each of us—family members, doctors, nurses, social workers, palliative-care workers, chaplains, counsellors and advocates—needs to plan a survival program suited to his or her own needs and personality.

My own survival program is built around good friends and an understanding and tolerant family. It includes brisk walks and slow saunters as I enjoy one of my avocations—bird-watching. The style of treatment I prescribe for myself is determined by the time available to me and the specific situation. Let me share a small diversion with you.

A few years ago, Dying With Dignity was renting space on the second floor of a church in mid-Toronto. While the accommodations were not elegant as offices go, they served our purposes very well. The atmosphere was friendly, the people were charming and supportive and, most important, the view was therapeutic. There were large windows looking out on an ancient chestnut tree and an equally old apple tree, both of which attracted a stunning assortment of birds. As an amateur bird-watcher from way back, this was a special treat for me.

For some reason, perhaps because of the careful guardianship of that supreme power I know takes care of me, a mysterious relationship evolved between a pair of cardinals and myself.

I spent many days and evenings at my desk trying to work through an urgent crisis with a dying patient or the patient's family, or negotiating a sticky problem with other members of the health-care team. Frequently, when I was on the telephone concentrating very hard—perhaps trying to console someone in severe pain, perhaps just working through with them the endless minutes until their pain medication took effect, or listening to the latest sadness that was tearing into their aching spirit—I would glance at the window, often through a curtain of tears, to find one of the cardinals perched on the window-sill or on a branch just beyond the glass. Though I could never predict their comings and goings, it seemed that as long as I needed their presence, the lovely red creatures would be there, sometimes singing their unique call, at other times just perched—waiting patiently and quietly.

Then came the time when the church needed to undergo renovations and Dying With Dignity needed more space. We moved to different quarters, but while the new premises are roomier, more modern and more efficient, they lack one important amenity. Despite broad window-sills, there is no place nearby where birds can come and give moral support in my hours of need.

I was especially touched, then, that a thoughtful friend brought to our opening reception the gift of a sun-catcher in the form of a cardinal. Now when I look at it, it evokes the memory of friends who helped me through dark moments in the past and who continue to be a healing presence in the here and now.

So often it is friends that supply the spiritual nourishment so essential to sustain a sense of balance and one's sense of humour. Humour is, I believe, critical to survival. I deal with death every day of my life, for this is my chosen vocation. But to live and nourish others in an attitude of doom and gloom is impossible.

In the large network of caregivers there are many who graciously offer a shoulder and a caring heart, and who take the time to listen and nod and give an occasional hug. To be able to reciprocate these generous moments is, in itself, therapeutic. When Sheila or Kathleen, John or Harry or Robert, Mary or Joan call or turn up to seek support in their turn, the fact that I can offer help renews my energy to continue this work for yet another day.

On some occasions I feel nothing can exorcise the pain but a long and loud scream in the shower. So far my neighbours have never complained. Either the soundproofing is very good, or they understand the suffering behind that scream and say a small prayer of gratitude that "someone is out there who may be able to care for me some day". There are also times when I really do just need to cry to release the pent-up emotions inside me. At these times, "Dr. Marilynne" self-prescribes a three-hanky movie guaranteed to turn on the tap of healing tears.

The Case of Pam

Pam was a community nurse in a remote area of Canada. I had travelled to Alberta on a speaking tour in a number of cities as part of Dying With Dignity's mandate to educate and inform others about the rights of the dying and need for quality care at the end of life. As I was leaving the auditorium after the conference, a young woman approached me and asked if I would be in town the next day and if we could get together. I invited her to meet me for breakfast the next morning and then to take a long walk in the fresh snow that was falling softly outside.

During breakfast she talked a little about her family life and her decision to move to the north to pursue a career in public health nursing. She had thought she would feel more needed than she would working in a large city. And because she liked to concentrate on individual care, she thought the outreach sort of program would suit her.

Pam had been working in this setting for almost a year and was soon due for an "R and R" (rest and recreation) trip back south. She needed the break. Though she had chosen the style of nursing she had been doing, she now wondered if she had the strength to return to it when her holiday was over. Pam was feeling desperate, depressed and frustrated with her situation.

Her difficulties had come to a head when she had accompanied a young woman to a major health-care centre in the large city. The woman was not expected to recover from advanced tuberculosis. As Pam said, "I thought TB had almost been eradicated, but here I am surrounded by it in a country with supposedly one of the best health-care systems in the world. And not only TB, Marilynne. I'm also running into so many cases of venereal disease, a degree of alcoholism and drug use you could not believe and people dying from sheer neglect and lack of concern by the community leaders, or so it seems to me."

Pam was expressing feelings so many good nurses and doctors must cope with, especially when they are working alone, or isolated from colleagues they can talk with. The feeling of being a "lone voice in the wilderness" can make it hard to keep things in perspective.

We walked and talked for a long time until we were both emotionally and physically exhausted—Pam from shedding many months of private suffering and me from trying to hear not just the spoken but the unspoken message in her words. There was only one thing left to do at that point, and that was to give each other a huge hug. (I'm big on hugs and touching as a form of therapy.)

Gradually, we were able to sort out Pam's concerns in terms of priorities. What were the most pressing issues she had to deal with? Could we define some small goals that could be achieved fairly readily? (Pam needed to see at least a minor benefit in her work soon.) Were her expectations realistic? While many might want to be a Dr. Schweitzer or a Mother Teresa, few achieve such lofty goals.

I suggested she take her up-coming leave in a sunny climate, away from sick people, and try to get in touch with her personal values. Were her motives truly altruistic (a fact *I* did not doubt, but one that she needed to affirm for herself), and if so what price was she willing to pay to achieve her goals? It was appropriate and necessary, we both agreed, for her to take some time to care for Pam, have some fun and reassess her life. When we parted I was sure I would hear from Pam again, no doubt in a letter postmarked from northern Alberta. I had nothing special to offer this bold and courageous nurse except a warm heart and a sympathetic ear, but I think that was perhaps all she really needed.

"BUT THERE IS NO ONE I CAN TALK TO."

For those caregivers who live in small communities or work in rural environments, the stresses of caring and decision making are not only immense for their own complexity, but are augmented by isolation. As my monthly phone bill usually attests, sometimes these lone workers need a colleague, a friend with whom to share their uncertainties and confusion, a safety valve for the emotion and stress of coping every day with decisions of life and death.

Sometimes talking it out by long-distance telephone is not enough, and a personal visit is needed. For example, there may be a difference of opinion between a patient and the family or the health-care providers. A great deal of tension can build, egos can take over, and the primary objective (to serve the patient's wishes and best interests) can be lost sight of. When this happens an "objective third party" is needed, an "outsider" who may be familiar with the circumstances but who is viewed as neutral by the various parties.

Sometimes, however, caregivers, whether family members, volunteers, friends or professionals, just need someone to *listen*. We all need to feel that our concerns are known and our opinions are valued, and for this we need a sympathetic ear.

No one can do this work alone. Caregivers need opportunities to share the debate and the responsibility with others.

WHO CARES FOR THE CAREGIVERS AT HOME?

The amount of stress experienced by those providing care for a patient at home depends to a degree on the quality of home support, the extent and type of services available, and the financial resources of the family. And yet even under optimum conditions, those providing primary care at home can become prey to loneliness, isolation, fear, feelings of abandonment and irrational anger at the unfairness of it all.

One of the therapies prescribed by Dr. Elisabeth Kübler-Ross for patients suffering from great anger is to beat a pillow with a length of rubber hose. It is a harmless way to release the pent-up anger, fear and hostility that it is normal and natural to feel, without the risk of hurting another person. Does it matter whether the "beater" is a patient or a caregiver? I think not. Either may feel the need for physical release of unresolved emotions. Try it, or a variation of the same. You may find beating a pillow is a tremendous outlet for you, and it is certainly better than resorting to chemical tranquillizers or mood-altering drugs. If you can find no natural way to release your tensions, however, by all means speak to your doctor about a mild medication to help you through a particularly rough patch.

Another "therapy" I recommend highly is to build into your plan of caring a regular "time out", a time when you pamper yourself with whatever pleases you—a long, warm, scented bath; a brisk walk to smell the fresh air; a glass of wine—whatever helps. Discuss this with the person for whom you are caring and come to an agreement with him or her that at the same time every day or evening, for one hour, you are "off duty". I have found that if the terms of the agreement are clear from the start, both parties respect the agreement and both benefit.

With someone who is seriously ill but wishes to live independently and is capable of doing so, other types of support system are called for. Many ill persons desperately want privacy and independence but at the same time need the security of knowing that there is someone readily available. One solution is to make a mutually satisfactory arrangement to visit by telephone or in person at precisely the same time, and *never allow anything to interfere with this commitment.*

When I was very ill but able to go home from hospital for short periods, that time of privacy and revelling in my own personal space was something I jealously protected. And yet my family and other caregivers would legitimately worry if I failed to answer their attempts to communicate with me. We established a pattern of phone calls and visits that allowed me to feel in control of my environment and at the same time reassured them that my needs were being adequately met.

RESPITE CARE

Respite is a concept as old as "caring" itself. Man has always recognized, in theory at least, that every individual has physical, psychological and emotional limits. While we are all capable of enduring much more than we imagine, even the most dedicated, loving and committed caregivers must have a time away to replenish their energy reserves. When extended intergenerational families were more common, there were usually several members of the family available to take over the care of the sick child or granny for a while. With today's smaller nuclear families, however, there are fewer options of this kind, and new methods need to be explored.

Many nursing homes, some hospitals and many private nursing agencies can provide someone to relieve the primary caregiver for an agreed-upon period of time. Particularly when the illness is lengthy—for example, in cases of severe stroke, chronic degenerative diseases like muscular dystrophy, ALS, and AIDS, or long-term acute conditions such as some cancers, congestive heart failure, and emphysema—the demands on the caregiver are enormous. Even with the support of home care and visiting nurses, the day in, day out grind of always being present and ready to cope in a crisis wears down the most willing caregiver.

When "burnout" occurs it has negative consequences for both the patient and the caregiver. The quality of care may deteriorate. Loss of sleep, general fatigue from the pressure of being constantly "on-call", and lack of external stimuli can lead to a loss of perspective. The caregiver may lose his or her sense of humour, become depressed and find it more and more difficult to be patient and goodnatured. These symptoms of burnout send a signal to the patient that he or she is a burden, unloved and no longer of value, and the patient's morale suffers.

One remedy that is becoming increasingly popular in many communities is respite care. Under such a program, the caregiver may be removed from the situation for a specified period of time and replaced by a health-care provider. Or the patient may be moved to another location for care.

Some of the special-interest groups dealing with such illnesses as Parkinson's disease or Alzheimer's can also be very helpful. They may offer self-help programs or advice and assistance in arranging respite care. Caregivers should discuss the possibility of respite care with their social worker or home-care coordinator. Advance planning can make it easier to obtain help when you need it, since resources may not always be available at short notice.

Some communities also offer day-care arrangements for the elderly (the adult social day-care service at Kerby Centre in Calgary is an example). Hospice Calgary Society offers service to the families and caregivers of those in the later stages of cancer who have had chemotherapy or radiation. Edmonton has the Dickinsfield Day Program and the VON Adult Day Health Care. These are only a few of the options available in one part of Canada. Various hospital day-care programs are available for those who may require a more supervised regime. I have found these an excellent way to ensure a break for both the care provider and the ill person. For information about services in your area, start with the telephone directory or a visit to your local resource library or community centre.

Let us not forget the role friends and volunteers can play in respite care. When people say, as they often do, "I wish there was something I could do", or "Is there something I can do?", say "Yes. I really need to get away for a few hours (or an evening, or even a weekend). John (or Jennifer) has all the nursing care they need, but we still need someone to stay in the apartment and prepare simple meals and supervise his (her) medication. I would be pleased to give you guidance on what he (she) likes and needs. Could you do this for me?" You will be pleasantly surprised at how grateful others are to have something specific they can do to help. The break will help you to be a better caregiver, your friend will feel like a contributing member of your "extended family" and the ill person will almost always find the change a welcome diversion.

CHAPTER ELEVEN

Where Do We Go from Here?

B efore we can examine where we are going, we need to determine where we are. Every day I receive calls and letters from people from all parts of Canada asking for help in life-threatening or terminal situations. And just as often I hear from people who want information about advance planning to avoid an undignified end.

It is impossible to ignore such appeals, nor would I consider it ethical to do so. It cannot be said too often: We must learn to *listen* to each other and to hear—really hear—what is being said.

Death is inevitable. Dignified dying is not. A dignified death to me means a peaceful one, free from intolerable suffering, in a place I find comfortable and with the company of the family and friends who have made life such a joy. It is a private matter between the special people in my life, my physician and myself.

PUBLICITY VERSUS PRIVACY

When fighting for a cause—in this case, for a revolution in thinking and behaviour—you must decide on the principles and policies that you will be guided by, calculate a strategy and plan your route.

In any case I am involved in, I am guided above all by the principles of maintaining confidentiality and respecting the individual's right to privacy. These principles were soundly drummed into me as a student nurse and they have generally served me and my clients well during several decades of advocacy work. Each person and family with whom I am involved as either a counsellor or an advocate can be sure their privacy will always be respected. I expect no less from them. That is part of the agreement we make together.

Some critics maintain that the "right-to-die" movement would reach its goal more quickly if it were less scrupulous about people's personal privacy. I agree that dramatic scenes, the faces of suffering and the images of pain and desperation may make a louder public statement. However, I cannot believe that asking my clients (who usually come to me seeking a private resolution of their suffering) to endure the glare of publicity is a fair price to exact for my help.

The law provides another, equally compelling reason for discretion. Until either the courts or Parliament sanction compassionate, safe and dignified dying for all competent persons, there is always the threat of prosecution—not only for me but also for patients, families, friends and other health-care providers. While criminal prosecutions are few and far between, the cases I have discussed show how the courts wrestle with the letter of the law and the underlying issues of justice and compassion such cases raise.

Those who counsel and comfort people in distress, myself included, cannot be effective if our energies are dissipated in fighting legal battles or avoiding potential lawsuits. There are anti-choice activists in Canada who would like to obstruct our work. I do not choose to allow them that satisfaction, nor does their presence make me less than fully committed to helping those who call on me in their time of crisis.

As this book is about free choice, it is my choice not to offer myself as either target or victim of the unthinking bigotry that seeks to deny choice. Clearly, feelings about the issues of suicide, assisted suicide, autonomy and self-determination run very high. One only needs to look at the abuses perpetrated in Canada by the so-called right-to-life campaigners—many of whom have threatened and tried to coerce through immoral and even violent means those who think differently from themselves.

When "Nancy B" received the authority of the court to pursue her lawful and moral right to refuse further treatment, there were people who asked to be allowed to spend ten minutes or so with Nancy in the belief that they would get her to change her mind. What incredible arrogance! As if this young woman had not had all reasonable arguments presented to her innumerable times. In my opinion, the fact that she chose to expose herself and her loving family to the ordeal of a court trial proved beyond any doubt that she had thought through the question from all possible angles before making her choice—to be free from the tyranny of life-support machinery.

In Sue Rodriguez we recognize and applaud a courageous and strong pioneer in the fight for physician-assisted dying. Along with Terry Fox and Rick Hansen, who also sacrificed their privacy to champion very different but equally important issues, she belongs among the great heroes of Canada. We admire these people and bless their generosity.

But not everyone is so inclined. Most still prefer to pursue their personal goals in privacy, if not in silence. Those who do go public in their search for a remedy often do so out of desperation. When they do, they may find that the public and the media can be a fickle lot. What is a *cause célèbre* today may be simply yesterday's news tomorrow.

The Case of Analise

One day I received a call from a young woman who was obviously quite distressed. She told me she had been referred to me by a television reporter on the condition that neither of us ever revealed the reporter's name. Berta said her mother was slowly dying of lung cancer and was now so debilitated that she was dependent on a ventilator to breathe and a gastrostomy tube surgically implanted in her stomach to receive

A GENTLE DEATH

nourishment. The mother, Analise, had lost the use of both arms in an automobile accident three years ago, and now at the age of sixty-three wished to be released from the prison of a body that was falling apart bit by bit. Analise spoke only through a signing board, but she had made it very clear to the doctors, nurses and her family that she wished all the tubes to be removed to allow her to die.

Analise's husband and her six children had discussed the matter with her, and after a great deal of energetic debate had agreed that she deserved to be granted her wish. Together they approached the hospital staff. The initial reaction was a definite no. "We will not discuss this further. Your wife and mother is here in our care and we intend to do everything possible to keep her alive as long as we can."

This is frequently the first, spontaneous reaction of many caregivers, who are intensely involved in trying to improve the quality of life for the suffering. It is not usually an intransigent stand, and if one allows time for the dust to settle before returning to the subject, perhaps from a different angle, quite often a more sympathetic response is forthcoming. But how is a desperate family supposed to know that?

Instead, this family, reacting instinctively, contacted the most sensationalistic newspaper they could think of and told their story to the press. The newspaper loved it. They took pictures of the mother and anyone else available and made it a front-page story—for two days.

Everyone was the villain—the hospital, the doctors, the nurses. The whole medical system was conspiring to keep this patient a prisoner. The effect of the publicity was to cause the medical team to close ranks and refuse all further talks with the family. Everyone felt exposed, vulnerable and victimized.

Most of all, however, it was Analise who paid the price. Her family's action cost her dearly.

It took six weeks of diplomacy and negotiation for me to

216

allow a peaceful and dignified death for Analise. I am pleased to reveal that this final mercy occurred with the full support of the original doctor, all of the nurses on the care team, the social worker, the pastoral care counsellor, the hospital administrator and all the family.

The main steps in the process of negotiation were: helping the family to work through their concerns; ensuring that family members were all of one mind and speaking with one voice, as so eloquently expressed by Analise; getting the family to select one person, and only one, to be the official spokesperson for all of them (thus reducing the chance of communication breakdown between the family and the health-care staff); meeting in a non-confrontational manner with the attending physician and the nurse coordinator, who gradually involved the whole staff; avoiding language and behaviour that would be unacceptable to the Canadian Medical Protective Association (the insuring body of physicians) and the coroner's office. By these means we were able to establish a foundation of mutual respect and understanding that allowed us to work together toward an acceptable resolution for Analise.

For the patient and family it was a very long struggle. But it was only after the media were removed from the situation that we could get to the real issue at hand—a compassionate death for Analise.

I am not implying that reporters and journalists are heartless people. Far from it. Most people, media persons included, have great compassion and sympathy for patients in such situations. It is nevertheless not usually appropriate for the public to be invited into what is normally a very private matter.

As with any other type of work, of course, a few insensitive and thoughtless individuals can reflect badly on the whole profession. Such as the young man who phoned me at home at six in the morning to say in a breathless voice, "Nancy Cruzan just died. Could you find me someone like that in Canada to interview for my nine o'clock show?" Or the publicity hound who called and asked me to find him a candidate for Dr. Kevorkian's machine to help launch the latter's book in Canada. These persons shall stay nameless, and in my view they should choose a different career.

I believe that Dr. Kevorkian, a retired Michigan pathologist known in the news media as "Dr. Death", did begin his crusade with good intentions. Though I disliked his approach, when he assisted Janet Adkins to die I believe it was a merciful end to her intolerable suffering. Latterly, however, his openly provocative stance has in my opinion done more damage to the cause of legitimizing rational, planned death than otherwise. I am repelled by his publicity seeking, which flies in the face of the need to respect each person's right to privacy and compassion. Such behaviour simply makes a spectacle—a circus—out of the desperation and despair of vulnerable people in our otherwise civilized society.

THE HIDDEN WORLD
OF NEGOTIATION

Countless times a doctor, a nurse or a coroner has said to me, "We understand each other. Let us demonstrate our mutual respect by not saying or doing anything that could be misconstrued or push the other party into an awkward position."

Yes, there is a covertness but also a correctness to our actions. We all understand the law, but ethics and humanity sometimes must take precedence over a too-literal interpretation of the cold words of law. The principles of justice and compassion demand that we recognize the individual's autonomy and right of self-determination in this matter.

A time of dying is a time for peace and tranquillity, not for game playing. If we are forced to live and act in a framework of hypocrisy, then I must accept it—for the time being. Many advocates and caregivers for those at the end of life feel they cannot endure the status quo much longer. We bear it for the sake of the suffering human beings who wish for and need our courage. But our patience is not infinite. To the over-zealous, self-styled arbiters of society's morals who oppose change, we say, "Do not test us too long!" Perhaps they believe they are driven by humanitarian principles, but to me it looks like a need for control and power, and a self-righteous conviction that they have a better knowledge of the will of the Almighty than others. By what authority do these few dare to dictate how much suffering a person must endure? Enough is enough! It is time for the voices of reason and caring to be heard in Canada on this all-important issue of the quality of dying.

PHYSICIAN-ASSISTED DEATH

I prefer to use the term "physician-assisted death" because it is more inclusive than "physician-assisted suicide" and not as burdened with confusing associations as "euthanasia." There are too many definitions of euthanasia, and it has such a controversial history, that a beautiful concept (literally translated "euthanasia" means "a good and gentle death") has become frightening, controversial and the source of confusion.

"Physician-assisted suicide" is too limiting a term. To take one's own life first requires the physical capacity to act; consequently the act of suicide is impossible for a great number of people. While these persons might choose to end their own life instead of enduring a prolonged, protracted death, they can't. This was the case with Hans, described in Chapter 1, a quadriplegic, unable to use or control his limbs, and therefore unable to feed himself or take drugs without someone's assistance. An individual in the advanced stage of Lou Gehrig's disease would be similarly incapacitated. While the mind is clear and the decision-making ability fully rational, the physical ability to swallow medication may be absent. In this case, too, the individual may have lost control and the strength to manipulate his or her limbs.

Physician-assisted dying would include all those who, either by their own hand, or with the direct intervention of their physician, would choose to have their life ended by merciful means before nature dictates.

Modern medicine has become so "successful" in interfering with nature that it is frequently almost impossible to choose the time and manner of death. As previously discussed, however, for many individuals the quantity of life is of much less value than its quality. Each person must be able to make such a determination, without fear and without judgement by others.

I believe that physician-assisted death is acceptable in certain circumstances. Should it be legally sanctioned in Canada? Yes: with proper safeguards to protect the vulnerable, it is time to legitimize a practice that is already taking place. We desperately need to have physician-assisted dying available, for those who would choose it, as a natural extension of medical practice. I also believe that doctors can and should be trusted to act in this matter. In most cases, they have the skill, the judgement and the compassion to act appropriately.

Some would say that for physicians to assist patients who wish to hasten their dying is to break the Hippocratic Oath. According to a 1991 report in the *New York Times*, however, medical schools now use different forms of oaths when their students graduate. Only 6 per cent ask new doctors to swear the classic fifth-century Hippocratic Oath (which forbids abortion and euthanasia), and 42 per cent offer a modified version. The declaration of Geneva, written by the World Medical Association in 1948, is used in 28 per cent of medical schools. Some use the oath written by Dr. Louis Lasagna in 1964: "Most especially I must tread with care in matters of life and death. If it is given to me to save a life, all thanks. But it may also be within my power to take a life; this awesome responsibility must be faced with great humbleness and awareness of my own frailty. Above all, I must not play God."

Most Canadians will probably never consider physician-assisted dying as a choice for themselves. Many have emotional, psychological, philosophical or religious reasons for not seeking such an end for themselves. But a significant majority do feel that others should have the right to choose it if they wish.

Many in our society find the suffering they are enduring intolerable. They cannot be cured, and we cannot offer them sufficient relief to make them wish to continue living. I am not talking here only about the limited concept of physical pain. I am talking about a much broader concept of suffering. For such people, if they choose it, the option of a merciful death with dignity should be available.

For the sake of such people, of the health-care professionals involved in such acts and of society in general, we must have a regulated means of providing assistance in dying. To say that this devalues human life is hypocritical. I believe most adamantly in the sanctity of life, but I also believe each person has the right to define what he or she can personally accept as "life". Allowing people the right to choose is an affirmation of their humanity, a recognition of their right not to be completely subject to the whims of fate and abstract authority and of their right to determine for themselves the meaning of quality of life. Without that right we are not fully alive. Without it we are not fully persons. To be denied the right to live and die in dignity, with a peaceful and generous heart, because of a provision in the Criminal Code that dates from more than a century ago is beyond reason.

At the beginning of Chapter 1, I called this book the "story of a journey". A rather long journey it has been, and yet as I continue to travel the road I realize more and more that though it has many sad turnings, I can also look forward to many joyous ones.

We have many goals to achieve and innumerable friends who help us every day in this noble cause. The debate continues, but more and more people are realizing that action on this matter is long overdue. The freedom to choose assisted death must be a legal alternative for all persons who wish it.

The Case of Henri

He was bone weary, exhausted—too tired to eat when he came home from work, too tired to take the kids out to play, too tired even to stay awake during a ball game on TV. Henri's stomach ached almost all the time. Headaches, bouts of dizziness, mood swings, depression, anxiety and a "short fuse", disturbed sleep—these problems plagued him almost constantly. He began having occasional nosebleeds and pains in his chest. Finally, after a particularly severe chest pain, he collapsed at the dinner table one night.

Jacqueline called the ambulance, arranged for a neighbour to keep an eye on the kids and rode with Henri to the hospital. The doctors were puzzled. It looked as if Henri had suffered a heart attack, but there were no other indicators or previous symptoms. It certainly was not a typical heart attack. In fact, Henri had been seeing doctors for a couple of months about his various ailments. He had never been really ill before and certainly was not a complainer or a malingerer by nature. The only answer the family physician seemed able to give was, "I don't know." So they would run a new series of tests. Yes, a few of the results were a bit peculiar, but nothing that could be pinned down to a specific diagnosis. So, Henri listened to more of the "I don't know" kind of answers, and then finally it came. "Well, Henri, maybe you are just depressed about something—maybe it is all in your head and you should just thank God you have such a wonderful wife and children and a job you like, and forget about feeling sick. Just get on with things and stop feeling sorry for yourself. Stop looking for problems and in no time you'll be your old happy self again." He called me that night. "It is one of the worst nights of my life," he said, and then went on to explain.

Henri tried. And tried. And tried some more. We were as close as friends can be, and when he was home alone he

222

would call me to elaborate in detail how very hard he was trying. "Can it really be all in my head, Marilynne? I feel so bad, yet I go to work every morning thinking if I can just be positive I will be able to ignore all the aches and hurting and get on with the day and do my job well." He agonized over the persistent inability to feel better.

We met over the holidays and I was shocked at the change in him. He suddenly looked five years older, with bags under his eyes and a haunted look behind them. The worry and suffering poured out of him, pleading for resolution, for an answer—any answer—just to know what was wrong. When we went for a walk that evening, with gentle snow falling about us, he could barely put one foot in front of the other, but he needed to talk plainly.

"I'm afraid, Marilynne. What if I am really ill? Even worse, what if I am not physically ill but going crazy? No one can find an explanation for how I feel. Surely some time soon people are going to lose patience with me and maybe give up. Jacqueline is fantastic. I know how worried she must be, and she tries so hard never to let it show. When I can't make it off the sofa, there's Jacqueline taking the boys to hockey practice. She and the boys automatically have taken over my share of the household chores. And nobody ever complains. Marilynne, how will Jacqueline and the boys manage if something serious happens to me? I'm just plain scared and I don't know what to do about it."

We stopped and we put our arms around each other and he sobbed as though his heart was breaking. All the pent-up fear and agony of these past few months just poured out of him. What could I say? I could only hold him and reassure him his family and friends loved him very much and had confidence that he had the strength to endure whatever came along. I begged him to phone me whenever the pressure built up, or just to say hello. His family was wonderfully supportive, but there were times when he needed another ear to listen. There are also times when even the most caring family can feel impatient—especially when the doctors say there is nothing wrong. Like me, Jacqueline was a nurse, and we had recognized in each other a special relationship over the years, but neither of us really understood Henri's suffering or the why of it.

The night of the ambulance ride was only ten days after my walk and talk with Henri, and it marked the beginning of many such races to one hospital or another. Within weeks he had suffered two serious heart attacks followed by a stroke that left him aphasic (without speech) and paralysed on one side—helpless as a new-born kitten.

It was during this episode that I first visited him in hospital. He would be sleeping or slipping in and out of consciousness for long periods. I sat quietly at his bedside and continued working on material I had brought with me so I could stay away from Toronto for a longer stretch. I was preparing a program for TV on the subject of how healthcare workers deal with a patient's death. Dr. Rob Buckman had a book due to be released soon, and I was working from the "galleys" (a great heavy pile of proofs that fell across both sides of my lap) for my research. As I sat reading I felt someone watching me and I looked up surprised, to see that Henri's eyes were open and he was trying hard with his half-paralysed mouth to smile "hello". He still could not speak, so he poked the manuscript with his unparalysed hand and drew a question mark. What was I reading? What was I working on? I hesitated to tell him, for I thought he might relate it to his own condition and be upset. But, knowing Henri, I knew there was no dodging it.

I explained about the show and the book I was reading. With his good hand he wrote me a note. "Can you leave it with me tonight? I'd like to read it too." I knew he could not focus enough to read by himself, so I said I would read him a few chapters. Over the next couple of days we read the whole book together, and it both confirmed the value of the book and illustrated Henri's needs so acutely. In fact, when I returned home, I left the manuscript with Henri. In desperate moments of frustration with the hospital staff, he would flip to the page he needed and nag the staff to read the appropriate section to try to understand what concerned him. It became another voice for him.

This funny, virile, energetic, loving young man of thirty-nine was the victim of a disease so rare no one could even guess at a diagnosis. At the large teaching hospital he was poked, prodded and examined many times over by every kind of specialist. His symptoms were fed into a highly sophisticated computer system that compiled cases, symptoms and patient profiles from across North America. Finally, there was a hint of what the problem might be. The diagnosis could only be confirmed through a painful procedure, but Henri instructed the doctors to please "get on with it". Anything was better than just lying in hospital not knowing.

Gradually his speech started to return, and the physiotherapy was helping him to get back on his feet again. In fact, everyone was amazed at the progress he made. Most people who have had a stroke of such severity do not respond so quickly or so well. No one could even have imagined that Henri would walk out of the hospital a few weeks later using only a walker, able to remember and speak most of the words he needed to communicate and recalling more each day. He was still very unsteady on his feet, of course, and he needed help in dressing and sometimes even to eat. Jacqueline and the children rallied around without ever making a fuss about it, so that someone was always there to help him lower himself into a chair or get up from the sofa. Automatically his coffee or soft drink appeared at his place, served with a straw. These things were not discussed; they were just done. Soon he called to tell me he had "graduated" to using two canes, and eventually he could manage with just one cane.

And oh, the day I came to visit and he invited me to walk with him to the doctor's office—without any cane. "Free," he said. "Look, no hands."—the sort of thing kids shout to each other when they ride their bikes down the driveway without touching the handlebars. "If you walk beside me and we take it slow, I know I can make it." "Now Henri," spoke the mother instinct in me, "quit being a show-off. You don't have to prove anything to me." "I know that," he said. "I have to do it for myself." I shut up, having been properly put in my place.

Then, our conversation took on a more serious note. Henri looked me squarely in the eye and said, "If the time ever comes when I have no quality of life, when I cannot manage my own future, when life is more of a burden than a blessing, will you help me to die? Do we have a bargain?"

I returned his direct look and stated firmly, "Yes, Henri. We have a bargain."

One day in early spring I was able to visit their city and invite Jacqueline and Henri for lunch at an elegant restaurant, just the three of us. Henri had the reputation all his life of being full of fun. In fact he was a terror at teasing his younger brother when they were children. That sense of fun was popping out of him again. "Look, Jacqueline," he would say, "I can eat all by myself—no straws, and with my 'gimpy' hand, too. I'm really well—a whole person again." He looked wonderful. What utter joy to see that mischievous grin again, as though he had not a care in the world.

And yet, we wondered aloud, seeking reassurances from each other, about the unknown and whether Henri would ever really be totally well again. We wondered when the test results would come back. (It had been ten weeks since the tests had been done and sent for analysis.) What would the results tell us?

The worst, I thought, would be to confirm that Henri had a disease called hypereosinophilic syndrome (HES). There was very little known about it, but I had called in all my "markers", plaguing some specialist friends in Toronto to find out all they could tell me about the disease. They had regretfully revealed that the prognosis was very poor. Only a few dozen cases had even been diagnosed. A few persons had lived for up to ten years, but these were older people, and usually the younger the person the more virulent and fast-moving the disease. So far, no one had had a complete remission. Henri knew this, for we always spoke the truth to each other. His response was, "No, Marilynne, the worst thing they can tell me is that they don't know what is troubling me. That is the worst thing to live with—the not knowing."

I understood what he meant so clearly, recalling my own experience just a few years before when I had undergone routine surgery. For three and a half years I existed, most of the time in hospital. More than a dozen operations had been performed to heal the wounds. All had failed. I just kept deteriorating more and more every day. No one could tell me why. I had heard those terrible words, "I don't know," and "Wait and see" so many times I could sense them coming before the doctors opened their mouths. I wanted to scream at them not to say it. Sometimes I did scream—not at the doctors so much as at the uncertainty—the suffering for which there was no rational answer.

So, yes, I certainly understood and empathized with what Henri was telling us. Please. Anything. Even tell me that I am dying—just give me an answer. Give me a name for this condition so I won't have to feel guilty about it any more. Irrational though it may seem, people do at times feel guilty that they have "failed" to respond to treatment. What am I doing wrong? Perhaps I'm not fighting hard enough. Perhaps if I could think more positively I could beat this thing.

And yet all the time your rational self is telling you that you are doing the best you can. You know how much there is to live for and you want so much to be well again. Why is this not working for you? Without consciously meaning to,

I'm sure, sometimes the doctors and nurses give you the same message. The look of impatience that says, What is it now? So you decide to bear the pain this time, to hang on an hour longer. But then half an hour has gone by and you are screaming inside and you have to push the bell and ask, "Please, could I have some more medication now?" You apologize for disturbing them, and you chastise yourself for not being stronger, when all the time you have no resources left to be strong with. They are all used up just fighting the pain between injections or between treatments.

Finally, even before the test results were in, Henri felt so strong and healthy he decided to go on a holiday to the family cottage with his parents. Not only that, he went out to play nine holes of golf with his best buddy. When he returned to the cottage after the game he simply said, "Mom, Dad, I think you had better drive me to the hospital. I feel pretty bad and I can't breathe very well." When they arrived at the small but efficient local hospital, the doctor immediately saw that Henri's condition was serious, far beyond the capability or resources of the available facilities. Henri was rushed by ambulance to a larger hospital forty miles away. They too saw that his rapidly deteriorating condition was beyond their ability to cope with and had him quickly air transported to the teaching hospital that had cared for him previously.

Henri was in congestive heart failure, the drugs he was taking to control some of his symptoms had become toxic in his system. He was very seriously ill but not critical, and the medical team felt they could reverse this. And so they did— for a while. Just a few days later Henri phoned me at the office. "Marilynne, I'm dying. Please come."

Immediately I called his primary-care doctor and was informed that they were sure Henri would recover. Always in such situations I accept the patient's instinct. Most of us possess a second sense that tells us when death is near. If Henri believed death was close, it was true, much as it hurt me to accept that fact. Taking the next plane, I arrived at his bedside a few hours later.

He was pale, bloated and bright red from the prednisone, weak and short of breath. But he still had that grin on his face—and tears in his eyes. "Thank you, thank you. You remember our bargain. I think I will die soon, and I need you here."

It seemed a long time since we had first talked about "our bargain". It had been in the spring, and this was only mid-August but it seemed very far away because I had deliberately chosen to suppress the memory. After all, I reasoned, Henri could not die. But it was true. I had promised Henri if the time ever came when he believed he could no longer live with dignity and for the best interest of his family, I would help him to die at a time and in a manner of his choosing. He had expressed his wish to die at home.

He recognized that the latter request could not be met, given his present state. It was not even remotely feasible to keep him comfortable at home, and it would also be too hard to try to care for him there. He needed the "high-tech" facility to manage his symptoms. In fact, he did not now ask to go home.

During the next four days, Henri, Jacqueline and I met with his health-care team. Doctors, nurses, the social worker and various therapists were always available to us. For the first couple of days, everyone but the three of us was convinced that he would go into remission again. It was just a matter of time. Henri, however, still needed that sense of control and insisted on a meeting with the doctor to discuss whether or not it would be beneficial for someone in the future if he gave his body to the medical school for study. The doctor thanked him most humbly, and then told him that equal benefit could be obtained if the family would allow an autopsy and permit three sets of tissue sections (thin slices of all vital organs) to be taken and frozen for later study when more was understood about this mysterious condition. Henri and Jacqueline both agreed.

The next few days were a roller-coaster ride. One minute Henri would be sitting up in a chair laughing with his kids and other family who came to visit. The next hour he would be rushed to intensive care. A little while later there he was, sitting on the edge of the bed, smiling and saying how good a cold beer would taste. The nurse brought one in for him. We did not know whether to leave him at night or not, but Henri would say, "It's okay—take the boys home to bed. It won't be tonight."

"No," he said, "I'm going to die on Sunday morning, after the family has been to church. It will be a nice sunny day, and that will make it less scary for the kids. I don't want to die at night. According to some of the books on death, it can cause children to fear the dark and unknown of the night. Sunday morning will be the best time."

By now all of the family had gathered except one. It was hard for the brother to make appropriate arrangements for his own young family and to travel from a long distance away. In fact, he could not accept that his brother, at the young age of thirty-nine, was really dying. But Henri was adamant. "Marilynne, get him here. Do whatever you have to do. I need to say goodbye to him." Finally Pierre did arrive, barely in time; they had only a few brief minutes together. But perhaps it was enough.

On Sunday morning there were seventeen people—family and friends—quietly and respectfully keeping vigil at the hospital, reassuring ourselves and each other that the time was now and the manner was fitting. I noticed Henri's wife and sons huddled together holding each other tightly outside the intensive care room where their husband and father lay so still. His parents, siblings and extended family all sat quietly, praying or thinking their own thoughts but at the same time sending forth their private wishes to Henri for a peaceful journey.

The morphine that had been used to keep Henri sedated and pain-free through the night was reduced so that he would regain consciousness and be able to recognize each person in a last farewell. Singly or in pairs, most of those waiting took turns being with Henri, saying their personal goodbyes. Some found it more than they could bear and chose to hold onto their memory of the laughing, healthy Henri from earlier days.

Finally, the time came—the time Henri had chosen. Jacqueline and I spent a little time with him and asked the boys if they wanted to see their dad one last time. At first each said no. Then first one and then the other came to the ICU door. They donned gowns (much too big for them) and came to be with their father. We instructed them to touch his face, to stroke his cheek, for this was the only place he now could feel human contact.

In order to keep him comfortable through the night and free from pain, it had been necessary to sedate him with high doses of morphine and insert a ventilator tube to help him breathe. He was not dependent for life on these interventions, but for comfort.

Everyone left the room except Jacqueline and myself. The nurses had created a private little corner of the room for us. This was to give Henri and his family some personal space and also to allow the least disturbance for the other patients in the unit. In fact, we were all so quiet and discreet, I do not think the other patients were aware of us. Even our tears were silent.

At last one of the many doctors and nurses who were present in the room handed a tray to us and asked simply, "Do you know what to do?" "Yes," we answered. The curtain was closed around the bed and all was private. After a final kiss and blessing the bargain was kept. Henri smiled ever so calmly, and, with a "thank you" in his eyes, gradually died. Through my tears I was aware of nothing but his peaceful face until I felt two arms enfold me. I glanced back and saw one of the nurses holding my shoulders saying, "It's okay, Marilynne." Only then did I raise my eyes to look around the room and see that more than twenty people surrounded Henri—mother, father, wife, sons, brother, sisters and their spouses, in-laws, a boyhood friend and his family, nurses, doctors and the priest. Almost all were touching some part of our dear friend with one hand and comforting the person next to them with the other.

Dignity. There is no more perfect word for it.

APPENDIX A

GLOSSARY

Acupressure: compression of blood vessels by means of needles in surrounding tissues.

Acupuncture: technique for treating certain painful conditions and for producing regional anaesthesia by passing long thin needles through the skin to specific points. The free ends of the needles are twirled in some cases to conduct a weak electrical current.

AIDS (acquired immune deficiency syndrome): the syndrome of opportunistic infections that occur as the final stage of infection by the human immunodeficiency virus (HIV).

ALS (amyotrophic lateral sclerosis; also called Lou Gehrig's disease): a syndrome marked by muscular weakness and atrophy with spasticity and hyperflexia due to degeneration of motor neurons of the spinal cord, medulla and cortex of the brain. There is no specific treatment. Prognosis is very poor, and while some patients have survived for ten to twenty years, most live for six months to five years.

Alzheimer's disease: a chronic, organic mental disorder; a form of presenile dementia due to atrophy of the frontal and occipital lobes of the brain. It involves progressive, irreversible loss of memory, deterioration of intellectual functions, apathy, speech and gait disturbances and disorientation.

Analgesia: absence of a normal sense of pain.

Angina pectoris: severe pain and a feeling of constriction about the heart.

Aphasia: absence or impairment of the ability to communicate through speech, and sometimes through writing or signs, due to dysfunction of brain centres.

Cardiopulmonary arrest: sudden cessation of the respiratory and cardiovascular systems.

Cardiopulmonary resuscitation: treatment used to try to restore heart and lung function.

Cardiovascular failure: an inability of the heart and blood vessels to function adequately to sustain life for any period of time.

Chemotherapy: the use of chemical reagents that have a specific and toxic effect on disease-causing micro-organisms.

Compression fracture: a broken vertebra caused by pressure along the long axis of the spine.

Cordotomy: incision of the spinal-cord section of lateral pathways to relieve pain.

Dialysis: a process of diffusing blood across a semipermeable membrane to remove toxic materials and to maintain fluid, electrolyte and acid-base balance in cases of impaired kidney function.

Emphysema: a cardiopulmonary disease characterized by increase beyond the normal in the size of air spaces distal to the terminal bronchiole with destructive changes in their walls.

End-stage renal disease: the extreme stage of kidney failure.

Euthanasia: the act of bringing about a peaceful and gentle death at the person's request.

Gastrostomy tube: a tube surgically implanted into the stomach for the purpose of introducing food or, in some instances, extracting waste products that have accumulated in the gastrointestinal system.

HES (hypereosinophilic syndrome): a rare world-wide disease more common in men than in women in which the eosinophils increase in abnormal amounts. Almost any organ can be affected, but most sufferers have bone-marrow, cardiac and central-nervous-system involvement.

Homeotherapy: treatment or prevention of disease with a substance similar to but not identical with the active causative agent of the problem.

Hospice care: an interdisciplinary program of palliative care and supportive services that addresses the physical, spiritual, social and economic needs of terminally ill patients and their families.

Lou Gehrig's disease. See "amyotrophic lateral sclerosis".

Lumpectomy: surgical removal of a tumour from the breast.

Multiple sclerosis: an inflammatory disease of the central nervous system that affects the myelin sheath of nerves.

Nasogastric tube: a plastic tube introduced through the nose into the stomach for the purpose of either introducing fluid (usually food) to the stomach or removing fluid from it.

Neuropathy: any disease of the nerves. This is a common side-effect of diabetes and other chronic diseases.

Osteoporosis: a hereditary condition marked by excessive calcification of bones, causing spontaneous fractures and marblelike appearance.

Palliative care: a philosophy of care that serves to alleviate untoward symptoms in the terminally ill rather than to cure the underlying disease. It is usually approached from an interdisciplinary concept of care.

Persistent vegetative state: a continuous state in which a person was previously comatose and may give the appearance that he or she is now awake. The person may or may not respond to stimuli. It is properly characterized by severe dementia.

Physician-assisted dying: assistance by a physician that enables a person to die mercifully and quickly at the person's own request.

Physician-assisted suicide: provision of advice and or means by a physician for a person to end his or her own life at the person's own choosing.

Respirator: a machine for prolonged artificial respiration.

Respiratory failure: a condition wherein there is a marked drop in oxygenation of the blood that, if it continues, is fatal.

Respite care: a system of providing relief for those caring for an ill person.

Rheumatic fever: a systemic fever resulting from streptococcal infection and frequently followed by serious heart and kidney disease, as well as other lifelong complications.

TENS (transcutaneous electrical nerve stimulation): a procedure that can be helpful in managing pain and stimulating muscle activity.

Ventilator: a mechanical device used for artificial ventilation of the lungs.

APPENDIX B

SELECTED READING

Buckman, Robert. *I Don't Know What to Say: How to Help and Support Someone Who Is Dying*. Toronto: Key Porter Books, 1988.

Buckman, Robert. *Magic or Medicine?* Toronto: Key Porter Books, 1993.

Callwood, June. *Twelve Weeks in Spring*. Toronto: Lester and Orpen Dennys, 1986.

Cunningham, Alastair J. *The Healing Journey*. Toronto: Key Porter Books, 1992.

Frank, Arthur W. *At the Will of the Body: Reflections on Illness*. Boston: Houghton Mifflin Company, 1991.

Hill, T. Patrick, and David Shirley. *A Good Death: Taking More Control at the End of Your Life*. Reading, Mass.: Addison-Wesley, 1992.

Horne, Jo. *A Survival Guide for Family Caregivers*. Minneapolis: ComCare Publishers, 1991.

Humphry, Derek. *Final Exit*. Eugene, Or.: Hemlock Society, 1991.

Humphry, Derek, and Ann Wickett. *The Right To Die: Understanding Euthanasia*. Eugene, Or.: Hemlock Society, 1992.

Kübler-Ross, Elisabeth. *On Death and Dying*. New York: Macmillan, 1969.

Ley, Dorothy C.H., and Harry van Bommel. *The Heart of Hospice*. Toronto: NC Press, 1993.

Malcolm, Andrew. *Someday*. New York: Alfred A. Knopf, 1991.

Malcolm, Andrew. *This Far and No More*. New York: New York Times Books, 1987.

Martin, John D. and Frank D. Ferris, *"I Can't Stop Crying": It's So Hard When Someone You Love Dies*. Toronto: Key Porter Books, 1992.

Rachels, James. *The End of Life: Euthanasia and Morality*. Oxford: Oxford University Press, 1986.

Rollin, Betty. *Last Wish*. New York: Warren Books, 1985.

Roth, Philip. *Patrimony*. Toronto: Simon and Schuster, 1991.

van Bommel, Harry. *Choices: For People Who Have Terminal Illness, Their Families and Their Care-Givers*. Updated edition. Toronto: NC Press, 1993.

van Bommel, Harry. *Dying for Care: Hospice Care and Euthanasia*. Toronto: NC Press, 1992.

Wylie, Betty Jane. *New Beginnings: Living Through Loss and Grief*. Toronto: Key Porter Books, 1991.

Books for Health-Care Professionals

Beauchamp, Tom L., and Seymour Perlin. *Ethical Issues in Death and Dying*. Englewood Cliffs, N.J.: Prentice-Hall, 1978.

Brody, Baruch. *Life and Death Decision Making*. Oxford: Oxford University Press, 1988.

Buckman, Robert. *How to Break Bad News*. Toronto: University of Toronto Press, 1992.

Cohen, Cynthia B. *Casebook on the Termination of Life-Sustaining Treatment and the Care of the Dying*. Briarcliff Manor, N.Y.: Hastings Center, 1988.

Colt, George Howe. *The Enigma of Suicide*. Toronto: Summit Books, 1991.

Hamel, Ron P., ed. *Choosing Death: Active Euthanasia, Religion and the Public Debate*. Philadelphia: Trinity Press International, 1991.

Kilner, John F. *Who Lives? Who Dies? Ethical Criteria in Patient Selection*. New Haven: Yale University Press, 1990.

Kluge, Eike-Henner W. *Biomedical Ethics in a Canadian Context*. Scarborough, Ont.: Prentice-Hall, 1992.

Levine, Howard. *Life Choices: Confronting the Life and Death Decisions Created by Modern Medicine*. New York: Simon and Schuster, 1986.

Momeyer, Richard W. *Confronting Death*. Bloomington: Indiana University Press, 1988.

Quill, Timothy E. *Death and Dignity: Making Choices and Taking Charge*. New York: W.W. Norton, 1993.

Rozovsky, Lorne E., and Fay A. Rozovsky. *The Canadian Law of Consent to Treatment*. Toronto: Butterworth, 1990.

Scully, Thomas, and Celia Scully. *Making Medical Decisions*. Toronto: Simon and Schuster, 1989.

Sneiderman, Barney, John C. Irvine and Philip H. Osborne. *Canadian Medical Law*. Toronto: Carswell, 1989.

Thomas, John E., and Wilfred Waluchow. *Well and Good: Case Studies in Biomedical Ethics*. Peterborough, Ont.: Broadview Press, 1987.

Weir, Robert F. *Ethical Issues in Death and Dying*. New York: Columbia University Press, 1986.

Wennberg, Robert N. *Terminal Choices: Euthanasia, Suicide, and the Right to Die*. Grand Rapids, Mich.: William B. Eerdmans Publishing Co., 1989.

Winslade, William J., and Judith W. Ross. *Choosing Life or Death*. New York: Free Press, 1986.

World Federation of Right to Die Societies. *Right to Self-Determination: Proceedings of the 8th World Conference, Maastricht, June, 1990*. Amsterdam: VU University Press, 1990.

World Federation of Right to Die Societies. *The Living Will in the World: Participants' Lectures*. Kyoto, Japan: Japan Society for Dying With Dignity, 1992.

A LIVING WILL

THE LIVING WILL

(An Advance Health Care Directive)

To My Family, My Physician and All Others Whom It May Concern,

INTRODUCTION

1. Death is as much a reality as birth, growth, maturity and old age. It is the one certainty of life. However, I do not fear death as much as I fear the possible indignity the dying process may impose on me.

   I realize it is possible that accidental sudden illness may bring death quickly and gently. I also realize that other circumstances may arise in which a lingering illness, or the gradual deterioration of mind and body would impose a condition or quality of life that I would find unacceptable in light of my personal values and beliefs.

   After careful and thoughtful consideration I wish to state my wishes for my health care in the event I should become physically or mentally incapacitated.

   Therefore, now, while I am able to exercise my right to choose the type and extent of health care which I want, I sign this Living Will as an advance directive for those who will be in a position to influence the health care to be given to me.

RIGHTS

2. I know that when I am rational and able to express my wishes, I have the right to accept or reject any specific medical treatment. My fear is that should I lack the capacity to express my wishes, medical treatment which I do not want may be given to me.

DECLARATION

3. *If the time comes when I lack the capacity to give directions for my health care, this statement shall stand as an expression of my wishes and directions.*

CIRCUMSTANCES

4. *I direct that, in any of the following circumstances, I receive only such care as will keep me comfortable and that my dying not be prolonged.*

Initial

____ *a) An acute life threatening illness of an IRREVERSIBLE nature, or,*

____ *b) Chronic debilitating suffering of a PERMANENT nature, or,*

____ *c)* _____

____ *d)* _____

____ *e)* _____

DIRECTIONS

5. I specifically direct the following:

____ a) Give me all medication necessary to control pain even if such medication might shorten my remaining life.

____ b) Give me physical care to keep me warm and sufficiently hydrated to maintain continuous comfort.

TREATMENT REFUSED

6. In the circumstances set out in section 4, I specifically refuse the following:

____ a) Electrical, mechanical or other artificial stimulation of my heart.

____ b) Use of respiratory ventilation to assist breathing.

Initial

___ c) Artificial feeding "i.e." by tube, intravenous or central line, other than for basic hydration

___ d) Transfer to an intensive care or similar "high tech" facility.

(Add here any other specific medical treatment that would be unacceptable to you.)

___ e) _____

___ f) _____

___ g) _____

DIE AT HOME

___ 7. If it will not impose an undue hardship, I would prefer to die at home.

LIABILITY

8. It is my wish that no legal action be taken against any person because they

   a) acted in good faith, in accordance with the wishes expressed in this health care directive, or

   b) acted contrary to the wishes expressed in this health care directive if the person did not know of its existence.

TRANSFER TO ANOTHER HEALTH CARE PROVIDER

9. If I should be under the care of a health care provider who, for any reason, cannot give effect to my wishes, I ask that my care be transferred to another health care provider who will respect my wishes.

TRANSFER TO ANOTHER HEALTH CARE FACILITY

10. If I should be a patient of resident in a health care facility which, for any reason, cannot give effect to my wishes, I ask that I be transferred to another health care facility.

_____   _____
Signature   Date

_____
Print name

_____
Witness signature

_____
Print name and address

_____
Witness signature

_____
Print name and address

© Dying With Dignity, 1992.

For more information on obtaining an original document, please contact:

Dying With Dignity
600 Eglington Avenue East, Suite 401
Toronto, Ontario
Canada M4P 1P3

APPENDIX D

CANADIAN SUPPORT GROUPS

Dying With Dignity:
A Canadian Society Concerned With the Quality of Dying (DWD)
600 Eglinton Ave. E., Suite 401
Toronto, Ont. M4P 1P3

Fondation Responsable Jusqu'à la Fin
10150 de Bretagne
Quebec, P.Q. G2B 2R1

Goodbye:
A Right-to-Die Society
P.O. Box 39149, Point Grey RPO
Vancouver, B.C. V6R 4P1

The Right to Die Society of Canada
P.O. Box 39018
Victoria, B.C. V8V 1B1

Saskatchewan Action Committee for Death With Dignity
Box 23043
Saskatoon, Sask. S7J 5H3

APPENDIX E

SOURCES FOR INFORMATION ABOUT FEDERAL AND PROVINCIAL LEGISLATION ON ADVANCE HEALTH CARE DIRECTIVES

Alberta

Attorney General's Department
2nd Floor, Bowker Building
9833 109 Street
Edmonton, Alta. T5K 2E8

Department of Justice
Edmonton Regional Office
Room 928, Royal Trust Tower
Edmonton Centre
Edmonton, Alta. T5J 2Z2

British Columbia

Department of Justice
Vancouver Regional Office
Royal Centre
2800-1055 West Georgia Street
Vancouver, B.C. V6E 3P9

Ministry of the Attorney General
910 Government Street, 5th Floor
Victoria, B.C. V8V 1X4

Manitoba

Department of Justice
Winnipeg Regional Office
Centennial House
310 Broadview Avenue, Suite 301
Winnipeg, Man. R3C 0S6

Ministry of the Attorney General
9th Floor, Woodsworth Building
405 Broadway
Winnipeg, Man. R3C 3L6

New Brunswick

Ministry of the Attorney General
Room 416, Centennial Building
P.O. Box 6000
Fredericton, N.B. E3B 5H1

Newfoundland

Ministry of the Attorney General
Confederation Building
P.O. Box 8700
St. John's, Nfld. A1B 4J6

Northwest Territories

Department of Justice
Iqaluit Sub-Office
P.O. Box 1030
Building 163
Iqaluit, N.W.T. X0A 0H0

Department of Justice
Yellowknife Regional Office
11th Floor, Precambrian Building
Box 8
Yellowknife, N.W.T. X1A 2N1

Nova Scotia

Ministry of the Attorney General
P.O. Box 7
Halifax, N.S. B3J 2L6

Ontario

Department of Justice
Toronto Regional Office
2 First Canadian Place
Suite 3400, Exchange Tower
Box 36
Toronto, Ont. M5X 1K6

Ministry of the Attorney General
11th Floor, 720 Bay Street
Toronto, Ont. M5G 2K1

Prince Edward Island

Department of Justice
P.O. Box 2000
Charlottetown, P.E.I. C1A 7N8

Quebec

Department of Justice
Montreal Regional Office
Complexe Guy Favreau
200, René Lévesque Ouest
Tour Est, 9e étage
Montréal, P.Q. H2Z 1X4

Ministère de la justice
1200 rue de l'Eglise
2e étage
Sainte-Foy, P.Q. G1V 4M1

Saskatchewan

Attorney General
Department of Justice
1874 Scarth Street
Regina, Sask. S4P 3V7

Department of Justice
Saskatoon Regional Office
7th Floor, Churchill Building
229 4th Avenue South
Saskatoon, Sask. S7K 4K3

Yukon Territory

Department of Justice
Whitehorse Regional Office
Main Floor, Financial Plaza
204 Lambert Street
Whitehorse, Y.T. Y1A 1Z4

APPENDIX F

MEMBERS OF THE WORLD FEDERATION OF RIGHT TO DIE SOCIETIES

Australia

South Australia Voluntary
Euthanasia Society (SAVES)
P.O. Box 2151
Kent Town Centre 5071
S. Australia

Voluntary Euthanasia Society of
New South Wales (Inc.)
(VES of NSW)
P.O. Box 25
Broadway, NSW 2007
Australia

Voluntary Euthanasia Society of
Queensland
GPO Box 2041
Brisbane, Queensland 4001
Australia

Voluntary Euthanasia Society
of Victoria (Inc.) (VESV)
Unit 1/71 Riverside Rd, Hawthorn
Victoria 3122, Australia

West Australian Voluntary
Euthanasia Society (WAVES)
P.O. Box 7243
Cloisters Square
Perth
Western Australia 6850

Belgium

Association pour le Droit de
Mourir dans la Dignité (ADMD)
rue du Président, 55
B-1050 Bruxelles, Belgium

Recht op Waardig Sterven (RWS)
Constitutiestraat 33
B 2060 Antwerpen, Belgium

Britain

The Voluntary Euthanasia
Society (VES)
13 Prince of Wales Terrace
London, W8 5PG, England

The Voluntary Euthanasia
Society of Scotland (VESS)
17 Hart Street
Edinburgh EH1 3RN
Scotland, UK

Canada

Dying With Dignity (DWD)
600 Eglinton Ave. E., Suite 401
Toronto, ON
M4P 1P3, Canada

Fondation Responsable
Jusqu'à la Fin (FRJF)
10150 de Bretagne
Quebec, PQ
G2B 2R1, Canada

Goodbye: A Right-to-Die Society
PO Box 39149, Point Grey RPO
Vancouver, BC V6R 4P1, Canada

The Right to Die Society
of Canada (Provisional)
P.O. Box 39018
Victoria, BC V8V 1B1, Canada

Colombia

Fundacion Pro Derecho a Morir
Dignamente (DMD)
A.A. 88900
Bogotá, Colombia, S.America

Finland

EXITUS (Provisional)
c/o Mrs. Margareta Hohenthal
Bredavaegen 8 D 20
2700 Grankulla,
Finland

France

Association pour le droit de
mourir dans la dignité (ADMD)
103 rue Lafayette
75010 Paris, France

India

The Society For The Right
To Die With Dignity (SRDD)
127, Mahatma Gandhi Road, Fort
Bombay 400 023, India

Israel

The Israeli Society For
The Right To Die With Dignity
P.O.B. 21751
Tel Aviv, Israel 61217

Japan

Japan Society For
Dying With Dignity (JSDD)
Watanabe Building 202
2-29-1 Hongou Bunkyo-ku
Tokyo 113, Japan

Luxembourg

Association pour le Droit de
Mourir dans la Dignité (Letzebuerg)
(ADMD-L)
50 Bd. J.F. Kennedy
L-4170 Esch-sur-Alzette
Luxembourg

Netherlands

Nederlandse Vereniging voor
Vrijwillige Euthanasie (NVVE)
Postbus 75331, 1070 AH
Amsterdam, Nederland

New Zealand

Voluntary Euthanasia Society
(Auckland) Inc.
P.O. Box 10-351
Dominion Road
Auckland 3, New Zealand

Voluntary Euthanasia Society
(VES)
95 Melrose Road, Island Bay
Wellington 2, New Zealand

Norway

Landsforeningen Mitt
Livstestament (Provisional)
c/o Ms. Unni Bohmer Lybekkv
9b, 0385 Oslo
Norway

South Africa

SAVES—The Living Will
Society/Die Lewende Testament
P.O. Box 1460, Wandsbeck 3631
Republic of South Africa

Spain

Derecho a Morir
Dignamente (DMD)
Apartado 31, 134
08080 Barcelona, Spain

Sweden

Ratten Till Var Dod (RTVD)
Hoganasgatan 20, 753 30
Uppsala, Sweden

Switzerland

EXIT (Deutsche Schweiz) Vereini-
gung fur humanes Sterben
Ch-2540 Grenchen, Switzerland

United States of America

Americans for
Death With Dignity
87 E. Green St., #303
Pasadena, CA 91105, U.S.A.

Euthanasia Research and Guidance
Organization (ERGO)
(Provisional)
24829 Norris Lane
Junction City, OR 97448-9559
U.S.A.

Choice in Dying
200 Varick St.
New York, N.Y. 10014
U.S.A.

The National Hemlock Society
P.O. Box 11830
Eugene, OR 97440-4030
U.S.A